THE
FIRST BUCKINGHAMSHIRE
BATTALION

1914—1919

LT.-COL. L. L. C. REYNOLDS, D.S.O., T.D.   [*Frontispiece*

The First Buckinghamshire Battalion

1914—1919

BY

CAPTAIN P. L. WRIGHT, D.S.O., M.C.

With a Foreword

BY

MAJOR-GENERAL SIR ROBERT FANSHAWE
K.C.B., D.S.O.

The Naval & Military Press Ltd

Published by
The Naval & Military Press Ltd
5 Riverside, Brambleside, Bellbrook
Industrial Estate, Uckfield, East Sussex,
TN22 1QQ England

Tel: +44 (0) 1825 749494
Fax: +44 (0) 1825 765701

www.naval-military-press.com
www.nmarchive.com

In reprinting in facsimile from the original, any imperfections are inevitably reproduced and the quality may fall short of modern type and cartographic standards.

FOREWORD

BY

MAJOR-GENERAL SIR ROBERT FANSHAWE
K.C.B., D.S.O.

THE 1st Bucks Battalion of the Oxfordshire and Buckinghamshire Light Infantry was trained and modelled on the traditions of the Light Division of Peninsular fame, and served through the War in the 145th Brigade of the 48th South Midland Division. The Battalion went out to the War with that great fighting asset—a strong *esprit de corps*. This they maintained; and whether it was training, " holding the line," marching, or the attack, I, as their Divisional Commander, felt confident that their task would be thoroughly done, and carried through with the determination, endurance, dash, and with that proper use of initiative for which the Light Division officers and men were noted a hundred years ago. The officers, N.C.O.s, and men could be relied on to act as the occasion required, in carrying out what they knew to be the general plan.

In no case was this confidence misplaced, whether the affair was that of a patrol or post, or for the whole Battalion.

Amongst the officers were many fine leaders of men, none more so than Lieutenant-Colonel Reynolds, who led the Battalion through most of the War. He was backed by many officers imbued with the same spirit and energy.

Amongst the N.C.O.s and men were always many

ready ably to second this good leadership, and determined to make the Battalion a name of which their whole county might be proud.

The engagements during my command of the Division which to my mind stand prominently out were first on July 23, 1916, during the Battle of the Somme, when the 48th Division were carrying out an attack to break the German line of defence which linked Pozières to Thiepval, in order to assist in the capture of the former place, and pave the way towards the capture of the latter. The Battalion was in brigade reserve when the battle started. The Brigade Commander had been warned that, if his initial attack did not succeed everywhere, a fresh attack would be made to secure our objective. I well remember my conversation on the telephone during the attack, and being assured that the Battalion would be ready by the time the Artillery said they would be.

The right of the Brigade attack succeeded, but that on the left was checked, and to the Bucks Battalion was given the task, at short notice, of capturing the point, without which the gains on the right of the Brigade could not have been held for long. The success of the attack is well told in these pages. The difficulty of the Battalion's task is only to be appreciated by those who, in the long war, have seen how seldom a fresh attack of this sort could be organised and carried out successfully by the immediate use of troops in reserve. The attack cost the Battalion a heavy price—Captain E. V. Birchall, the brilliant company commander who led his company in the attack, being mortally wounded.

The second occasion was the capture of Tombois Farm on the night of April 16–17, 1917. The task of the Division was to keep such continual pressure on the enemy opposite, that he should feel that that part of the Hindenburg Line in our front was really being worked up to. The advanced posts of Epéhy—Lempire—Ronssoy in front of his outpost line had been captured, and a footing gained in his outpost line, which was covered by a belt of wire, south of Tombois Farm. The object of the attack on this night was to gain this line of wire and the fortified outposts along it on the rest of our Division front, which was on a very wide one. The operation is accurately described. It was a case where good arrangement, determination to win, and the initiative of those on the spot led to success in spite of all obstacles.

It was said that on this occasion the Army Commander called up the Corps Commander on the telephone, and asked whether the operation would be carried out in such weather. The Corps Commander's reply showed his confidence in, and knowledge of, the troops employed, when he replied in the affirmative without even asking the Division.

The third occasion was on August 16, 1917, at St. Julien, during the Third Battle of Ypres, when the Battalion and certain battalions of the 145th Brigade completed the capture of St. Julien, and only circumstances over which the Battalion had no control prevented their success being still more complete.

The last occasion was on June 15, 1918, when the Austrians made their great attempt to break our line along the Asiago Plateau. Although, as the history relates, the Battalion was only holding the rear line on that day, yet by its action it enabled the troops fighting in front of this line to carry out their difficult task, showing what confidence they felt in the Bucks Battalion. The initiative with which the Battalion, finding that the right of the 1/4th Oxford & Bucks Battalion was exposed by the line being left unoccupied beyond our own posts, pushed out to close this gap, was of especial value to their side.

FOREWORD

During the first few days of November, the same year, the Battalion showed how it could play its part in that last phase of victory, when, after the long and arduous struggle, the enemy finally broke, and the fruits of victory had to be gathered by a vigorous pursuit. Truly has the Battalion played a great and glorious part in this great War.

R. FANSHAWE,
Major-General.

July 1, 1920.

CONTENTS

CHAPTER I
FROM MOBILISATION TO PLOEGSTEERT . . 1

CHAPTER II
HÉBUTERNE 13

CHAPTER III
THE SOMME 24

CHAPTER IV
THE SOMME 36

CHAPTER V
LE SARS—CAPPY 45

CHAPTER VI
THE GERMAN RETIREMENT . . . 54

CHAPTER VII
THE THIRD BATTLE OF YPRES . . . 69

CONTENTS

CHAPTER VIII
THE THIRD BATTLE OF YPRES—VIMY . . 83

CHAPTER IX
ITALY 91

CHAPTER X
THE AUSTRIAN ATTACK OF JUNE 15 . . 103

CHAPTER XI
RAIDS 115

CHAPTER XII
THE AUSTRIAN DÉBÂCLE. 123

CHAPTER XIII
AFTER THE ARMISTICE—THE END . . . 138

APPENDIX I
OPERATION ORDERS 144

APPENDIX II
ROLLS OF OFFICERS WHO TOOK PART IN THE MAIN ACTIONS OF 1916—1917—1918 . . 163

APPENDIX III
HONOURS AND DECORATIONS GAINED BY OFFICERS OF THE 1ST BUCKS BATTALION . . . 172

APPENDIX IV

Honours and Decorations gained by Warrant Officers, N.C.O.'s, and Men of the First Bucks Battalion while serving with the Battalion 176

APPENDIX V

Roll of Officers who served with the 1st Bucks Battalion during the Period March 1915—December 1918 . . . 179

APPENDIX VI

Nominal Roll of Warrant Officers, N.C.O.'s and Men who served with the Battalion during the Period March 1915—December 1918. 197

APPENDIX VII

Translation of the Italian Diploma . . 215

ILLUSTRATIONS

LT.-COL. L. L. C. REYNOLDS, D.S.O., T.D. *Frontispiece*	
	FACING PAGE
BATTALION OFFICERS, CHELMSFORD, MARCH 1915 .	4
A TYPICAL FLANDERS ROAD	8
THE 1ST BUCKS BATTALION CEMETERY, PLOEGSTEERT	8
COY. H.Q. IN THE " KEEP " AT HÉBUTERNE . .	16
HÉBUTERNE CHURCH, 1915	16
OUR TRENCHES IN FOREGROUND. GOMMECOURT WOOD IN BACKGROUND, WITH Z HEDGE IN FRONT OF IT	18
REST BILLETS, COUIN	18
LT.-COL. F. O. WETHERED, C.M.G., V.D.; LT.-COL. C. P. DOIG, D.S.O.; LT.-COL. L. C. HAWKINS, T.D. .	20
THE 1ST BUCKS BATTALION CEMETERY, HÉBUTERNE .	22
FRONT LINE COY. H.Q., LE SARS	48
REPRODUCTION OF A FRENCH POSTCARD OF PÉRONNE AFTER GERMAN EVACUATION IN MARCH 1917. (WITH CRUDE TRANSLATION)	54
PÉRONNE CHURCH	58
RONSSOY SUGAR FACTORY	58
CHEDDAR VILLA, ST. JULIEN	72

ILLUSTRATIONS

	FACING PAGE
THE STEENBEEK	76
THE BATTLE-FIELD NEAR ST. JULIEN, YPRES	76
RESERVE BATTALION H.Q., KABERLABA N.	120
THE C.-IN-C. PRESENTING MEDALS TO THE BATTALION AT GRANEZZA, AUGUST 1918	120
THE LAST QUARTER GUARD, ITALY, 1919	140
THE CADRE, 1919	142
ITALIAN MEMORIAL CERTIFICATE	216

MAPS AND PANORAMA

MAP No. 1.	SOMME OPERATIONS, JULY TO SEPTEMBER 1916	28
„ No. 2.	ATTACK ON TOMBOIS FARM, NIGHT 16/17, APRIL, 1917	60
„ No. 3.	THIRD BATTLE OF YPRES, JULY TO OCTOBER, 1917	80
„ No. 4.	ITALIAN OPERATIONS	*In pocket of cover*
„ No. 5.	AREA RAIDED ON NIGHT 26/27 AUGUST, 1918	116
PANORAMA FROM MT. TORLE		128

IMPORTANT NOTE

On the eve of publication, and too late for mention in the text, the officer commanding the 1st Bucks Battalion has received a letter from the War Office enclosing a translation of an Italian diploma and a facsimile in bronze of a gold medal presented to H.M. the King of Italy. Copies of the letter and diploma will be found printed in Appendix VII to this Record, and will be read with pride.

It will be seen that, out of all the Infantry Battalions engaged on the Italian Front, the 1st Bucks Battalion, the 1st Battalion Royal Welsh Fusiliers, and the H.A C. are the three selected recipients of this high honour.

THE
FIRST BUCKINGHAMSHIRE BATTALION
1914—1919

CHAPTER I

FROM MOBILISATION TO PLOEGSTEERT

August 1914 *to June* 1915

IT seemed almost incredible news, too good to be true, when on March 28, 1915, we received orders to proceed overseas. The 48th Division, of which we were part, had been mobilised on August 4, 1914, immediately on the outbreak of war. From that day our thoughts and hearts had been at the Front—and how we longed to follow them; if war news sometimes seemed bad it only made us the keener to be given our chance, more confident that we should help to turn the tide. Since then eight months had all but gone, long months of waiting, full of hopes and expectations so often to be disappointed, but now to be realised.

The Division was commanded by Major-General H. N. C. Heath, C.B., and consisted, as regards Infantry, of three Brigades—the Warwick, the Gloucester and Worcester, and the South Midland, which later became known as the 143rd, 144th, and 145th Infantry Brigades respectively. The 145th Infantry Brigade, commanded by Brigadier-General W. K. McLintock, consisted of four battalions: the 1/5th Battalion Gloucestershire

2 FIRST BUCKINGHAMSHIRE BATTALION

Regiment, the 1/4th Battalion Oxfordshire and Buckinghamshire Light Infantry, our own 1/1st Buckinghamshire Battalion, and the 1/4th Battalion Royal Berkshire Regiment.

Our Battalion was at first commanded by Lieutenant-Colonel F. O. Wethered, T.D., but this officer was taken ill in January 1915, and shortly afterwards the command was taken over by Lieutenant-Colonel C. P. Doig, Seaforth Highlanders.

Before mobilisation, the Bucks Battalion had not adopted the four-company system, but on outbreak of war this was at once organised. The following table shows how it was effected, and from what districts each company drew its recruits:

A Company	.	Marlow	}	A Company.
B ,,	.	High Wycombe		Captain L. L. C. Reynolds.
C ,,	.	Buckingham	}	B Company.
D ,,	.	Aylesbury		Captain L. W. Crouch.
E ,,	.	Slough	}	C Company.
F ,,	.	Wolverton		Captain G. E. W. Bowyer.
G ,,	.	Wolverton	}	D Company.
H ,,	.	High Wycombe		Captain E. V. Birchall.

The order to mobilise was received at Battalion Headquarters at Aylesbury at 6.30 p.m. on August 4, 1914. With the exception of the Wolverton Company, whose train was put into a siding owing to some misunderstanding, the whole Battalion was concentrated at Aylesbury before midnight on the 4th/5th. On the evening of the 5th we entrained for Cosham, the Battalion's war station, where transport was drawn, and three days were spent in digging trenches on the hills overlooking Portsmouth harbour.

Entraining again on August 9, the Battalion journeyed to Swindon, where a week's hard training was carried out, and after this a succession of moves, partly by rail, but mostly on foot, carried us via Dunstable,

Hitchin, Ware, Harlow and Great Dunmow to Chelmsford, where we arrived on August 25. Here, with the exception of a most bitterly cold fortnight in November spent under canvas at Great Totham, where the Battalion was employed digging defences of the East coast, we remained for seven months, training vigorously and praying for our early dispatch to France.

After so long a sojourn in Chelmsford we had become part and parcel of the town, and even rumour, who for four months had been sending us out " in two days' time," had given us up as hopeless. Some had even started wondering whether, after all, the war could not be won without the Bucks Battalion winning it.

However, here at last was the order we had longed for, and this time there seemed to be no mistake about it.

Officers, who had spent six months buying useless things for their kit, now bought more feverishly and imprudently than ever. The men took it all very quietly, on the principle, no doubt, that " an order is an order, but it's got to be cancelled at least twice before being carried out." For once they were wrong, and on the afternoon of March 30, 1915, the Battalion paraded for the last time on the Chelmsford parade-ground and marched to the station.

Chelmsford turned out *en masse* and gave us a first-rate send-off. Not a few had become fond of us and we of them, but we were too cheerful and thankful to be off to allow our farewells to damp our spirits. At 5.30 p.m. the train steamed out of Chelmsford Station and we were on our way to the war. The detrainment and embarkation at Folkestone were carried out without difficulty, and at 11 p.m. we were at Boulogne.

The few *Boulonnais* who were about did not

appear to rate our arrival nearly so highly as we did ourselves. In fact, to be honest, they were not interested. They had seen thousands of British troops already, and confidently counted on seeing millions more.

Eventually, we got formed up and on the move, being told that there was a march of four or five miles ahead of us. After following a very winding road for some two hours, we scaled a young mountain and found ourselves at Ostrehove camp. Why the wind invariably blows icy blasts, from all directions, on to this peculiarly unattractive spot, is not known, but apparently it always does. However, the majority of the tents remained standing throughout the night, though few of us got much sleep, on account of the cold. Anxiety to see France in daylight turned us all out of our tents early, and breakfast brought with it rumours of moving which proved to be correct.

At 3.30 p.m. on March 31, 1915, the Battalion paraded and marched down another tortuous road to Pont de Briques, where it entrained. We had not thought much about the composition of a French troop-train, but our first sight of one was, to say the least, a disappointment. It consisted of some twenty cattle-trucks, each marked to hold between forty and fifty men. This particular train, being a novelty, did not have such scathing remarks passed on it as those which later had the honour of carrying us, but even this one was not spoken of nicely. When, finally, the guard blew his penny horn, and " puffing Billy " (as the engine was immediately dubbed) got busy, laughter knew no bounds, and French railways were put down as a bad show.

After some five hours of this very crowded travelling, we arrived at Cassel, and detrained at 11 p.m. A three-hour march brought us to Terdeghem, where our billets lay. Accommodation being very scanty, many of us

Back Row: G. M. A. Hampden. J. B. Hill. A. S. Vernon. F. D. Earle. P. L. Wright. J. W. Backhouse. R. G. Ellis. E. L. Wright. G. G. Jackson. O. V. Viney. N. S. Reid. H. V. Combs. B. Green.

Centre Row: G. R. Crouch. E. V. Birchall. L. L. C. Reynolds. L. C. Hawkins. Lt.-Col. C. P. Doig. A. J. N. Bartlett. L. W. Crouch. G. E. W. Bowyer. P. A. Hall

Front Row: E. N. C. Woollerton. G. V. Neave. A. D. B. Brown. N. B. Williamson. F. G. B. Reynolds. L. E. Hughes.

BATTALION OFFICERS, CHELMSFORD, MARCH 1915.

spent the warm night in the open. The wind changed during that night, with the result that we heard the guns for the first time in the morning. We had arrived in the neighbourhood of the war.

We were expecting to move hourly closer up to the line, but for three nights we remained at Terdeghem, the only event of importance being an inspection on April 2 of the Brigade at Steenvoorde by General Sir H. Smith-Dorrien, who was at that time commanding the 2nd Army. We then moved to billets on the Oultersteene-Bailleul Road (S.E. of Méteren), where two more nights were spent, and on April 7 the Battalion marched via Bailleul and Armentières to Le Bizet, for trench attachment to the 4th Division. These two marches, although only some twenty-five miles, were formidable ones. Feet, in spite of the number of route marches carried out at home, started to blister on these cobbled roads. Heat, dust, and the monotony of the Flanders country, increased the discomfort. Billeting parties, sent on in advance on bicycles, had not yet learnt that it was no kindness to meet the Battalion five miles from billets and assure them that twenty minutes would see them in.

On April 8, all companies were attached to different units of the 4th Division (2nd Monmouthshire Regiment, 2nd Battalion Lancashire Fusiliers, 2nd Battalion Essex Regiment), for instruction in the method of holding trenches. It is doubtful whether our brains ever worked again so feverishly and incontinently as they did on that first march up to trenches. The march was carried out in pitch darkness, along a road which ran up to and through the British front line. Guides met us five or six hundred yards behind the line, and escorted us as far as the trenches. These guides, treating us like the ignorant children that we were, kept the pace as slow as possible, knowing quite truly that we liked that the least.

Several of them, not content with this, insisted on telling one how the Boche was in the habit of raking that road with machine-gun fire at that hour precisely, and how two men had met their end there the previous evening. We arrived therefore with nerves highly strung.

The number of questions put to our hosts during that night must have seemed to them phenomenal. How far away was Fritz ? Did he do much shooting ? Was he likely to attack ? Had there been many casualties ? And a thousand more such questions, all of which were asked for curiosity and with the object of acquiring knowledge, but could well be taken to mean we were frightened out of our lives.

Dawn enlightened us considerably and interested us no less, and by nightfall we thought ourselves veterans at the game. There was, in fact, a tendency to treat the Boche with much less respect than he was entitled to, under the circumstances. Sniping was active, and the Germans were no mean shots at the 50 to 150 yards which separated their trenches from ours.

On the morning of the second day, April 9, the 4th Division exploded a mine under the enemy trenches. This very naturally nettled the Boche considerably, and he retaliated by shelling our line. One shell entered and burst inside the remains of an old house, containing our A Company headquarters. By a miracle everyone escaped unhurt, though many of their possessions were never seen again.

Our attachment for instruction lasted four days, two of which were spent in the front line, and two in support.

On April 12, the Battalion marched to billets at Steenwerck, some eight miles distant. Here, although all companies were again very scattered in farms, the inhabitants were most tolerant to us. Provided their manure was left alone, and their pigs allowed to move

FROM MOBILISATION TO PLOEGSTEERT

about as they wished, no objection would be raised to us. The importance in life of owning large quantities of manure speedily became evident. One might almost say that a man's riches were gauged by the size and aroma of the heap he possessed.

On the 14th the Commanding Officer, Adjutant and company commanders received orders to reconnoitre the line with a view to the Battalion relieving the 1st Battalion Somersetshire Light Infantry, who were in support in Ploegsteert Wood.

As one tour in the line was so like another, it is proposed to give a general outline of our life during the next two months, which were spent at Ploegsteert or in billets at Romarin.

The weather, during the first few days we passed in reserve in the wood, was gorgeous, and one felt grateful to those who had been responsible for choosing this spot for us to carry on our war. Our quarters were certainly not luxurious, consisting chiefly of what cover could be made with a waterproof sheet. But with the whole wood at our disposal, comfort of a kind was quite obtainable, provided one made the effort. Some Canadians who had been there before us had indeed started building operations, and erected a magnificent log hut, known as Plugstreet Hall. C Company were fortunate enough to secure this as their company headquarters at first, to the complete astonishment of D Company, who had no notion that such a palpable error could be made.

To enhance our enjoyment of those first few days in the wood, we were troubled with very few shells, but few of us will forget the distant thunder, which reached our ears coming from the direction of Hill 60, on the evening of the second or third day we were there. It was the first real, continuous roar of bombardment we had heard, and it impressed us mightily, suggesting to our minds that we were living in a fool's paradise.

The trees had been damaged very little, and the fresh green foliage and undisturbed bird life made it most difficult to believe in the existence of a war, and that at no great distance. Paths had been cleared in all useful directions through the wood, and duck-board tracks laid down to prevent the paths becoming mud channels in wet weather. The majority of these tracks were known by London names, such as The Strand, Rotten Row, Hyde Park Corner, but here and there names like "Dead Horse Corner" appeared. All the houses behind our lines had names, those which received the most attention from the German gunners being the best known: Hull's Burnt Farm, Three Huns, St. Yves Post Office, are names which conjure up innumerable memories.

The trenches most frequently held by the Battalion in this area were situated in front of the village of St. Yves, the line being held with three companies in the firing line and one in support. The 1/5th Battalion Gloucestershire Regiment relieved us every four days, when we were in the habit of moving either into the wood or back to billets at Romarin.

The trenches consisted of sandbagged walls, a duck-board bottom, a host of large flies and an enormous smell. The flies were kindly quiescent at night, but the smell—never; presumably because it had so many sources to draw upon that the wind could never really help us.

Our fire trench ran about 200 yards from the German front line, though in places the two trenches approached to within 100 yards of each other. To show one's head over the top of the parapet was therefore risky, in view of the enemy snipers, who were really first-rate shots and always on the look-out for a target. Desultory rifle fire was kept up by both sides throughout the twenty-

A TYPICAL FLANDERS ROAD.

THE 1st BUCKS BATTALION CEMETERY, PLOEGSTEERT.

four hours, always increasing in volume at "stand to," each morning and evening, and generally reaching the most absurd pitch about one hour after darkness. The lunacy of expending thousands of rounds of small arms ammunition per diem, in this way, had yet to be fully realised.

Shells were not nearly so plentiful on either side. Certainly the Boche fired considerably more than did our gunners, who—poor souls—had next to none to fire. The main targets for German gunners were:

(1) Any new sandbagging in the front line;
(2) St. Yves Post Office and Hull's Burnt Farm;
(3) Battalion Headquarters.

His dislike for the last-named was often intense. On one memorable afternoon he put 67 six-inch high-explosive and incendiary shells within a 70-yards radius of their domain. This shoot was watched by our front line with enormous interest, bordering with a callous few on satisfaction.

Rifle grenades were used extensively by the enemy, and as far as possible by us. But the German grenades had a far greater range than our own, which could only be employed where trenches were within 170 yards of each other. One German grenade, fired into the rear of A Company's trench, wounded two company commanders, another officer, a company sergeant-major, and five other ranks.

On occasions when anything in the nature of an attack was taking place on some other part of the front, we received orders to make a demonstration. Some idea of what these demonstrations consisted of should be given here, not only to suggest their utter futility, but to show the gradual way in which we learnt to play the game of frightfulness. The demonstration would be carried out by all units who happened to be holding the Divisional front.

9 a.m.—Long-range rifle fire directed on roads in rear of enemy trenches.

11 a.m.—Artillery bombard a certain section or sections of enemy trench with the object of breaching their parapet. (Nothing was ever to be seen taking place at the spot indicated, but on more than one occasion shells did reach the war zone, and went dangerously near breaching *our* parapet.)

11.5 a.m.—Whole of front-line garrison open five minutes' rapid fire on German front line.

1.45 p.m.—A few rifle grenades fired by companies within range of enemy.

4.15 p.m.—A trench mortar fired; three rifle grenades fired at same time from either side of it.

6.15 p.m.—Long-range rifle fire directed on roads in rear.

The enemy seldom paid the smallest attention to these demonstrations, except possibly by spending five minutes in flooding our trench with rifle grenades.

Soon after one of our demonstrations, however, the Boche pulled our leg quite successfully. He had been very quiet during one afternoon, and also during "stand to" in the evening. About an hour after "stand down" every German in that part of the world started shouting at the top of his voice. The immediate result (as had been anticipated by the enemy) was to draw all our men on to their fire-steps; men who were working in the trench, and those carrying rations, with one accord set aside their work, took up their rifles, and manned the parapet to see what was happening. They at once became good targets for the Hun, who opened rapid fire on our parapet, and hurled at us every available grenade he could lay his hands on. Twenty minutes later silence reigned again. We had sustained several casualties, for although it was dark and no shots could be aimed ones, a few of them succeeded in finding homes.

It is permissible perhaps to give one illustration of the fact that our gunners were at this time not too well supplied with shells, and that gunnery had not yet attained that high standard of proficiency which it afterwards reached. A house which was occupied by a listening post from our centre company by night and by a German sniper by day, was causing us considerable annoyance, as it was placed so that from a window in the gable end the sniper could fire at anyone entering or leaving our right company headquarters, unless the movement was carried out on hands and knees. Captain Reynolds, who was commanding the centre company, applied for some sappers to come and blow the house up at night. That was refused, but he was told that the gunners would knock it down. This idea was not received enthusiastically, as the house was at so short a distance from our line. However, a battery of 15-pounders was ordered to carry out the shoot, and at 10 o'clock one morning, after we had carefully cleared that portion of our trench which came in the line of fire, the excitement started. Several gunner officers superintended the shoot. Twelve rounds were fired; only one hit the house, and that one caused no damage. One penetrated our own trench. We were then informed that the battery had expended their ration of shells for one week (12 rounds), and that they would have another go next week.

The company, however, were quite determined that the gunners should have no further "go's." The next morning, at "stand to," Captain Reynolds gave orders that one platoon was to open rapid fire at the gable end. This soon brought down the entire gable end, exposing the whole attic of the house. The sniper had lost his nest, and never fired from there again.

We were fortunate in our sector to be rather too far away from the enemy for mining operations, though in the sector on our right the 1/4th Battalion Oxford & Bucks L.I., who owned a section of trench known as the Birdcage, were blowing up or being blown up most days.

So much for our trench conditions and little excitements. Our billets lay at Romarin, a village about two and a half miles from Ploegsteert. Days here were spent in a variety of ways—making roads, digging rear lines, writing and censoring letters, kit inspections, baths, etc. Here also was enacted one of the real tragedies of the war, the surrender of our cameras.

The last period we spent in the line in these parts was in the Douve trenches facing Messines, after which we began on June 24 a four-day march to other climes.

Our casualties while in the Ploegsteert area were:

Officers:	Killed	None
	Wounded	5
Other ranks:	Killed	9
	Wounded	57

In the middle of June, owing to illness, Major-General H. N. C. Heath, C.B., handed over command of the Division to Major-General R. Fanshawe, C.B., D.S.O. (52nd L.I.).

CHAPTER II

HÉBUTERNE

June 1915 to June 1916

THERE followed a series of three night marches, via Vieux-Berquin, Merville, Busnettes, to Allouagne, which lies five miles west of Béthune. The night's march of June 26/27, from Vieux-Berquin to Busnettes, was a particularly unpleasant one, for we moved as a Division, and those who have taken part in a divisional march, on a dark night, will know that the constant but inevitable checking is apt to become very tiring. In addition, we arrived at Busnettes to find that a Brigade which should have left those billets that evening had decided not to move, with the result that we were forced to bivouac in a very damp orchard for the remainder of the night. We were far too weary to grouse, however, and were quite compensated the following morning on finding ourselves surrounded by cherry trees, the fruit on which was quite ripe. Colossal deals were at once done with the natives, and there were but few cherries left in the neighbourhood when we marched off.

The billets at Allouagne were the best we had yet seen, and quite a happy fortnight was spent here. Training was strenuous and carried out mostly in a neighbouring wood, called the Bois de Maraquet. This wood was said to resemble closely one with which we were to have more serious dealings, and many sinister rumours got about in regard to it.

On the morning of July 8, 1915, the Brigade rose early and lined a portion of the Lillers-Chocques road, down which Lord Kitchener was to pass together with Field Marshal Lord French and the Prince of Wales. Four cars passed hurriedly by. These well-known officers were probably inside them.

On the 12th, the Battalion was moved in to bivouacs close to Nœux-les-Mines, every man available during the two succeeding days being put on to digging a new rear line. It was quite thought that the Division was to take over new trenches in these parts, but not a bit of it : on July 16 we suddenly got orders to move, and marched the whole of that night, in a deluge of rain, to billets in Lières, passing again within a stone's throw of Allouagne. Everyone was wet through after the first twenty minutes, and, as the whole march occupied six hours and the rain was continuous, our entry into Lières may well be pictured. Night marches had previously been carried out more or less in silence, but at the end of some two hours of this march, word was passed down the line that the men could sing. Instead of having a really good grouse, and declaring that they were of course allowed to sing when the conditions were such as to make any lightheartedness impossible, they saw only the humour of the situation and sang lustily for several hours.

Our probable destination entirely baffled us, and there appeared good grounds for believing any, or all, the following rumours which were at this time prevalent : (1) The Dardanelles, (2) Dunkirk, (3) Ypres, (4) attachment to the French at Arras. The fourth appeared the least probable, as we were marching so very hard in the opposite direction. However, on the 18th this situation became a trifle less obscure, as we were put into a train at Berguette, in which we slowly proceeded to Doullens. A two hours' march from here took us to some woods at Marieux, where we arrived at 4 a.m. to bivouac.

HÉBUTERNE 15

On July 20, the Division started to relieve the French in the line in front of the village of Hébuterne, the Battalion being in reserve, with two companies at Sailly-au-Bois and two companies at Bayencourt. Both these villages were then a mass of flies, owing to the general filth everywhere, and, as the weather was extremely hot, life in these billets was none too pleasant.

The trenches, which the Battalion took over on July 24, lay some 100 to 300 yards east of Hébuterne, and were at this time good and quiet. Unlike the front line at Ploegsteert, where the trenches consisted of sand-bagged barricades, these trenches were dug down about 6 feet deep all along. The parapets were low, and consequently little visible to the enemy. What there was of them had no pretence of being bullet-proof, though this was apparently a matter of small importance, bullets being so rare owing to our line being anything from 300 to 1,000 yards distant from the Boche trenches.

Our dugouts had the outward appearance of real luxury, owing to a large portion of the furniture of Hébuterne having been imported into them. Four-poster beds existed in quite a number, but owing to the quantities of small vermin and mice which had made their homes in them, they proved to be most undesirable, and were almost all scrapped before we had been a week in the line.

For the first fortnight the Division was supported by French guns, with apparently no shortage of ammunition. Their gunners were most obliging, and took endless trouble to do everything in their power for our front-line infantry. If asked to retaliate when our front trenches were being heavily shelled, they would throw at least three times as many shells back—and then ring up to know if we were entirely satisfied with their work. Satisfied indeed—we revelled, for the first time in our lives, in the sight of the Boche receiving far more in return than what he had hurled at us.

Brigade and Battalion headquarters were both in the village, and for some time occupied quarters above ground, though they were compelled eventually, when the shelling of the village became more frequent, to take to cellars and dugouts.

Company cookers were housed in the village, and from them all food was carried up to the front line through communication trenches.

The Battalion in Brigade reserve occupied billets above ground in Hébuterne, and of this one company was detailed as garrison of a large portion of the village defences, in case of attack. This company had considerably the best of the billets, living in what was known as the " keep," a really charming spot amongst orchards and trees; and all those who were then present with the Battalion and still live will cherish happy memories of it.

As will be gathered, it was a very quiet war that was waged round Hébuterne when we first arrived, there being a tacit agreement, between ourselves and the Germans opposite, that provided they would leave Hébuterne quiet, we would not entirely destroy Gommecourt, and again, if they decided to leave Sailly alone, we in our turn would keep our hands off Bucquoy and Puisieux. For all that, it was not pleasant to reflect on the fact that, should the enemy choose, he could perfectly well destroy our billets, and with them ourselves, in the short space of an hour. What actually occurred was a gradual warming up of artillery fire on the villages by both sides, and it became just as gradually evident that life above ground was not only unwise, but exceedingly foolish, with the result that, after several months' work, dugouts had been constructed for the entire garrison of Hébuterne.

COY. H.Q. IN THE "KEEP" AT HÉBUTERNE.

HÉBUTERNE CHURCH, 1915.

HÉBUTERNE

During the first six weeks, reliefs of this sector of the front line, by the 5th Battalion Gloucestershire Regiment and ourselves, took place every eight days. These reliefs were really only notable on account of one particular incident, which created not a little feeling at the time, and has for ever since been the cause of constant good-natured banter between the two Battalions concerned.

When the 5th Gloucesters took over the front line from the French, the latter were generous enough to hand over to them, with the line, a good milking cow, which was duly passed on to us on our taking over the front line. It transpired afterwards that the Gloucesters surrendered the cow to us not because they regarded her as belonging to the Battalion which happened to be in Hébuterne (as we considered should be the case), but because they thought she would not appreciate the continual move to and from Sailly, where the rest billets lay. After some four weeks of this periodical change of ownership, instead of our being sent back to Sailly on relief, we were only sent as far as the western outskirts of Hébuterne, so that the field wherein the cow grazed lay just midway between the Gloucester headquarters and our own. Now came the trouble—the Gloucesters discovered the cow to be dry every morning at the usual milking hour. Accusations poured forth against our Adjutant, and he alone is able to say whether these were justified. In any case the cow was never again handed over to us, on taking over the line, and it is believed that she eventually died of excessive exercise taken between Sailly and Hébuterne, and from the overanxiety on the part of all ranks in the Gloucesters to extract their full share of milk. This at any rate was our explanation of her disappearance, though it is by no means certain that it will accurately coincide with the official account to be given by that Battalion.

18 FIRST BUCKINGHAMSHIRE BATTALION

Throughout the six months during which our Battalion held K sector, patrolling was most active ; this was very necessary if we were to prevent the enemy establishing control of the extensive " No Man's Land " which lay between us. With the exception of a Z-shaped hedge, known as the Z hedge, which lay out in front of the left company, " No Man's Land " was very featureless. This hedge, however, provided no end of excitement, for it was most difficult at night for either side to locate and dislodge a party which had got out first and taken up a position in it. But the enemy were seldom, if ever, permitted to do this owing to our constant patrolling, and after some months they gave up all except periodical visits.

Having gained supremacy of the hedge at night, it proved of some value to us in pushing larger patrols along it towards the German lines. On one night Captain N. S. Reid, who had previously carried out some daring patrols, succeeded in reaching the enemy wire and crawling into it with his party. Four German sentries could be distinguished along a stretch of about 80 yards of trench. Gradually our patrol approached one of the sentries, who was occupying a sap-head which we knew as " Y " sap. The sentry challenged when our men were within a few yards of him. For answer Captain Reid fired his revolver, and the sentry was seen to fall across his parapet. An excited buzz of conversation rose from the trench, and while this was going on our patrol was able to retire into some dead ground before the enemy opened rapid fire. Eventually our men returned without a casualty, having ascertained accurately the position of at least four German sentry posts.

About September, the 5th Gloucesters took over the trenches on our right, and from then onwards to December we were relieved by the 6th Battalion Gloucestershire Regiment (144th Infantry Brigade) every eight days.

OUR TRENCHES IN FOREGROUND. GOMMECOURT WOOD IN BACKGROUND, WITH Z HEDGE IN FRONT OF IT.

REST BILLETS, COUIN.

HÉBUTERNE

Each Battalion on relief went back some four miles to the village of Couin. There was nothing particularly attractive about this village on the hill, but owing to the regularity of our visits to it and the duration of our stays there, we became almost part of the place, with the result that we became fond of it.

On the way back to these billets from the trenches during the evening of January 27, 1916, the Commanding Officer, Lieutenant-Colonel C. P. Doig, D.S.O., sustained severe injuries through a fall from his horse, and Major L. C. Hawkins assumed command.

Towards the middle of the month the Battalion had to bid good-bye to K sector. We had done so much work on it in the way of defence and comfort that the order came as a bitter blow, the more so as the trenches we were to take over were in the last state of decay and were rapidly falling in everywhere. They lay more to the S.E. of Hébuterne, in very much lower ground than K sector.

We were warned that a bad state of affairs existed in this, G sector, and were told that the Battalion had been singled out for bettering it. The result was that every man was out to do his utmost with the spade and show some substantial improvement, and it was not long before a very marked change had been effected, and life was made a little more possible. But it must be admitted that when frost gave way to heavy rains, it became impossible to keep every trench in the sector open, and on several occasions long lengths of even the front line became impassable. Our efforts to keep open the communication trenches Jena, Jean-Bart and Vercingétorix were positively heart-rending, and the results achieved, even in good weather, were in no way proportionate to the amount of work put on to them.

In addition, the enemy artillery became daily more active, and their shooting, which was most exceptionally good, accounted for quite a number of casualties, including amongst the killed Captain J. W. Backhouse and 2/Lieutenant R. B. Furley, the last-named having only joined us two weeks previously.

During the period that the Battalion held G sector, the enemy undertook several raids, though on no occasion did he succeed in entering the Battalion's trenches. All these raids were preceded by extremely heavy bombardments, usually of about an hour's duration. In one of these attacks, which the Germans delivered at 2 a.m. on March 19, they employed a great number of gas shells, but owing to the amount of practice the men had been given in adjusting their gas helmets quickly, these shells did us little harm; in fact, in one way they did us good, as the bombardment tended to increase our confidence in gas helmets for the future.

In this same bombardment, the use and importance of yet another protective appliance was brought out for the first time. This was the steel helmet, which had not as yet been made a general issue, but which had been sent to us in very small quantities to test and report on. Two men who were wearing these helmets had them struck by large fragments of shell. In one case the helmet was merely badly dinted, and in the other, although the steel was ripped open, the shell fragment lost its sting and failed to penetrate the man's head.

In all these bombardments our trenches invariably suffered considerably, the more so when *Minenwerfers* were employed in large numbers, as these shells made the most gigantic craters, which completely obliterated all traces of dugouts and trench.

At the beginning of April the Battalion was relieved in G sector, and took over trenches between G and K sectors. These were better but by no means good.

Fighting patrols, with the coming of better weather, were now sent out more frequently, and brisk fighting

LT.-COL. F. O. WETHERED, C.M.G., V.D.

LT.-COL. C. P. DOIG, D.S.O.

LT.-COL. L. C. HAWKINS, T.D.

HÉBUTERNE 21

in " No Man's Land " resulted. The most successful of these were undertaken by B Company (Captain L. W. Crouch), and were carried out under the leadership of Captain H. V. Combs. The main road from Hébuterne to Puisieux ran through this company's line across " No Man's Land." At some distance before it reached the German line a sunken road branched from it. This road also crossed the enemy trenches. In the sunken road, close to the junction and about 100 yards from the German front line, were sixteen poplar trees. Our reconnoitring patrols had heard the enemy digging here at night very regularly, and it was considered a good opportunity for a fighting patrol to take up a position before the enemy's working party came out, and engage them with fire, while another party endeavoured to cut off their retreat.

Captain Combs with twenty-one N.C.O.'s and men reached the Sixteen Poplars soon after 7 p.m. on March 6. At 10 p.m. some Germans came up, entered the Poplars and started to work with shovels. No scouting had been carried out by them previously, which made it appear that some further enemy party had done this without being seen by our patrol. The latter was now split up, one party being sent to engage the workers with bombs, the other being sent down the road to intercept the enemy should they retire.

Everything worked according to plan, except that a larger number of the enemy existed in the Poplars than had been seen to enter them. Efforts were made to get them to surrender before bombing, but they preferred to fight. Our bombs played havoc in their midst, and caused those who remained to fly down the road towards their line. Our second party further diminished their numbers, L/Cpl. R. Colbrook, Ptes. J. Goldswain and H. Hazzard standing in the middle of the road to hold up the rush. Of the Germans who escaped the bullets and bayonets of these men the majority made off across country in a southerly direction. Large parties of the enemy now appeared from out of their wire, but our patrol were able to save themselves just in time from being overwhelmed. As a result of this encounter, at least twenty of the enemy were killed, while our casualties consisted of three slightly wounded.

Efforts were made to repeat this performance the following month, Captain H. V. Combs going out during the evening of April 1 with 2/Lieutenant R. Aitken and twenty-five other ranks. On this occasion the Germans were before us, and in much larger numbers. A great fight ensued and casualties occurred on both sides.

The following account of the action appeared in the VIII Corps summaries of April 3 and 4:

April 3.—" A patrol of two officers and twenty-five other ranks advanced during the night of April 1/2 in the direction of the Sixteen Poplars, with the intention of intercepting or capturing an enemy patrol. The enemy, apparently becoming early aware of this patrol, sent out a strong party of fifty men to oppose them. Our patrol after putting up a good fight retired safely behind our wire. Our casualties were four killed and two wounded, all of whom were brought in. Casualties to the enemy are unknown, though several of the bombs and rifle grenades fired were seen to burst well amongst them."

April 4.—" With reference to the patrol report in yesterday's summary, attention is drawn to the fact that the enemy were robbed of any possible identification by the calmness and resource shown by the patrol in getting back the killed and wounded to our trenches. The behaviour of all ranks was excellent. The withdrawal was slow and deliberate, and the men were well in hand.

THE 1st BUCKS BATTALION CEMETERY, HÉBUTERNE.

HÉBUTERNE

"Although it is difficult to distinguish one man's services from another, Sergt. W. J. Baldwin, L/Cpl. Goldswain, and L/Cpl. Jennings are deserving of special notice. Although Sergt. Baldwin was wounded, not only did he assist in carrying back one of the dead men, but came back again to help the covering party, when the enemy were almost on top of them. During the fight, several of the grenades which were thrown amongst the enemy caused considerable havoc, loud cries and groans being heard."

Our killed included L/Cpl. R. Colbrook and Pte. H. Hazzard, both of whom had distinguished themselves in the previous fight.

In May 1916, the Battalion was withdrawn from the front area, and sent back to rest at Beauval, where a fortnight was spent before moving to Agenvillers for a week. The most strenuous training was undertaken at these two places, and all manner of attacks practised, with a view to the coming British offensive.

During the march from Beauval to Agenvillers on June 2, the Commanding Officer, Lieutenant-Colonel L. C. Hawkins, was unfortunate enough to meet with a similar accident to that which befell Lieutenant-Colonel Doig, being thrown from his horse and seriously damaging his shoulder. Major L. L. C. Reynolds then assumed command, Captain A. B. Lloyd-Baker being appointed second in command.

On June 9, we moved back to the line, and held the Hébuterne trenches during the preparations for the coming big offensive. But for these operations it had been decreed that the 48th Division was to be in VII. Corps reserve, with the result that zero day (July 1, 1916) found us no nearer to the line than Couin Woods.

CHAPTER III

THE SOMME

July 1916

JULY 1, that day full of hopes and expectations, dawned at last. The previous week had been so noisy that away in Couin Woods one hardly noticed the increased bombardment denoting zero hour. Our departure for Mailly-Maillet had been fixed for 9 a.m., and by that time no rumours had reached us, let alone accurate news. However, after marching for about half an hour, word was passed down the column that Gommecourt Wood and Serre were ours and the attack was going well. This, although it proved later to be quite inaccurate, more than satisfied us at the time.

Our bivouacs, in the plantations to the south-west of Mailly-Maillet, did not tend to allay our restlessness, and listening to rumours and the 15-inch gun just below us was our only occupation.

In the afternoon, commanding officers and adjutants were summoned to Brigade Headquarters. They returned with plans for a proposed attack by the 8th, 144th and 145th Infantry Brigades. For this attack, which was to be a night operation, the Battalion was to be in Brigade reserve. Officers and N.C.O.'s were sent forward to reconnoitre the ground, so as to be able to support the assault, should assistance be necessary. The attacking battalions had actually formed up when, at ten minutes before zero, operations were cancelled.

There had been a change in the situation, and it had been decided that the VII. Corps should withdraw to the line it had held previous to attacking that morning. If this didn't spell failure, nothing did, and our hopes, which had been running sadly too high, crashed to the ground.

The Battalion remained in these bivouacs until the evening of July 8, when a move was made back to our old huts in Couin Woods. We were destined to carry out one further tour in the Hébuterne trenches, before our next move, which took place in motor lorries, after handing over our camp on July 14, at the Bus-Bayencourt-Sailly-Coigneux cross-roads, to the 11th Battalion Middlesex Regiment.

The attack farther south, commenced on the 1st inst., had been pressed forward satisfactorily during the days following and, when the news of the 13th that several more villages had been taken together with numerous prisoners was succeeded by our hasty dispatch in motor lorries to Senlis, our spirits rose once more. At Senlis we remained two days, during which time company commanders carried out useful reconnaissances of the ground round La Boisselle, with a view to ascertaining the best routes up to the line.

Orders having been received that the Battalion was to carry out a reconnaissance in force of the enemy line, which now ran between Ovillers and Pozières, a move was made on the evening of July 17 to some bivouacs on the Albert-Bapaume road, and as soon as it was dark we started up to the line, marching by platoons. Our orders were to ascertain whether the enemy was holding four certain points. If these points were not held by him, they were to be occupied by us and made into strong points. Heavy fighting was not to be undertaken.

The tasks were allotted to A and D Companies, each

company detailing one platoon for each of the points in its sector. B and C Companies supplied carrying parties.

At 1 a.m. during the night of July 17/18 the attacking platoons advanced in two lines of sections in file, with a point patrol immediately in front, led by the officer in charge. All points were found to be strongly held, and only one was occupied by us, viz. the most easterly, which was rushed by a platoon of A Company under 2/Lieutenant B. C. Rigden. This platoon, after driving off several bombing attacks and starting to consolidate, was ordered to withdraw, owing to the other points not having been taken. The reconnaissance, however, succeeded in its object, for the positions and strength of the German dispositions in this area were established.

The Battalion received the thanks and congratulations of the Divisional Commander. Our casualties were :

Officers :
Died of wounds . . 2/Lieutenant C. Hall (wounded severely in the head whilst bringing in casualties).
Missing . . . 2/Lieutenant R. C. Norwood (afterwards presumed killed).

Other ranks :
Killed 2
Wounded . . . 29
Missing . . . 27 (all later presumed killed).

Efforts on the part of search parties, who were sent out to find the missing, were fruitless, on account of the extreme darkness of the night.

THE SOMME

It was daylight when we started to move back, for the evacuation of the wounded had taken some little while. The trench which led us back presented one of the most gruesome sights we had yet seen, the floor being literally paved with the bodies of dead Englishmen. Nor was this all. Bodies lay over the parapet with rifle and fixed bayonet still held in the hand. Others were seated or lying on fire-steps in most lifelike positions. All had been killed at least a week previously, but burial parties had been too much occupied farther back to reach them as yet. It was not difficult to picture how these men had come by their end—a German machine gun skimming the parapet of the trench with deadly accuracy at the moment when our men were going over the top of it.

Although our orders were to move back to billets at Bouzincourt, we were under no delusions as to our fighting in this area being finished. The next blow to be struck was certain to be on a very much larger scale, and would probably affect the whole Battalion. Sure enough, the following day brought out the plans of Divisional Headquarters for an attack, which included the 145th Infantry Brigade.

The objectives of the Bucks Battalion were points A and B (Map No. 1) and the trenches adjoining these points. The 1/5th Battalion Gloucester Regiment were to attack on our left, and the 1/4th Battalion Oxford & Bucks Light Infantry on our right.

On July 19, the Battalion marched through Albert, and took over bivouacs from 1/5th Battalion Royal Warwickshire Regiment by the side of the Albert-Bapaume road. The following day was a busy one, what with the issuing of detailed orders, explanatory lectures to the N.C.O.'s and men, and the drawing and distribution of stores such as small arms ammunition, grenades, Verey lights, ground flares, shovels, all of which would have to be carried into the attack. C Company were most unlucky to have an accident, while detonating their bombs, which caused several casualties, and did not help them towards making a cheery start.

By 10.30 p.m. company commanders had given their final instructions to the men, and off we started for the front line, which lay some two and a half miles distant.

The Battalion (Lieutenant-Colonel L. L. C. Reynolds) was to attack in four lines, on a front of two companies, each in line of platoons in column of sections,—two sections in first line, one in second and one in third,— C Company (Captain G. G. Jackson) on the right, A Company (Captain N. S. Reid, M.C.) on the left. B Company (Captain L. W. Crouch) was in immediate support to both companies in one line, and formed the fourth wave. The enemy trench was situated about 325 yards distant from our front assembly trench (known as Sickle Trench), but a tape was laid by the Royal Engineers 175 yards from the German line, for the Battalion to form up on.

Zero was fixed for 2.45 a.m. on July 21, and at 2.15 a.m. our companies left Sickle Trench to form up on the tape. D Company (Captain E. V. Birchall) moved up to garrison Sickle Trench, as soon as the other three companies went forward to their tapes. Although no unusual amount of gunfire had as yet started, the enemy appeared to be very nervous, starting at 2.30 a.m. to send up large quantities of flares. This was disconcerting, as it showed too plainly that he was very much on the *qui vive*. A few minutes later, red flares went up from his lines. Whether these were a signal to his machine guns to open fire is not known, but open they did—and to some tune. So long as the hands of the watch did not point to 2.45 a.m. it was possible to lie flat, though even so some few were hit. The moment to go forward, however, arrived, and still the German machine guns chattered

MAP No. I.

SOMME OPERATIONS
JULY TO SEPTR 1916.

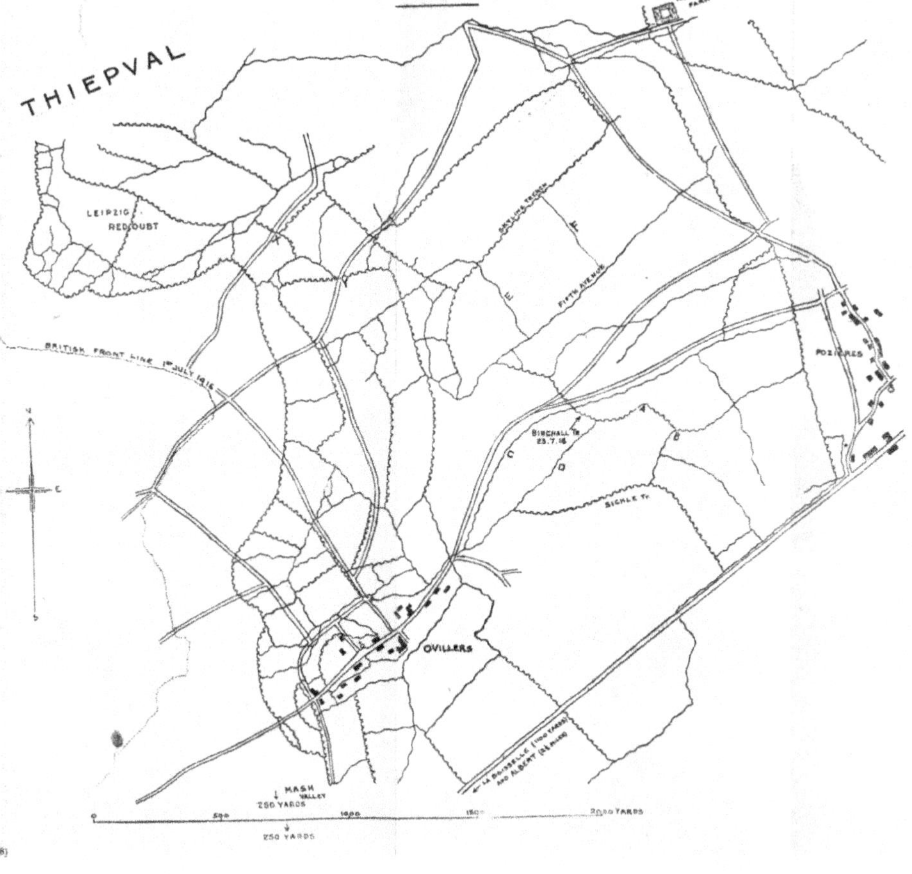

unceasingly. At 2.45 a.m. our guns opened with a roar, and shells flew just over our heads by the thousand, bursting their shrapnel in a line of flashes along the trench opposite us. It was the signal to advance. Few, however, were able to do so, for as men rose the machine guns of the enemy, upon whom our barrage appeared to be having no effect, scythed them down. Officers especially were dropping on all sides. A few isolated men reached the objective, but of these hardly any returned. The attack, including that portion of it made by the Gloucesters and Oxfords on our flanks, failed, and there seems little doubt that the enemy were aware of our intentions, probably owing to the bright moonlight. Casualties were heavy and included :

Officers.—Killed. Capt. L. W. Crouch.
2/Lieut. J. P. Chapman.
2/Lieut. C. G. Abrey.
2/Lieut. C. W. Trimmer.
Wounded. 2/Lieut. H. C. E. Mason.
2/Lieut. B. C. Rigden.
2/Lieut. H. V. Shepherd.
2/Lieut. A. P. Godfrey.
Wounded and prisoner. Capt. G. G. Jackson.

Other ranks.—Killed—8.
Wounded—96 (including 9 sergeants).
Missing—41 (all afterwards presumed killed).

Thus of the thirteen officers who were present with the three attacking companies, only four were unhit. Captain L. W. Crouch, who was killed, had for many years taken an active part in the training of his Aylesbury Company, and had rendered the Battalion great service during the period overseas. His death was felt most keenly by all ranks.

The failure of this attack was a great blow to the whole Battalion, as it was our first serious attack, and it was as disappointed and sadder men that we made our way back to the bivouacs: nearly everyone had lost a real pal, temporarily or for always.

For the survivors, sleep was the first consideration, for we were worn out; after that, reorganisation, with a view to the next attack, orders for which might arrive at any moment. We were terribly short of officers and short of N.C.O.'s, but fortunately, four officers had been left out of the attack with a view to coping with this emergency in case it should arise.

At 3 p.m. the following day (July 22), when our greatest efforts were concentrated on refitting, cleaning up, tracing the missing and the thousand things necessary after a battle, orders arrived to the effect that the Battalion was to move forward at 10 p.m. to some disused trenches, about two miles north. Here we were to stay for the night, in support of the remainder of the Brigade, who were to attack about midnight.

The attack was to be general along the greater part of the front held by the Fourth Army, while the Australians were to capture Pozières, with the 145th Infantry Brigade on their immediate left, in the order from right to left—1/4th Battalion Oxford & Bucks Light Infantry, 1/4th Battalion Royal Berkshire Regiment, 1/5th Battalion Gloucestershire Regiment, with the Bucks Battalion in reserve in the Mash Valley behind Ovillers.

Thus, at 10 p.m., we once more left our bivouacs and moved to these support positions.

At zero, half an hour after midnight (July 22/23), the host of guns all around us broke forth in one monstrous roar. The flashes of them were on all sides, and overhead we heard the shells, shrieking, whistling and whining through the air, on the way to German trenches. Gunfire and bursting shells lit up the country in fitful starts, giving sudden pictures of ridges of ground, ruins and woods, revealing their shapes. Rockets of every colour soared up from the German lines, in an endeavour to give to their guns, and headquarters in rear, some indication of the storm and trouble that assailed the garrison. A more wonderful or more terrible picture it is impossible to imagine.

News of the attack filtered back to us slowly, but it was soon after 3 a.m. that a message reached us from Brigade Headquarters that the Commanding Officer was required to report there immediately. He returned about 4 a.m. The 1/4th Oxfords and 1/4th Royal Berks had gained a footing in their objectives, but had suffered heavy casualties. They were cut off from the Australians by a large stretch of trench, which remained in enemy hands. On the extreme left, the 5th Gloucesters had been unsuccessful, thus leaving the Berks in a very perilous position.

Our orders were to attack and seize at all costs that portion of the line which had been attacked by the Gloucesters (Birchall Trench Map No. 1). Zero had been fixed for 6.30 a.m. on July 23, and as we had two miles of strange country to cover before reaching the "jumping off" trench, no time could be lost; orders were necessarily scanty, and much was left to the initiative of company commanders.

The attack was one of very great difficulty, owing to the run of the trenches. The enemy position was a stretch of trench approached by two communication trenches, C and D, each about 400 yards long. The right-hand one was in good condition, and met the enemy's trench at right angles, but the enemy had a bomb-stop about 50 yards from the junction. The left-hand communicator was badly damaged, and ran at an obtuse angle into the enemy's line.

B (Captain O. V. Viney) and D (Captain E. V. Birchall)

Companies were detailed for the attack. B Company assembled in the left communicator, D Company in the right.

Both companies, at zero, were to leave their trenches and to form inwards on the intervening space, which was about 200 yards. A Company (Captain N. S. Reid) were to be in support at the bottom of the communicator. C Company (Captain P. A. Hall) were to provide the necessary carrying parties, after the attack had been launched.

While moving up into position along the left-hand communicator, B Company suffered a very grave misfortune. Our heavy guns, which had been ordered to bombard the objective before zero, were shooting very short, and many of their shells fell right in the ranks of the company. Many casualties resulted, the trench being blocked with them in several places. Progress under these conditions became difficult in the extreme, and, in spite of the energy shown by the officer in command, the company just failed to reach their forming up positions in time to take any real part in the assault.

D Company, however, under the splendid leadership of Captain E. V. Birchall, were able to carry out their orders to the letter, and by dint of following our barrage so closely as to be almost in it, captured the whole position single-handed. A Company were immediately sent up to assist D Company in the work of consolidation and the clearing of prisoners, who were appearing in considerable numbers, coming over the top. These prisoners soon repented of this, however, as a battery of German guns, either intentionally or thinking they were our men, landed several shells in their midst and " dropped " quite a number ; the remainder took to the trenches. In all, the prisoners collected numbered two officers and about 150 men. One of these officers stated that the assault had taken them entirely by surprise, as they were waiting for the barrage to lift, before manning the parapet; and declared his opinion that the success of our assault, where two previous ones had failed, was due entirely to the way in which we had hugged the barrage.

Consolidation proceeded apace, thanks largely to the efforts of Captain N. S. Reid, and, at the end of a very short time, we were able to report that a bombing section had got in touch with the 4th Royal Berks on our right.

The enemy made frequent attempts during the day to retake the trench by means of bombing attacks, but they were in all cases successfully driven off. It was not till midnight of July 23/24 that he put down a heavy barrage on the captured line, though, to our great surprise, no attack developed, and at 12 noon the following day we were enabled, very thankfully, to hand over the position intact to the 5th Gloucesters and return to our bivouacs near Albert. Our casualties in this action were :

Officers.—Wounded (died of wounds) Capt. E. V. Birchall.
Wounded . Capt. O. V. Viney.
Lieut. E. N. C. Woollerton.
2/Lieut. R. E. M. Young.
2/Lieut. F. Niall.

Other ranks.—Killed—7.
Wounded—68.
Missing—8 (all later presumed killed).

The death of Captain Birchall was a very real loss and sorrow to the whole Battalion. Probably no company ever had a better, fairer or more capable commander, and no officer a truer friend. A large number of most valuable senior N.C.O.'s were also casualties in this action, including C.S.M. R. Read and Sergt. F. Barrett, both of whom were killed.

The success of this action amply compensated for the failure of our previous one, and the Battalion was proud indeed to receive the following letter from its Brigade Commander, Brigadier-General H. R. Done, D.S.O.:

To Lieutenant-Colonel L. L. C. Reynolds
" Please give my heartiest congratulations to all ranks of the regiment under your command, on their gallant and entirely successful attack on July 23. By this success, which was obtained in spite of heavy loss, you enabled the Brigade to carry out the whole of the task allotted, and also made secure the position of the troops who had already gained a footing in the enemy's position on your right."

The following was also received:
" The Army Commander wishes to thank all ranks of the 48th Division for their excellent work during the past ten days. By their exertions they have greatly extended our hold on Ovillers and have directly contributed towards the ultimate capture of Pozières."

As may well be imagined, the last ten days had left their mark on the Battalion. Our strength was reduced to a very low figure, and even this included a draft of sixty-eight privates, who had arrived on the evening of July 21, and of whose capabilities we did not know sufficient to warrant our taking them into action. As regards officers and N.C.O.'s the shortage was acute.

It was now decided that the Division should be withdrawn, and on July 26, at 7 a.m., the Battalion marched back to temporary billets at Arquèves, moving via Bouzincourt, Hédauville and Varennes. Here we remained forty-eight hours, before resuming the march to Beauval, via Raincheval and Beauquesne. The Battalion marched exceedingly well during these two moves, which one may safely say was distinctly creditable, considering the strenuous days of the past fortnight, the insufficient sleep, and the fact that full marching order was being carried.

The following day, however, saw us started off on a seventeen-mile march to Domléger, by way of Candas, Fienvillers and Bernaville. This proved too much for the new draft which had joined us on the 21st, and, after the first twelve miles, considerable difficulty was experienced in getting them along! The old hands marched into Domléger as cheerily as they had left Albert, and great was the delight of everyone at the prospect of a few days' complete rest and some measure of comfort.

CHAPTER IV

THE SOMME

August 1916

DOMLÉGER proved to be a real haven of rest. Training was carried on without interruption, and life was made to resemble peace time so far as it was possible. Courses of all kinds were arranged by the higher authorities, in particular for the training of junior officers as company commanders and for N.C.O.'s. The maintenance and further improvement of discipline was always the first consideration, as this could do so much to counterbalance the unavoidable discomforts to which all ranks were so often subjected.

Every effort was made to prevent the troops becoming tired or stale under training. Physical rest was a necessity, and it was only by adequate periods of relaxation in rest billets that the troops could recover from the heavy moral strain and nerve themselves for the next effort. We were now reinforced by a draft of ninety-seven men, mostly drawn from the Hunts Cyclist Battalion. These were the first "strangers" sent to us, but they proved to be an excellent lot, and many afterwards became N.C.O.'s.

Our stay in these comfortable billets was all too short for the amount of work to be done, for on August 9 the Battalion started marching back to the line by the way it had come, and on the 11th we were once more in the neighbourhood of our old friend Bouzincourt,

THE SOMME 37

which did not appear to have become any more attractive in our absence. The Battalion from whom we took over informed us that the Boche had lately taken to shelling the camp, and had burnt out one of the huts on the previous evening by registering a direct hit on it. No sooner had that Battalion left us than a covey of seven or eight shells came over and landed in or around the camp, demolishing yet another hut. This appeared to be no spot for a so-called rest, and we were not long in finding more healthy surroundings.

At 6 a.m. on August 13, the Battalion moved forward through Albert, and took over a line of gunpits a little to the west of Usna Redoubt. Here we were in reserve to the remainder of the Brigade, who were holding a line immediately west of Pozières and on the extreme crest of the ridge. The front trench was known as Sixth Avenue or Skyline Trench (Map No. 1). The Australians were on the right, round Pozières Windmill.

A heavy attack delivered by the enemy during the early part of the night of August 13/14, drove the 1/4th Oxfords out of Skyline Trench. At 3 a.m. on the 14th C and D Companies were hurriedly sent up to the old German front line at Ovillers, and were placed under the orders of O.C. 1/4th Royal Berks, to be in reserve while two companies of that regiment were engaged in making a counter-attack on Skyline. The forming up for this attack was observed by the enemy, and the assault proved a very costly failure.

The Bucks Battalion was then ordered to retake this trench, and in the afternoon of August 14 moved up and relieved the 1/4th Oxfords in the positions they were then holding, namely Fifth Avenue.

The expression " moved up and relieved " does not give quite the picture of what actually occurred, for in reality it was one of the most uncomfortable proceedings ever taken part in. The ground all round was going up

38 FIRST BUCKINGHAMSHIRE BATTALION

like a bank of earth due to the enemy's 5·9's, and progress was distinctly difficult. There certainly were casualties, but not one quarter the number that one would have expected.

The position to be attacked consisted of a trench about 800 yards long, approached from Fifth Avenue by two badly damaged communicators, E and F, each about 250 yards long. It was decided to carry out a bombing attack up these communicators, for which C Company (Captain P. A. Hall) was detailed. Shortly after 10 p.m. bombing sections from this company worked their way up the right-hand communicator and succeeded in gaining Skyline Trench. They then worked outwards. A Company established a T head at the top of the left communicator.

The operation was completely successful, and only slight opposition was met with, the enemy running away down the north slope of the hill after throwing a few bombs. Contact was regained with the Australians on the right, and the whole of Skyline Trench, with the exception of about 100 yards, was in our hands by 5 a.m. the next day (August 15).

About 8 a.m. A Company (Captain N. S. Reid, D.S.O., M.C.) were sent back for a few hours' rest to the west entrance to Ovillers, and C and D (Lieutenant F. D. Earle) Companies took over the line, B Company (Captain G. R. Crouch) being in immediate support to them.

This was the situation on the morning of August 15. At 11.30 the enemy opened heavy shell fire on the right of Fifth Avenue. At mid-day he started on Skyline Trench with an intense enfilade bombardment carried out mostly with heavy guns up to 12-inch, though a fair number of trench-mortars and several *Minenwerfers* which fired from Mouquet Farm also took part. It seemed as if all the power of destruction in Germany had suddenly got to work on this trench, and that the enemy were determined that, since they were not able to hold it themselves, no other men should either. Every size of shell was flung with unerring accuracy, so that one great volume of smoke rose from the ridge and covered the trench in a dense black pall. This terrific bombardment continued for nine consecutive hours, systematically destroying everything.

By 3 p.m. the Battalion was only holding the tops of the two communicators and a few posts in between, and casualties from the two companies had been very heavy. That men lived at all in such a place of death, when shells were bursting above them, under them and round them, was nothing less than a miracle. There were but few unwounded, and when at 8 p.m. it became necessary to send up B Company to relieve the remnants of C and D, the survivors were found to be dead-beat, both physically and mentally.

But no attack ensued, and at 9 p.m. the situation became quieter. It was then decided, in order to reduce casualties, that the remains of the ploughed-up trench should be evacuated, and that posts should be pushed out in shell-holes in front of it.

By night the whole Battalion was tired out, but a still further effort was required of it in order to complete the work of the previous morning. At midnight of August 15/16, in conjunction with the 5th Battalion Gloucestershire Regiment, a bombing attack was delivered by A Company against that portion of Skyline Trench on the extreme left which was still in enemy hands. The attack was pressed with great determination, and casualties were heavy, but success could not be attained owing to the exhaustion of the supply of bombs, which could not be kept up by the efforts of the worn-out remnants of C and D Companies.

The shelling in Skyline Trench and Fifth Avenue was undoubtedly the heaviest and most prolonged that the

Battalion had ever undergone, and the endurance of all ranks throughout was of the very finest. Our casualties were :

Officers.—Wounded. Capt. V. C. Heathcote-Hacker.
Lieut. F. D. Earle.
2/Lieut. F. C. Dixon.
2/Lieut. D. Fallon.

Other ranks.—Killed—8 (including 1 sergt.).
Wounded—165 (including 8 sergts.).
Missing—20.

It is certain that all the missing were killed, and so killed that no trace could be found of them. The casualties included many of our best N.C.O.'s, among whom may be mentioned Sergts. H. Watts, C. Fowler, A. J. Hart and W. G. Cartwright. The greater part of the losses were borne by C and D Companies, especially the former, who were now a mere handful of men.

At 11 a.m. on the 16th, the exhausted Battalion was relieved by the 4th Oxfords, and moved back to a new camp of bivouacs, trenches and smells between Bouzincourt and Albert. On our way out of the front trenches we passed the Divisional General, who, as usual, was one of the first on the spot after a show, and had a cheery word for everyone.

The forty-eight hours allowed us in this camp was no great rest, as there was so much to be done to prepare ourselves for action again. A lot of equipment had been lost during the bombardment of Skyline, much of it having been blown to pieces. The exact deficiencies of each article had to be ascertained, and returns which would satisfy the Quartermaster, the Staff Captain and D.A.D.O.S., made out. In addition there were fresh drafts to be inspected and posted, and a thousand inquiries to be made as to when all the missing had last been seen and what had been their probable fate. This, if it did not make everyone busy, supplied the Adjutant and company commanders with more than sufficient work.

At the end of forty-eight hours, we received sudden orders to move at once to the neighbourhood of Usna Redoubt. This we did, bivouacking for the night in the open, without blankets. The 143rd Infantry Brigade were attacking at dawn on August 19, and we had been sent up to be in support and to be ready to exploit any success.

The attack was a complete success, and when the Divisional General, who passed us on the roadside as he was going up to an O.P. at Ovillers, instructed us to " get all the rest you can," qualifying it by " You'll want your arms and your legs to-night," we made sure we were in for more trouble. This, however, did not mature, and by the evening of the 20th we were back in Bouzincourt again for another forty-eight hours, before being once more sent up to Ovillers Post to support the 144th Infantry Brigade.

A day later we ourselves received orders for an attack to be made by the Battalion the following afternoon on the enemy's forward positions between Pozières and Thiepval. The attack was to include the capture of a trench shown as X—Y on Map No. 1, and was to be carried out in conjunction with the 7th Infantry Brigade, 25th Division, who were to assault other trenches on our left.

Accordingly the Battalion took over the line from the 6th Battalion Gloucestershire Regiment. A and C Companies were detailed for the attack, zero being fixed for 3.5 p.m., August 23. A bombardment was carried out by the Heavy Artillery from 1 p.m. to 2.45 p.m., which not only had no effect on the enemy trenches, but served merely to define the precise limits of the objective. At 3 p.m. an intense bombardment was put down for five minutes by the field guns, under cover of which the attack was launched. The barrage was good but a trifle short, as when it lifted the attacking troops had still some way to go, and the enemy was manning his trench thickly, apparently very little affected by it and firing hard on our men. In addition the enemy barrage came down immediately after our own. The result was that casualties were heavy and progress almost impossible. 2/Lieut. E. G. H. Bates, who was commanding C Company, ran forward to try to rush the position, but was instantly killed. C.S.M. F. Smith endeavoured immediately afterwards to do the same thing, but was severely wounded. The only other officer in this company was also wounded.

On the left, A Company's fate was much the same, 2/Lieut. W. R. Heath being killed and Lieut. M. Bowen wounded. A few N.C.O.'s and men of C Company reached their objective on the extreme right, but all were at once either killed or wounded, Sergt. S. G. Bishop alone getting back. The remnants of the two companies had to lie out in No Man's Land until dark, during which time more became casualties through shell fire and sniping.

Very great gallantry was displayed by the officers and N.C.O.'s, but the losses in both companies were irreparable, coming on the heels of previous fighting, and in 2/Lieutenants Bates and Heath the Battalion lost two very able and gallant officers. No real gain resulted except that we captured almost the whole of a diagonal trench running from our centre to the enemy's right, and on the left advanced our bombstop some 50 yards.

Out of a total of four officers and 150 other ranks who actually went over the top, our casualties were :

THE SOMME

Officers.—Killed. 2/Lieut. E. G. H. Bates.
2/Lieut. W. R. Heath.
Wounded. Lieut. M. Bowen.
2/Lieut. H. M. Breton.
Other ranks.—Killed—24.
Wounded—71.
Missing—13 (all subsequently presumed killed).

The Battalion spent three more nights in these trenches before being relieved by the 5th Gloucesters on August 25. During this time every effort was made to improve our position, and to gain certain points by means of bombing attacks.

Some sort of revenge for the failure of the attack on the 23rd fell to the Battalion early one morning, when an enemy relief was spotted coming over the open and heavy casualties were inflicted on them with Lewis-gun fire.

Constant patrols, too, were sent out at night and gathered much useful information concerning the enemy's dispositions, and a German prisoner, belonging to the 28th I.R., confirmed much of this, and added more. This information was handed over to the 5th Gloucesters, and assisted them in making a most successful attack on the position on the 27th.

On the 28th the whole Division was relieved, and started moving back to Bus-les-Artois via Hédauville, Forceville and Bertrancourt.

Throughout this month's fighting on the Somme, the Battalion had been greatly handicapped by a shortage of thoroughly trained men, more especially in bombing and Lewis-gun work. Bombing had proved itself to be all important in this kind of fighting, and it was really necessary that every man, as far as possible, should be a trained bomber:

merely to have been taught to throw a Mills bomb was not sufficient. In clearing Skyline Trench, eight bombing sections were absorbed in a few hours through casualties and the manning of bomb-stops.

It was found essential to collect a very plentiful supply of bombs and rifle grenades at several advanced dumps before bombing operations were undertaken, for they were used up at an incredible rate. The replenishing of these forward dumps was often a great difficulty, unless a permanent party had been detailed for the purpose, as troops in support, if they had been relieved recently from the front line, were often far too exhausted to be detailed for carrying, which is one of the most fatiguing duties a soldier has to perform.

It must be said, however, that although great importance was rightly attached to bombing, it was found later that the men had come to rely overmuch on this form of weapon, and were apt to forget that the rifle is, and always will be, their main weapon of defence.

It would not be right to fail to add here some word of praise for our gunners. Their shooting had by this time won the entire trust and confidence of the Infantry. As for our own divisional gunners, they were the best, and there was not a man in the ranks of the Battalion whose *moral* was not the better, when going forward to an attack, for the knowledge that it was the 48th Divisional gunners who were supporting him.

CHAPTER V

LE SARS—CAPPY

September 1916 *to March* 1917

WE spent a week at Bus, before taking over trenches in front of Beaumont-Hamel. The Battalion held these trenches for four days, without any incident worthy of mention. The line here had not moved forward during the Somme fighting, as the attack on July 1 had failed in that sector, and no subsequent one had been delivered.

We had considered ourselves a little ill used in not being taken back and given a proper rest, with the chance to refit after our recent exertions, so our delight was great when, after spending a night or two in Mailly-Maillet and a day in the Bois de Warnimont, we were moved back to Beauval on September 11.

It was not the first time we had been in Beauval, and the Battalion was becoming increasingly popular in that part of the town in which our billets lay. As a billeting area, it was an ideally proportioned place, holding without much difficulty an entire Brigade of Infantry. There were good billets, good mess-rooms and a few shops, and the town lay within easy reach of Doullens, where the shops were good. But the training facilities were bad, as the land was a mass of crops, which we had strict orders not to damage.

During the week we spent here, in addition to considerable drafts of men, we received a reinforcement of no less than thirteen officers of the Essex Regiment, who nearly all reported on the same day. The arrival of all these officers, belonging to another regiment, was, it must be admitted, something of a shock to us. The more credit to them then, when within a very few days we realised we had struck oil and been sent a most excellent batch of officers, many of whom afterwards greatly distinguished themselves, both in and out of action.

After a week at Beauval, on September 19 the Battalion moved to Berneuil, some nine miles distant, where the training area was decidedly better, though the billets were not so good. Intensive training was the order of the day, to such an extent indeed that many were only too glad to be inoculated and get forty-eight hours off duty.

On September 30 a twenty-mile march took us to Coullemont, and, after another move two days later to St. Amand, we found ourselves once again in the Hébuterne trenches on October 5. They had changed but little, though our disappointment was very great on finding that all the old familiar names of trenches in the K sector had been scrapped and new ones, all starting with the letter Y, substituted.

Rumour was rife that an attack was to be made on Gommecourt, and indeed with excellent reason, for everything pointed to something of the kind taking place at no very distant date. Orders for the attack soon made their appearance, and on October 7 we were taken out of the line and sent back to Souastre, about three miles behind, for a final " fatten up." Those who took part in that short march will not easily forget the scene that the road presented. It was one endless stream of horse and motor transport, moving up with every imaginable article on board. But, after all this material had been brought up, and everything appeared to be in readiness,

LE SARS—CAPPY

the attack was postponed, and we were sent still farther back to the village of Warlencourt. Here practice attacks of all kinds were exercised until about the middle of the month, when the Gommecourt attack was definitely given up and all orders cancelled.

This wandering about from place to place, spending a few days and sometimes only a few hours in each, was becoming a little tiresome, and we were not altogether sorry to find ourselves back in the line at the beginning of November, having spent the remainder of October in Warluzel, Talmas and La Houssoye. The part of the line to which we were sent, namely Martinpuich and Le Sars, proved, however, anything but pleasant; in fact, for a sector which was not taking part in active operations, it was the most miserable one the Battalion ever occupied.

From all sides, our line was under the most complete observation by the enemy—from Loupart Wood, Irles, the Butte de Warlencourt and other places, and this observation extended several miles behind the line. The trenches themselves were full of water and falling in; the ground all round them was pitted with shellholes, which also had filled with water, whilst every track was deep in glutinous mud. Movement in the dark was a nightmare, for it was impossible to struggle twenty yards without falling into a shell-hole, getting soaked through and plastered with mud. Ration-carrying parties, which had to manhandle the rations for almost a mile over this kind of ground, had the most bitter experiences; there were no landmarks, and men frequently lost themselves for a whole night. To add to our difficulties, the enemy shelling, particularly at night, was extremely heavy. His opportunities for observation by day enabled him to mark down all the tracks which our reliefs and carrying parties were in the habit of using by night, and to shell them accord-

48　FIRST BUCKINGHAMSHIRE BATTALION

ingly. He succeeded in making Le Sars quite uninhabitable, by shelling it for the greater part of the day and night, so that, as the place was of no tactical importance (the line running some half-mile in front), it was left severely alone. Destremont Farm, or rather the remains of it, which lay behind Le Sars, received the same attention; but it contained two large cellars which no shells could touch, and in these we quartered two platoons by day. This was the only semblance of accommodation in the sector, and even Battalion Headquarters had to be content with eight steps of a shaft of an incomplete mined dugout, started by the Germans and consequently facing the wrong way. These steps our Headquarters continued to occupy, for lack of a "better 'ole," even after a shell had landed in the entrance, blocking it up, and imprisoning the Commanding Officer, the Adjutant and Intelligence officers. Fortunately for them a meal happened to be long overdue, and the batman who brought it discovered them in this plight.

The strain and exhaustion of the Battalion, especially when holding the front line, were extreme, and the greatest difficulties were experienced by company commanders, struggling to make out written reports at night and endeavouring to prevent the appearance of "trench-foot" in their companies.

Reliefs varied, but on the average the Battalion were in the habit of doing three days in the front trenches, three days in support trenches and three days "at rest." Rest, so called, but which one never found. The camps lay round Contalmaison, and most unpleasant they were. The enemy knew their location exactly, and shot at them with unerring precision, usually having his greatest "hate" between midnight and 2 a.m., when a little sleep was helping us to forget, temporarily, the vileness of it all. A camp of huts known as Acid

FRONT LINE COY. H.Q., LE SARS.

LE SARS—CAPPY 49

Drop Camp used to catch the worst of the shelling, and two huts received direct hits at night whilst we were in occupation. In the other camps we were under canvas, chilled to the marrow in cold November nights.

During the periods spent " at rest," working parties were practically continuous; as many as 200 men had often to be found by day and the same number (if our strength allowed it) by night. Casualties were abnormally heavy, considering the fact that no active operations were undertaken, but the Battalion dealt most successfully with the trench-foot problem, having only one case up to the end of December.

Our transport in this area was quartered close to Bécourt, which lay some three miles behind Contalmaison, amongst a mass of old disused trenches, surrounded by a sea of mud. The conditions under which the transport lived, consequently, were miserable in the extreme, and it was due largely to the neverfailing energy of the transport officer, Captain J. B. Hill, who organised the erection of standings for the horses and shelters for the men, that living was made possible.

At this time there had been no leave open for some four months, so that the survivors of the Somme fighting were getting pretty well worn out, but after six weeks in the sector, the Division was relieved, and moved back to Bécourt, where a fortnight, including Christmas Day, was spent. Officers and men alike were determined to enjoy themselves thoroughly on this day, despite the very unfavourable conditions, and it speaks highly of the Quartermaster's branch that every man had a good whack of turkey with chestnut stuffing and vegetables.

On December 28 the Battalion moved about six miles west to the village of Bresle, where the Brigade was inspected on January 6, 1917, by Lieutenant-General Pulteney, commanding the IIIrd Corps.

A further move to Heilly took place on January 9,

where we entrained at 3.30 a.m. for Oisemont, arriving there at 12 noon. Here we were billeted in two small country villages, half a mile apart, A and B Companies being in Forceville, and Battalion Headquarters, C and D Companies, and the transport in Neuville. For three weeks most valuable training was carried out, and sports and games greatly encouraged. In the latter the Battalion distinguished itself by winning the Brigade football competition, the Brigade cross-country steeple-chase, and the majority of events in the boxing competition. The weather was good during the whole of this time, though a certain amount of snow fell.

On January 29 the Battalion entrained at Oisemont, preparatory to taking over a new area from the French south of the Somme. The detrainment was carried out at Cerisy, after nearly twelve hours' travelling in icy cold trucks. After spending three days at Hamel, we marched on February 2 to Cappy, taking over what was known as Camp 56, on the Cappy-Eclusier road, from a reserve battalion of the French. The few days we had here were occupied in reconnoitring the new forward area, and vainly endeavouring to extract a little heat from the French stoves which had been left in the huts.

So long as the frost lasted the trenches in this area were excellent, probably the best we had yet seen, but with the thaw, which made its appearance towards the end of February, their condition became very bad. The greatest possible precautions had once more to be taken to prevent " trench-foot." Arrangements were made for washing every man's feet in a special solution before the Battalion went into the line, and when in the line, for rubbing the feet and supplying every man with a dry pair of socks every twenty-four hours. Annoying as these precautions were to carry out at the time, it must be said that the result fully justified

LE SARS—CAPPY 51

them, for we had only one further case of trench-foot during the remainder of the winter, whereas many battalions suffered severely from this disease.

The trenches held by the Division crossed the river Somme and faced Péronne, half of the little village of Biaches being just included in our line. The sector was a quiet one, and the only missile used by the enemy which caused us any great inconvenience when we first took over, was one known as a " blue pigeon." It was a particularly effective form of mortar, which made a sort of shrill whistle as it proceeded through the air and caused us a considerable number of casualties.

Duration of tours in the trenches here was irregular, and the varying portions of the line held by the Battalion are well illustrated by the different elements of the whole of the 143rd Brigade to whom we handed over when we were relieved on February 9.

> Two left platoons on the Somme handed over to 1/8th Battalion Royal Warwickshire Regiment;
> Two right platoons on the Somme to 1/7th Battalion Royal Warwickshire Regiment;
> Garrison of Tr. Iglau and Battalion Headquarters to 1/5th Battalion Royal Warwickshire Regiment;
> Two platoons in Tr. Désirée to 1/6th Battalion Royal Warwickshire Regiment.

This relief occupied the whole night and did not proceed too smoothly, with the result that it was an irritated Commanding Officer who ordered Battalion Headquarters to move off just as daylight was appearing.

Towards the middle of February the Brigade took over the right of the Divisional line, north-east of the village of Barleux, which lay just inside the German lines. During the month that the Battalion took turns with the 7th Battalion Worcestershire Regiment in holding these trenches, patrolling was very active, especially when it became known that the enemy was evacuating his trenches farther north and effecting an organised retreat to some line in rear. Shelling was heavy on both sides, and on March 10 occurred one of the most unlucky events that had yet befallen us. About 4 a.m. on this date, a gas shell, fired from a German *Minenwerfer*, landed and exploded inside the entrance of the A Company Headquarters' dugout. There were at the time inside the dugout three officers (Captain J. D. B. Warwick, 2/Lieutenant S. Wiseman, 2/Lieutenant R. B. Cooper-Smith), C.S.M. Watts, two corporals, five orderlies, three signallers and four batmen. The first impression of those inside (presumably caused by the flash of the shell) appears to have been that the dugout was on fire, and a large dose of poison was inhaled before they adjusted their box respirators, while those who were asleep were killed without waking. Captain Warwick and 2/Lieutenant Wiseman, believing that a gas attack was taking place, together with their orderlies attempted to reach the front line, but the latter died just as he reached his platoon and the former not long after. The fate of the remaining occupants of the dugout was no less tragic, for, in spite of the utmost efforts to save them, the majority died within an hour of the bursting of the shell, and all were dead within six hours.

This sad event cannot be passed by without an allusion to No. 2535 Private Harry Topple, who was the company signaller on duty in the dugout at the time when the shell burst. Being under the impression that a gas attack was taking place, he refused to leave his post, and continued to endeavour to obtain communication with Battalion Headquarters, until forcibly dragged away by a rescue party half an hour later. He died in the trenches near the dugout about 7 a.m. the same day. By remaining at his post, this very gallant man undoubtedly sacrificed his own life in the hope of saving others.

Two days after this D Company were severely shelled in Flaucourt, which was the position of the reserve company, and suffered a number of casualties.

Our rest billets were usually Camp 56 at Cappy; this occasioned a long and weary march, usually taking place in the middle of the night, after a six days' tour in the line with a very inadequate ration of sleep. It was in this camp that we received news—about March 17—that patrols sent out by the Brigades holding the line had reported the enemy trenches opposite to be unoccupied. The retirement on our front had begun.

CHAPTER VI

THE GERMAN RETIREMENT

March to July 1917

THE excitement caused by the news of the enemy's retirement may well be imagined. The very idea of marching into his trenches without being fired at seemed almost too good to be true, and the possibilities opened up by the thought of marching for miles behind them appeared incalculable. One was very apt to forget during those first few days that the retirement was being carried out " according to plan," which meant that we could not pursue bald-headed the moment that we received news.

It was not, in fact, until March 20 that we received orders to move to billets at Péronne, which town had been entered by the 143rd Infantry Brigade on the previous day. The march through " No Man's Land," Biaches, and over the pontoon bridge, just finished by the Royal Engineers at Bazincourt, was one of exceptional interest. The area had been completely cleared of all stores by the enemy before his departure, and the most that one saw, in the way of material left behind, was a few coils of barbed wire. Péronne presented the most awful of pictures, being completely wrecked and a large portion of it still burning. An earthquake could not have produced a more appalling effect or a scene of greater chaos. House fronts in many cases had been blown completely out and had

REPRODUCTION OF A FRENCH POSTCARD OF PÉRONNE AFTER GERMAN EVACUATION IN MARCH 1917.
(WITH CRUDE TRANSLATION!)

THE GERMAN RETIREMENT 55

fallen right across the street, so that one looked from the street straight into the rooms of the houses. These rooms were bare of all furniture, every stick of which had been either carried away by the enemy or sent to Berlin as souvenirs. Everywhere lay huge masses of rubble and paper, and the work of tidying up appeared to be well-nigh hopeless. The only two buildings which remained more or less intact were the Town Hall and the Castle, and these we guessed must be mined. Battalion Headquarters were, however, billeted in the Castle for that night, and the remainder of the Battalion in cellars on the north-west side of the square. These cellars were selected, not from any idea of possible bombardment, but because they provided the only shelter left, and there was less fear of a wall falling on one there than above ground.

At 6.30 a.m. on March 21, B, C and D Companies moved off to relieve the 1/8th Battalion Royal Warwickshire Regiment in the outpost line, which then lay some three miles east of the town and embraced Doingt, Doingt Woods and Courcelles Wood, from a point about 500 yards south of Bussu to the Cologne River. In the afternoon, Battalion Headquarters and A Company moved up from Péronne, the former taking up quarters in Doingt.

In the evening, a flying column, known as "Ward's Column," and composed, roughly speaking, of one Infantry Brigade, drawn from elements of all Brigades in the Division, moved forward through the outpost line to Cartigny.

The line, which we took over on the 21st, remained the Divisional line of resistance until the 26th, though places well forward were occupied and held by us during this period. With the exception of a few Uhlans who were at times visible in the distance, no enemy was seen, and we were given a great opportunity of practising,

56 FIRST BUCKINGHAMSHIRE BATTALION

in real earnest and yet without molestation, open warfare, which was a complete novelty to us. Mounted officers were enabled to visit their outposts on horseback, and the free and open life, after trench warfare, was thoroughly appreciated. On the evening of March 26 we moved forward to Tincourt, taking over billets there from the 1/4th Battalion Oxford and Bucks Light Infantry. This village had not been completely demolished like the others, chiefly because it had been used by the enemy as a dumping ground for civilians, who had been collected there from all farms and villages in the neighbourhood. Our excitement at finding them was great, as they were the first we had seen.

The following day, March 27, the Battalion took over the outpost line, which now ran from Roisel (captured by 1/4th Battalion Oxford and Bucks Light Infantry) to Villers-Faucon (exclusive), Battalion Headquarters being at Hamel. At 5.30 in the afternoon, the 5th Cavalry Division attacked and captured Villers-Faucon. At 7 p.m. that part of the line covering Roisel was handed over to the 2/4th Battalion Lincolnshire Regiment (59th Division), and B Company were dispatched to Villers-Faucon to assist the cavalry, who, in taking this village, had met with considerable opposition from the enemy rearguards, and suffered a number of casualties from their machine guns.

The following day the enemy shelled the village pretty heavily with 77 mm's. and 5.9's, and after dark the cavalry were withdrawn, being relieved by C Company. There can have been few darker or wetter nights than this one. Telephone lines were cut, and communication forward entirely broke down, owing to the difficulty of finding Company Headquarters in the dense darkness. Strong patrols were sent forward at dawn to ascertain whether the enemy were still holding St. Emilie, and they were found to be there in considerable numbers.

THE GERMAN RETIREMENT 57

In pouring rain on the 29th March, the Battalion marched back to Cartigny at dusk, on relief by the 4th Battalion Gloucestershire Regiment. Here we became part of what had been called " Ward's Column," but was now known as "Dobbin's Column." After four happy days with this column the Battalion was moved to Longavesnes, relieving the 1/4th Battalion Gloucestershire Regiment in Brigade reserve. This village, which had been attacked and captured by the 143rd Infantry Brigade on the 26th, was absolutely devoid of any accommodation or shelter, so completely had it been wrecked by the enemy and our shells.

On April 5, at 2 a.m., we marched to the railway cutting between Villers-Faucon and St. Emilie, acting as reserve to the remainder of the Brigade, who were to capture the villages of Lempire, Ronssoy and Basse-Boulogne (Map No. 2), attacking as follows :

1/4th Battalion Royal Berkshire Regiment, south and south-east of Ronssoy and Basse-Boulogne ;
1/4th Battalion Oxford and Bucks Light Infantry, south-west end of Ronssoy ;
1/5th Battalion Gloucestershire Regiment, the workhouse, Lempire and Basse-Boulogne.

Each of these battalions carried out the attack with three companies, keeping one in battalion reserve. Zero was at 4.45 a.m. The operation was completely successful, all objectives being taken, together with over thirty prisoners and six machine guns. The German dead numbered over 200. The prisoners, who belonged to the 237th Infantry Regiment, stated that one platoon from each of their companies had been holding the villages, but owing to our active patrolling the alarm had been given at 11 o'clock that night and the support platoons had been brought into the picquet line. They had received no orders to withdraw in case of a heavy attack, and had been told to hold the position to the last. All had the greatest confidence in the impregnability of the Hindenburg Line, and, though they were obviously tired of the war, their *moral* was not bad. They said that the Hindenburg Line near Bony had been occupied since the 28th of last month, and that their next outpost line ran in front of Tombois Farm and Malakoff Farm.

The Battalion moved back into Villers-Faucon for the remainder of the day, officers being sent up to reconnoitre the new line, with a view to relieving the 5th Battalion Gloucestershire Regiment that evening. The outpost line was held by A and B Companies, the 1/4th Battalion Royal Berkshire Regiment being on the right, and 1/6th Battalion Royal Warwickshire Regiment on the left. C Company were in support in cellars in Basse-Boulogne, and D Company in reserve with Battalion Headquarters in the railway cutting, just south of the Lempire-Epehy Road. The transport and quartermaster's stores had at this time been moved to the neighbourhood of Villers-Faucon.

No counter-attack developed on that night or the two succeeding ones, during which the Battalion held that line, and companies were occupied in consolidating the whole position, which it was decided should be the future Divisional line of resistance.

On the evening of April 7 we were relieved by the 1/7th Battalion Worcestershire Regiment, and marched back to cellar accommodation in Marquaix. Work was here concentrated on roads which the enemy had done everything in his power to make impassable. Additional parties were sent up to the outpost line on most nights, to help the forward battalions in the work of wiring and digging of new trenches.

On April 15 the Battalion took over the line again, receiving orders at the same time that we were to

PÉRONNE CHURCH.

RONSSOY SUGAR FACTORY.

THE GERMAN RETIREMENT 59

attack Tombois Farm on the following night. (See Appendix I A.)

This farm lay on the southern side of the Lempire-Vendhuille Road (Map No. 2), midway between the two villages, and about 1,000 yards from our nearest sentry post. At dusk on April 16, A Company (Captain N. S. Reid, D.S.O., M.C.) took over the whole of the Battalion outpost line, relieving B and C Companies for the attack. On our right, the 1/4th Battalion Royal Berkshire Regiment were to capture Gillemont Farm, and on our left, the 1/5th Battalion Royal Warwickshire Regiment were to attack Catelet Copse and Le Petit Priel Farm.

C Company (Captain J. B. Hales) had orders to form up just west of Sart Farm, and to direct their attack south and south-east of Tombois.

B Company (Lieutenant M. Bowen) were to form up on the northern side of the Lempire-Vendhuille Road, clear of Lempire, and to deliver their attack on the west and north of the farm; D Company (Captain R. Gregson-Ellis) to proceed in echelon behind C Company, occupying the trench in front of the farm, until satisfied that the leading companies had attained their objectives, when they were to go through and capture a small ridge lying some 200 yards beyond the farm.

Zero was fixed for 11.30 p.m., April 16.

The weather conditions could not conceivably have been more unfavourable for a night attack, over open country, with few landmarks. It was pitch-dark, with pouring rain, and a gale blowing in the direction of the enemy. That the attacking companies were able to find their forming-up position in such darkness was a creditable performance; that they should have kept direction and struck Tombois speaks very highly for their leaders.

At 11.45 p.m. the enemy opened with machine-gun and rifle fire, and sent up a great number of lights from

60 FIRST BUCKINGHAMSHIRE BATTALION

the farm and the trenches on either side of it. They also put down a moderate barrage well behind our attack, mostly on the outskirts of Lempire and on Sart Farm. All companies encountered a thick belt of wire in front of the enemy positions, which were strongly held, C and D Companies both being held up by this wire, which it was impossible to negotiate in face of the heavy enemy fire. All D Company's officers had become casualties, and at 12.30 a.m. Captain Hales decided to withdraw both companies to Sart Farm, and reform them there for another attack.

Meanwhile B Company, on the left, had attracted rather less rifle and machine-gun fire than the other two companies, and had succeeded in getting through a thinner belt of wire and penetrating the enemy trenches at a point just north of where the trench crossed the road.

In consequence of the failure of the two right companies, and in view of the fact that at that time no news had been received at Battalion Headquarters of the success of B Company's attack, three platoons of the support company (1/5th Battalion Gloucestershire Regiment) were ordered to advance on the farm, one platoon each side of the road and one in close support, in order to ascertain the situation as regards B Company and, if necessary, to attack. They arrived at the farm to find B Company in possession, but the enemy still holding out in the orchard south of the farm. Our men were finding considerable difficulty in clearing the orchard owing to the fire of the other two companies who had been held up.

By 3 a.m., however, both farm and orchard were clear, and a counter-attack, launched by the enemy down the road, was successfully broken up by B Company. C and D Companies, who had now reorganised, were at once sent up to help in the work of consolidation,

MAP N° 2.

Attack on Tombois Farm
Night 16/17 April 1917.

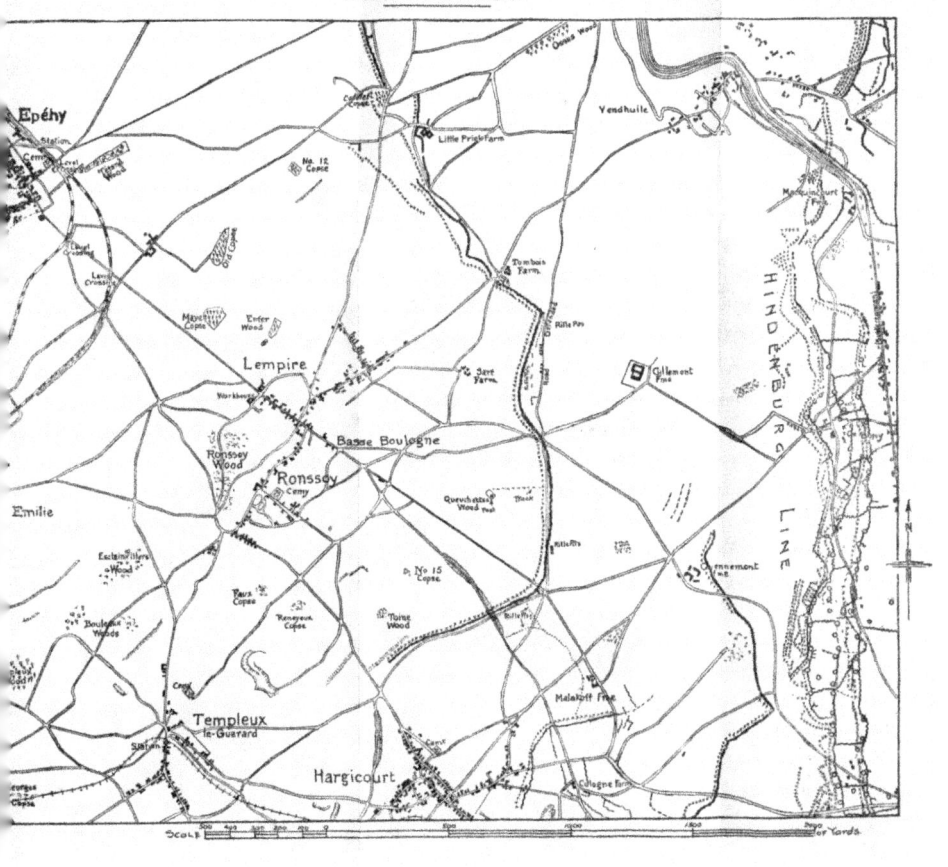

THE GERMAN RETIREMENT

and trenches were dug west of the road and north and east of the farm, Major A. B. Lloyd-Baker going forward to organise this work.

News was received that the 1/4th Battalion Royal Berkshire Regiment and 1/5th Battalion Royal Warwickshire Regiment had both failed to reach their objectives, on account of wire and heavy enemy fire.

At daylight on April 17, the Battalion was holding three or four hundred yards of trench on either side of the farm, with no sign of the enemy. Strong patrols were sent out to right and left, with orders to occupy every position possible, and by 7.30 a.m. one of these patrols, consisting of a platoon of Gloucesters, succeeded in entering Le Petit Priel Farm with little or no opposition. Another patrol from A Company (holding the old line), which had been sent forward to ascertain the left of our new line, found Catelet Copse unoccupied. This they reported to the nearest picquet of the Warwicks, who moved up and occupied it.

It would seem that at dawn the enemy, realising that he had lost Tombois, had decided to withdraw from the objectives which the battalion on our left had fought hard all that night to gain.

At least thirty dead Germans were found in and around the farm, and our captures were nine prisoners with one machine gun. Our casualties were:

Officers.—Wounded. Capt. R. Gregson-Ellis
　　　　　　　　　　(died following day).
　　　　　　　　　2/Lieut. J. Jack.
　　　　　　　　　2/Lieut. N. S. Flint.
　　　　　　　　　2/Lieut. B. C. C. Olivier.
　　　　　　　　　2/Lieut. R. F. Chatham.
Other ranks.—Killed—18.
　　　　　　　　Wounded—48.

The strengths of the attacking companies had been:

B Company—4 officers and 136 other ranks.
C Company—3 officers and 125 other ranks.
D Company—4 officers and 134 other ranks.

The following message was received from the Army Commander, General Sir H. Rawlinson:

" Please convey to 48th Division my admiration of their success last night. To have carried out a successful attack, on a wide front, in the midst of such a storm, reflects the highest credit on all ranks and especially on the leadership of subordinate commanders. My best congratulations and thanks to all troops engaged."

Tombois Farm, and the road running from the farm to Lempire, were shelled throughout the day, making our occupation of the new position and communication with the rear most unpleasant; but relief, in the shape of the 1/5th Battalion Gloucestershire Regiment, arrived that evening, and we tramped back, very wet and weary, to a camp in the neighbourhood of St. Emilie, only to be moved again two days later to huts and billets in Villers-Faucon.

Numerous mines, laid by the enemy in his retreat, had recently exploded in this village, the 1/6th Battalion Gloucestershire Regiment being unfortunate enough to lose the whole of their Battalion Headquarters, including their Commanding Officer, 2nd in Command, Adjutant, Intelligence Officer, Medical Officer, and a Chaplain attached to them. The mine exploded underneath a large cellar where these officers were all sleeping together. The Commanding Officer and Adjutant were brothers who had come out with the Division in 1915, and had become well known and popular. The result of this mishap was an order, issued by Division, that no officers were to live in billets in the town, and huts were erected to house them.

THE GERMAN RETIREMENT 63

On the 24th and 25th April the 144th Infantry Brigade made further attempts to capture Gillemont Farm, and these eventually proved successful. With this exception, no further active operations were undertaken by the Division in this area, and at the end of the month the Division was relieved, the Battalion marching back via Hamel to billets at Mons-en-Chaussée. Here we had ten days' strenuous training, though as usual this was partly interfered with by large working parties, which had to be provided about every other day for road-mending and filling up craters.

Those officers who were unable to ride—and there were at this time quite a number—will not have forgotten their first experiences on a horse in the fields behind this village. The Commanding Officer had been working up a " hate " for a considerable time against these unlucky individuals, and as he determined to be himself the riding master, the blow fell with full force. The result, however, was splendid, and a month later all officers in the Battalion were able to ride after a fashion.

Our ration strength at this time had fallen to 570 other ranks, and though we were hoping to receive reinforcements here, none arrived. Our officers numbered twenty-five, but many of them were always attending courses, of which a large number were held continuously.

On May 11 the Battalion started on the first of a series of daily marches up to a part of the line which we had not yet visited. These marches, which took us through Flamicourt (one night), Cléry, Maurepas (one night), Combles, Sailly-Saillisel, and Le Transloy (one night), were of exceptional interest, embracing as they did such a large part of the old Somme battle-fields. The roads had been entirely remade by the British Army and were excellent, but with this exception the whole country was one great stretch of shell-craters.

Over all these acres and acres of ground there was hardly a yard into which a shell had not fallen. The sites of the villages through which we passed were marked only by heaps of rubble, with a few charred tree-trunks standing like weary sentinels over them. A smell of dead pervaded the whole atmosphere.

On the night of May 14 we relieved the 7th Battalion South Staffordshire Regiment, 33rd Infantry Brigade, 11th Division, in the line between Hermies and Demicourt, the 143rd Brigade taking over the line on our left and the 1/4th Royal Berkshire Regiment on our right.

The Division spent nearly two months in this sector, the 143rd Brigade and 144th Brigade relieving each other on the left, and the 145th Brigade carrying out its own reliefs on the right. As regards the latter, two battalions held the line, a third was in support round the village of Beaumetz, while the fourth battalion was in reserve in Vélu Wood. The line held by the Bucks Battalion ran for the most part just in front of the village of Hermies, and consisted of a series of disconnected strong posts, separated from the enemy trenches by fifty yards on the right and some 300 yards on the left. The Germans were occupying the Hindenburg Line, their front trenches running mostly along the eastern side of the Canal du Nord, just in front of the village of Havrincourt, while opposite our left their line ran forward so as to include a large spoil-heap. This mound formed a magnificent stronghold for them and was a source of continual annoyance to us, harbouring as it did several machine-gun nests with splendid observation over our lines.

Our right post, well known as R3, was situated on either side of the Hermies-Havrincourt road, behind an old prisoners' cage which had been erected by the Germans before their retirement. Parties were at work nearly every night during the whole of our period in this area, digging trenches through and around this cage, to the intense displeasure of the platoon commander in charge of the post, who always had the most harrowing tales to tell in the evening of the hell which the garrison had endured in R3 during the day! The post certainly caught the bulk of the enemy trench-mortar and grenade fire, largely because of the close proximity of the two front trenches, which were practically separated only by the canal.

Artillery fire on points behind the lines was active on both sides, the chief targets for the enemy being the villages of Hermies, Demicourt and Beaumetz.

Aeroplane bombing, chiefly by night, was becoming increasingly popular with the enemy, and one bomb, which fell on the quarters of a field ambulance in Beaumetz, caused a number of casualties.

Our machine-gunners contracted a habit of pouring thousands of rounds of small-arms ammunition into enemy country each night, hoping no doubt to inconvenience the enemy infantry to an even greater extent than our own!

Only one operation, and this a small one, was undertaken by the Battalion during its tenure of these trenches. It had become apparent at the beginning of June that the enemy had established a night post amongst a cluster of bushes on our bank of the canal. The sniping from this post caused us considerable annoyance and some casualties to our working parties. It was therefore decided to capture it, and to dig a trench along the bank of the canal with a communicator running back to our present post. Two platoons of B Company (Captain M. Bowen, M.C.) were detailed to make the attack, forming up on a line parallel to the canal bank, each platoon being in two lines at fifteen yards' distance and on a frontage of fifty yards. Zero was fixed for midnight June 7/8, at which time a barrage from one section of field guns was placed on the enemy trenches. At zero plus five this barrage lifted, and the assaulting platoons charged with the bayonet. The enemy opened rifle fire before the assault, but was most effectually silenced by a Lewis gun posted on the right bank for the purpose of providing covering fire. This fact was confirmed by an *Unteroffizier* taken prisoner, who declared that the Lewis-gun fire forced them to take shelter behind the bank, and that the next thing they knew was that the English were on top of them. After the assaulting platoons got in there ensued a bombing fight which lasted for a few minutes, but the enemy soon gave in. No attempt at a counter-attack was made, but rifle grenades were fired from the opposite bank at intervals throughout the remainder of the night.

The report of this operation was afterwards issued for circulation throughout the IVth Corps, with the following minute added :

"*To 20th Division, 48th Division, Corps Mounted Troops, Corps Schools.*

" The Corps Commander considers this report should be circulated down to company and battery commanders, as it is a good example of the co-operation of all arms and of covering fire. The action of the Lewis guns in driving the enemy to take cover and thus letting our troops get in is especially good."

Our casualties were two killed and nine wounded. Eleven prisoners were taken by us and several of the enemy killed. The prisoners belonged to the 41st Infantry Regiment and stated that the previous artillery activity had led the picquet to expect an attack, and they had been ordered to maintain the greatest vigilance. They believed that the post in question was to have been finally withdrawn the following day as being tactically unsound. The average *moral* and physique of these men was second-rate, and they declared that the longing for peace in all classes was intense, the more so as it was firmly believed that the war would end in a draw. One of these prisoners was of special interest, as he had been on the Russian front in March, where he said there had been much fraternising between Germans and Russians, to such an extent indeed that whenever artillery shoots were planned each side warned the other of the danger zone to be avoided.

Another prisoner, who was a N.C.O., stated that the cage which has been mentioned above was called by them " Russenlager " (Russian Camp), because Russian prisoners used to be interned there within the danger zone, as an act of retaliation on the practice attributed to the English and French of requiring German prisoners to work within the range of German artillery.

On July 3 the Division was withdrawn from the line, the Battalion being relieved by the 4th Battalion Royal Fusiliers, 9th Brigade, 3rd Division. After a halt for one night at Vélu, we marched the two following days via Bihucourt, Achiet-le-Grand, Adinfer and Ransart to Bailleulval, where the most strenuous training was undertaken. Rumours of an offensive to be started by the British Army in the Ypres area had for some time been persistent, and it became increasingly evident during the first few days of our stay in this village that the Battalion was earmarked to take part in it.

Seconds in Command of battalions were detailed to attend a course at the XVIIIth Corps School, with a view to learning the general scheme of the operations and the rôles that the various Divisions in the Corps were to play in them. Points which required further training were brought out, but the special feature of the preparation was that every man should not only know his own job thoroughly but also be made acquainted with the jobs of all units near him, and not be " in the dark," as had been largely the case on previous occasions.

In other words, secrecy was to be to a great extent sacrificed with the hope of gaining greater efficiency.

Various changes were made in the headquarter staffs of battalions in the Brigade, and we had most regretfully to part with Major A. B. Lloyd-Baker, who was transferred to the 1/4th Battalion Oxford and Bucks Light Infantry as 2nd in Command, Captain P. A. Hall, M.C., being promoted to fill his place as our own 2nd in Command.

Two drafts were received on July 12 and 15, one of 196 other ranks and the other of 43 other ranks, which brought the Battalion ration strength up to about twenty-five officers and 920 other ranks. Two most instructive and interesting lectures were delivered by Major Hall, on his return from the Corps School, to all officers and N.C.O.'s, and in these he was able to state definitely the proposed objectives of the 48th Division.

The Second and Fifth Armies were to attack along the whole of their fronts. Our XVIIIth Corps was in the Fifth Army, and included the 11th, 39th, 48th, and 51st Divisions. So far as this Corps was concerned, the initial attack was to be made by the 39th Division on the right and the 51st Division on the left, with the 48th Division in reserve on the right and 11th Division in reserve on the left.

The Corps front ran roughly from Wieltje to the Ypres-Staden railway. The final objective on the first day was to include Pilkem Ridge on the left and St. Julien on the right, from which line the other two Divisions (11th and 48th) were to continue the attack, immediately guns could be got forward.

Every arrangement appeared to be so thoroughly thought out that it seemed impossible that the attack could be anything but a complete success, the results of which would eventually give us back the whole Belgian coast and, with any luck, finish the war.

CHAPTER VII

THE THIRD BATTLE OF YPRES

August 1917

Reference Map No. 3.

AT 5 a.m. on July 22 the Battalion left Bailleulval, marching to Mondicourt station, where we breakfasted and entrained for Belgium. After seven weary hours in the train we reached a village called Godewaersvelde (pronounced by the men " God help us "), and detrained. Hopes had been entertained that we might be allowed to pass the night here, but instead we were given a four hours' march to Houtkerque, eventually arriving there at 12.30 a.m. It had been a long day, and we were thankful to get into the very meagre accommodation that had been allotted to us, though before doing so most of us felt compelled to inform the billeting officer exactly how meagre we thought it. There never was, and perhaps never will be, a more thankless job than billeting, or one which bred unpopularity so certainly. The most suitable officer was found to be a senior one, capable of being intensely rude to anyone who showed signs of impoliteness to him.

Preparations for the coming battle reached their zenith during the week at Houtkerque. In consequence of an order that every officer and N.C.O. was to be in possession of a map of the battle area which would show at a glance the objectives and contours, mapping became a disease, and the most hideous productions in the way of colour schemes resulted.

It was laid down that the 2nd in Command, two company commanders, the assistant adjutant, two company sergeant-majors, with a proportion of platoon commanders and other ranks, should not be taken into action, but left at Houtkerque, in order that the Battalion might be reorganised quickly in the event of heavy casualties. This personnel was accordingly left behind when, at midnight on July 30/31, we moved to St. Jans-ter-Biezen, which lay just east of Poperinghe. No sooner had we reached the camp here at 4 a.m. than all the guns of the two attacking armies opened fire, and the Third Battle of Ypres had begun.

An intense desire for news of the attack filled the whole of that day. The weather was dull and cloudy, and towards evening rain fell, which continued unceasingly throughout the night. Official communiqués from General Headquarters informed us that the first three objectives had been gained, but, although it was not so stated, we inferred that our casualties had been heavy. This was confirmed when, on the following day, we were ordered to send one company (C) up to the line to assist the 39th Division in bringing in their wounded.

The rain continued in torrents during the whole of that day and the next, and the prospect of the operations being successful and working to plan grew dimmer and dimmer.

Reports from the line of conditions which prevailed there were depressing in the extreme. The whole area had become a quagmire, and the task of moving up guns an impossibility. Never had such appalling weather made its appearance at such an unfortunate time.

A continuance of the operations was therefore postponed until such time as the guns could be shifted and the movement of troops became possible. The enemy

THE THIRD BATTLE OF YPRES 71

meanwhile was presented with a priceless opportunity of reorganising, bringing up reinforcements, and making new positions preparatory to our next onslaught. He was, moreover, being driven back on to comparatively clean ground, while our armies were moving forward on to ground which had been shelled by our own guns for months past, and where roads no longer existed. For three days we watched the pouring rain and cursed the British Army's luck.

On August 4 the Battalion moved through Poperinghe to a spot known as Dambre Camp, which lay about a mile north of Vlamertinghe. After a day's reconnaissance of the line, the Battalion relieved the 1/1st Hertfordshire Regiment and a battalion of the Cheshire Regiment in support. These two battalions had suffered heavily in the attack and were dead-beat.

We found the conditions which prevailed even worse than the reports had led us to believe, for in addition to the sea of mud, which made movement almost impossible, enemy shelling was constant. Communication with companies was difficult in the extreme, as telephone wires were cut by shelling almost as soon as they were laid. At night, orderlies had a really terrible task, often under heavy shell-fire, to find the Headquarters of the Battalion and various companies. We were most fortunate to possess men so extraordinarily efficient for this ordeal, and it is safe to say that no body of men in the Battalion deserve more credit and praise for their magnificent work in the Ypres fighting than these runners. It was invariably of the most vital nature, including not only the carrying of important messages, but also the guiding of reliefs and ration parties. Rations, which had to be brought up to the line on pack animals (ponies and mules), were the cause of constant anxiety, and no one who has not accompanied those animals on a pitch-dark night, across open country pitted with shell-holes and with mud nearly to the knees, knows what difficulties the pack leaders experienced. Only too often an animal was killed on the way up, and its load had to be taken off and reloaded on to another, in the dark, with no possibility of showing a light.

It must not be imagined that our own artillery were quiet during these times—far from it. The majority of the guns were in position alongside a road or track, known as " Admiral's Road," which ran, roughly speaking, through the old " No Man's Land." Their positions were necessarily much exposed, and consequently received the enemy's earnest attention at frequent intervals throughout the day and night. This, however, did not prevent them from throwing back quite as much "stuff" as was hurled at us, and although conditions underfoot were easier behind the German lines, the enemy opposite us must have had a very thin time of it. His nervousness was most apparent at dawn and dusk, when he would often send up his S.O.S. signal for no good reason and put down an intense barrage. On several occasions our own gunners replied heatedly, thinking that an attack was on foot, and a terrific artillery duel would ensue, all owing to a misapprehension.

It was in this area too that we first made our acquaintance with the German concrete blockhouse. The large majority of these constructions had stood the test of the bombardment which preceded our original attack, and they now provided a few headquarters with good cover; but the insides of these blockhouses were in most cases too filthy for words, and several of them were half filled with stagnant water. Cover, however, was cover, and to get it one was prepared to put up with a good deal.

On August 7 the Battalion relieved the 5th Gloucester Regiment in the front line, on the western outskirts of

CHEDDAR VILLA, ST JULIEN.

THE THIRD BATTLE OF YPRES 73

St. Julien (Map No. 3). A and B Companies held this outpost line, while C Company was in support round Canopus Trench, and D Company in reserve in California Drive and Falkenhayn Redoubt. Battalion Headquarters was at Vanheule Farm, which now consisted only of a flooded blockhouse. D Company Headquarters, with one platoon and the Regimental Aid Post, occupied Cheddar Villa, which was a superior blockhouse to Vanheule, except that the Germans, when they built it, had made a particularly large entrance which, now that it was in our hands, was completely exposed to enemy shells. The accommodation being very limited, the platoon were, on the first night, packed closely inside the opening trying to get a little sleep. The very first shell which landed near the blockhouse arrived straight through the opening and burst in the midst of the slumbering platoon. The effect was appalling—many were killed, and of those who were not killed, several lost limbs, many their legs. Happily the Medical Officer (Captain L. E. Hughes) was unhurt, and, as usual on such occasions, excelled himself in the relief he gave and the amount of work he accomplished in the next few hours.

We were relieved on the following night by the 1/5th Battalion Royal Warwickshire Regiment, and moved back to Dambre Camp. The march from the line was exceedingly unpleasant, for the Battalion was literally chased out by shells of the 5·9 variety.

Considering that no active operations had taken place, and that the Battalion had only been twenty-four hours in the front line, with forty-eight hours in reserve, our casualties for the tour, amounting to two officers and sixty-seven other ranks, were certainly heavy, and they give a fair idea of the daily wastage due to shelling.

The weather had again turned wet, and, although it was known that the attack was to be resumed at the earliest favourable opportunity, it was not until the 13th that we got definite orders. From these, it transpired that the attack was to be carried on along the whole front of the Second and Fifth Armies, and that the XVIIIth Corps was to employ the 11th and 48th Divisions. The objective, so far as the 145th Infantry Brigade was concerned, was the high ground overlooking the valley of the Stroombeek; the order of battle of this Brigade was the 1/5th Battalion Gloucestershire Regiment on the right, the 1st Bucks Battalion in the centre, the 1/4th Battalion Oxford and Bucks Light Infantry on the left, with the 1/4th Battalion Royal Berkshire Regiment in Brigade reserve.

The British front line on the Brigade front lay immediately west of the Steenbeek, whilst the Germans were holding a line consisting of organised shell-holes and reinforced houses, along the ridge 200 yards east of the stream.

Full orders for the Battalion attack and the artillery programme are given in Appendix IB; it will therefore be sufficient here to say that the Battalion was to form up for the attack west of the Steenbeek, on a front of 500 yards immediately north of the St. Julien bridge (Map No. 3). The formation was to be: two companies in front, A (Captain G. R. F. Knight) on the left and B (2/Lieutenant E. H. Fawcitt) on the right, each in two waves of two platoons, with C (Captain G. V. Neave) and D (Captain H. J. Pullman) in artillery formation behind right and left respectively.

Tanks were to have co-operated, but, owing to the waterlogged state of the ground, were counter-ordered at the last moment.

On the morning of August 15, the Battalion (Lieutenant-Colonel L. L. C. Reynolds, D.S.O.) marched

THE THIRD BATTLE OF YPRES 75

from Dambre Camp to the canal bank. Here the afternoon was spent, and at 9.30 p.m. we began to move to the forming-up positions. It proved a most trying march, the greater part of the route being over ground a mass of shell-holes full of water, the night pitch-dark and enemy shelling heavy. There was, or had been, a trench-board track to guide us part of the way, but this did not help much, as in many places it had been completely blown away by shells. With nothing else to aid us in keeping direction, it was no real wonder that three platoons of C Company lost their way and failed to turn up in time to take part in the initial assault. The remainder of the Battalion reached the forming-up positions and were ready twenty minutes before zero, which was fixed for 4.45 a.m. on August 16, 1917.

At zero minus seven minutes, the two leading companies moved forward to cross the Steenbeek. At zero, the artillery barrage was put down 200 yards east of the stream and timed to creep forward at the rate of 100 yards every five minutes. The " going " was very bad indeed, as the ground was a mass of shell-craters and there were but few signs of dawn breaking. The result was that the barrage lifted off the enemy forward position before our leading wave could get up to it. A very heavy machine-gun fire was opened by the enemy from his concrete emplacements, and this was quickly reinforced by considerable rifle fire from his shell-hole positions. The fire almost entirely annihilated the leading wave of the right company, who instantly lost two out of their three officers. The second wave closed up and engaged the enemy with fire, while parties worked round the flanks, but the enemy kept up a very strong resistance, and until the leading platoons of D Company closed up and charged with the bayonet they showed no signs of giving in. This charge by the third wave was followed by a bout of hand-to-hand fighting around the blockhouses on the Hillock Farm-St. Julien road, until the garrison of one blockhouse put up their hands. After this the other garrisons soon followed suit. This was the situation on the right about 6 a.m.

The remains of B and D Companies were then quickly reorganised and pushed on in an attempt to overtake our barrage, which had by this time got well ahead of them. They could only succeed in advancing some 300 yards north-east of the outskirts of St. Julien, where they were confronted by a large sheet of water, with a blockhouse and two gunpits on the far side held by machine guns and riflemen. Every attempt made by these companies to get forward was stopped by a heavy cross-fire from these positions and others on the left.

The left leading company (A) met with less resistance at first, but on topping the slight ridge above the Steenbeek they came under a heavy cross-fire from Hillock Farm and two old gunpits west of it, as well as from positions away to their left, in front of the left Battalion, who had been held up close to the Steenbeek. The leading wave reached the gunpits with only sixteen men left. The second wave closed up, but its left platoon was completely stopped by fire from the direction of Maison du Hibou and Triangle Farm. The right platoon, carrying out their orders, continued the attack with the remains of the leading wave and succeeded in reaching their objective at Springfield at about 6.45 a.m. Many, however, were seen to fall as they passed Hillock Farm, and very few could actually have reached Springfield. After the first rush by this gallant party, every effort was made to reach the place and afford them assistance, but each attempt met with failure and many casualties, and at 9 a.m. the enemy

THE STEENBEEK.

THE BATTLE-FIELD NEAR ST. JULIEN, YPRES.

THE THIRD BATTLE OF YPRES

were seen to rush the house, three or four of our men being afterwards led away.

At 7 a.m. Battalion Headquarters was established in a blockhouse on the west side of the Hillock Farm-St. Julien road, and made itself responsible for that road, whilst the other troops that remained were sent to reinforce the more forward position on the right. In the meantime the 5th Gloucesters on the right had got about 300 yards west of the Steenbeek, where they too were finally held up.

Soon after 8 a.m. the enemy were seen coming over the ridge north of Springfield in considerable numbers and collecting in a trench below it. As by this time we had no communication with the artillery, this massing by the enemy continued, whilst our companies were hastily reorganised for defence, and three Vickers guns brought into suitable positions. One platoon of the 1/4th Royal Berks was also got up and placed so as to protect our left flank, which was quite in the air.

At 9 a.m. three thick waves of the enemy were seen to move down towards Triangle Farm, where they got under cover. At 10 a.m. the enemy counter-attacked us heavily from this farm and from each side of it. The fire from our machine guns, Lewis guns and rifles was, however, too much for them, for after a short time they commenced to retire over the ridge by which they had come.

Sniping and machine-gun fire were brisk throughout the day, and we had several casualties, mostly in the neighbourhood of Hillock Farm, where our men had little cover and the slightest movement was visible to the enemy.

At 7.30 p.m., as it was getting dusk, about a hundred Germans attempted to rush the gunpits we were holding on the left, but they were stopped and suffered heavily. No further counter-attack occurred until 9.30 p.m., when the enemy again launched a surprise attack from the direction of Triangle Farm, and succeeded on this occasion in driving in our posts very slightly round Hillock Farm.

Reconnoitring patrols, sent out during the night, reported the enemy to be holding the line of the Springfield road.

Owing to enemy sniping, it had been found quite impossible to collect the wounded during the day, and a great amount of searching and clearing had to be done that night. Enemy dead lay along the Hillock Farm road in large numbers, the majority having been bayoneted.

The captures by the Battalion were:

> 80 prisoners (mostly 7th Bavarian Infantry Regiment).
> 1 field gun.
> 3 machine guns.

Large quantities of equipment and medical stores were also taken.

The attack proved that our barrage had no effect whatever on the garrisons of concrete blockhouses, and that for future operations it was essential that these houses should be dealt with by the "heavies" prior to any assault.

For such a comparatively small advance, it had been a costly attack, but, as our flanks even now were largely in the air, it is difficult to see how we could have maintained positions farther forward, had we been able to reach them.

Our casualties were:

Officers.—Killed.   Capt. G. V. Neave.
　　　　　　　　　　Capt. G. R. F. Knight.

THE THIRD BATTLE OF YPRES

Wounded. Lieut. F. D. Ollard.
              2/Lieut. F. M. Passmore.
              2/Lieut. G. A. Johnston.
              2/Lieut. E. H. Fawcitt.
              2/Lieut. R. E. Norman.
              2/Lieut. A. T. Moyle.
              2/Lieut. F. C. Marshall.
Other Ranks.—Killed—54.
              Wounded—193.
              Missing—85 (14 afterwards reported prisoners of war).

2/Lieutenant G. A. Johnston showed remarkable gallantry during this action, in which he was very seriously wounded.

The Battalion was relieved the following evening by the 6th Battalion Royal Warwickshire Regiment, and as a result of this action the following congratulatory messages were received :

"*To the General Officer Commanding* 145*th Infantry Brigade.* August 19, 1917.

" In case the exigencies of the service prevent me visiting your battalions to-day, please tell them that I appreciate very much the stubborn and determined fighting spirit shown by you, and your officers and men, in the battle on the 16th. Although the fortunes of war, in the form of concrete shelters and an unexpectedly strong preliminary position, prevented us from gaining more than a portion of the objectives we want, we made a very valuable improvement to our position for future progress. Besides the capture of over 100 prisoners, very severe loss was inflicted on the Germans, one small field gun and several machine guns were captured.

" It is not the mere capture of positions which is going to bring us the final victory, but the determined fighting, in spite of all difficulties, like that of the Bucks Battalion, which shows the enemy that he is beaten and cannot hope to beat us and must give in.

" I have the fullest confidence in your Brigade, and know that they will continue to fight with the same spirit with which they have always done, in spite of difficulties.—(*Signed*) R. FANSHAWE, *Major-General.*"

" *To General Sir H. de la P. Gough, K.C.V.O., K.C.B., Commanding Fifth Army.*

" I wish to congratulate you personally, as well as the commanders, staffs and troops under your command, most warmly, on the successes gained by the Fifth Army yesterday, under conditions of great difficulty and in the face of the most determined opposition.

" The bad weather, which delayed the continuance of our offensive, enabled the enemy to bring up and concentrate considerable forces in reserve, and to make careful preparations to meet our attack yesterday. In spite of this, the determination and gallantry of the troops under your command succeeded in striking another of the successful blows, the cumulative effects of which are shattering the enemy's power of resistance and will ultimately lead to his complete defeat.—(*Signed*) D. HAIG, *Field-Marshal.*"

Eight days' rest in Dambre Camp was allowed us, before we again moved up to the line to take part in further operations. This time it was the turn of the 143rd and 144th Brigades to attack, the former on the right, the latter on the left, their objective being the red line shown on Map No. 3.

The 145th Brigade was to be in reserve until zero plus five hours, when it was to move through the leading brigades, and capture the line of farms included by the dotted blue line (Map No. 3). So far as this Brigade

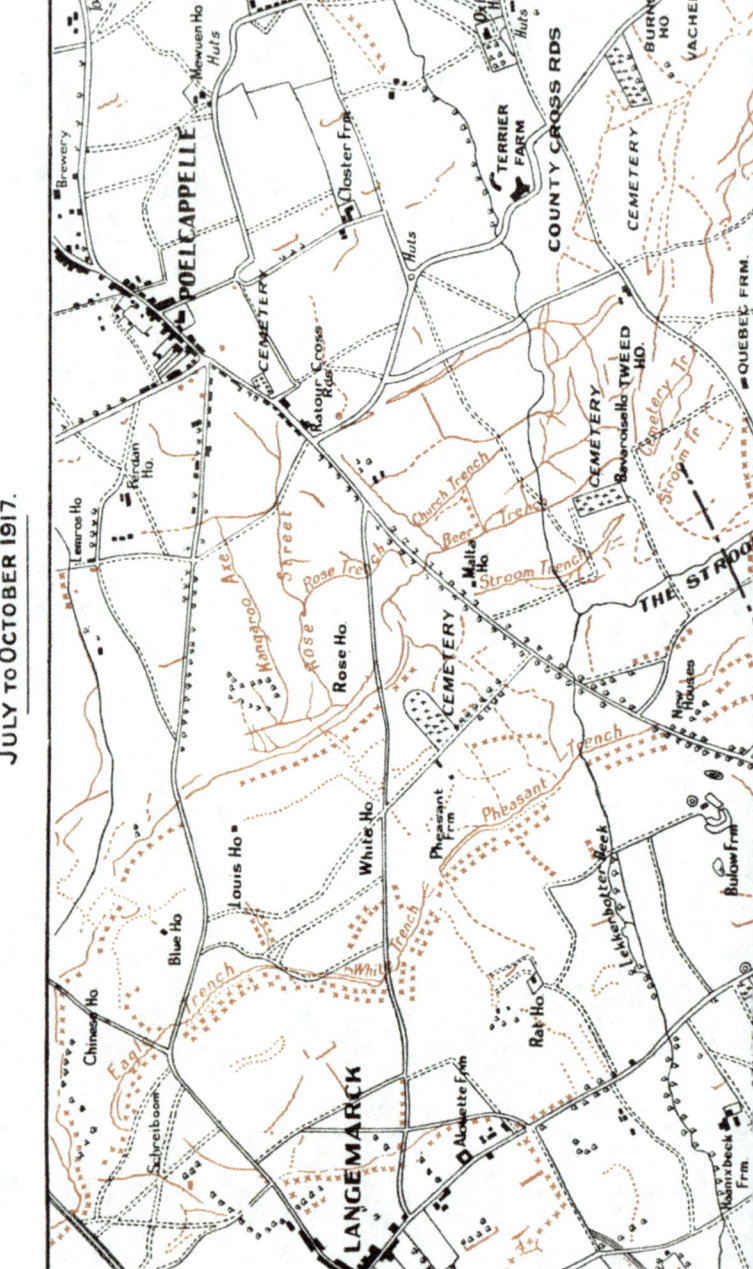

MAP No. 3.
Third Battle of Ypres
July to October 1917.

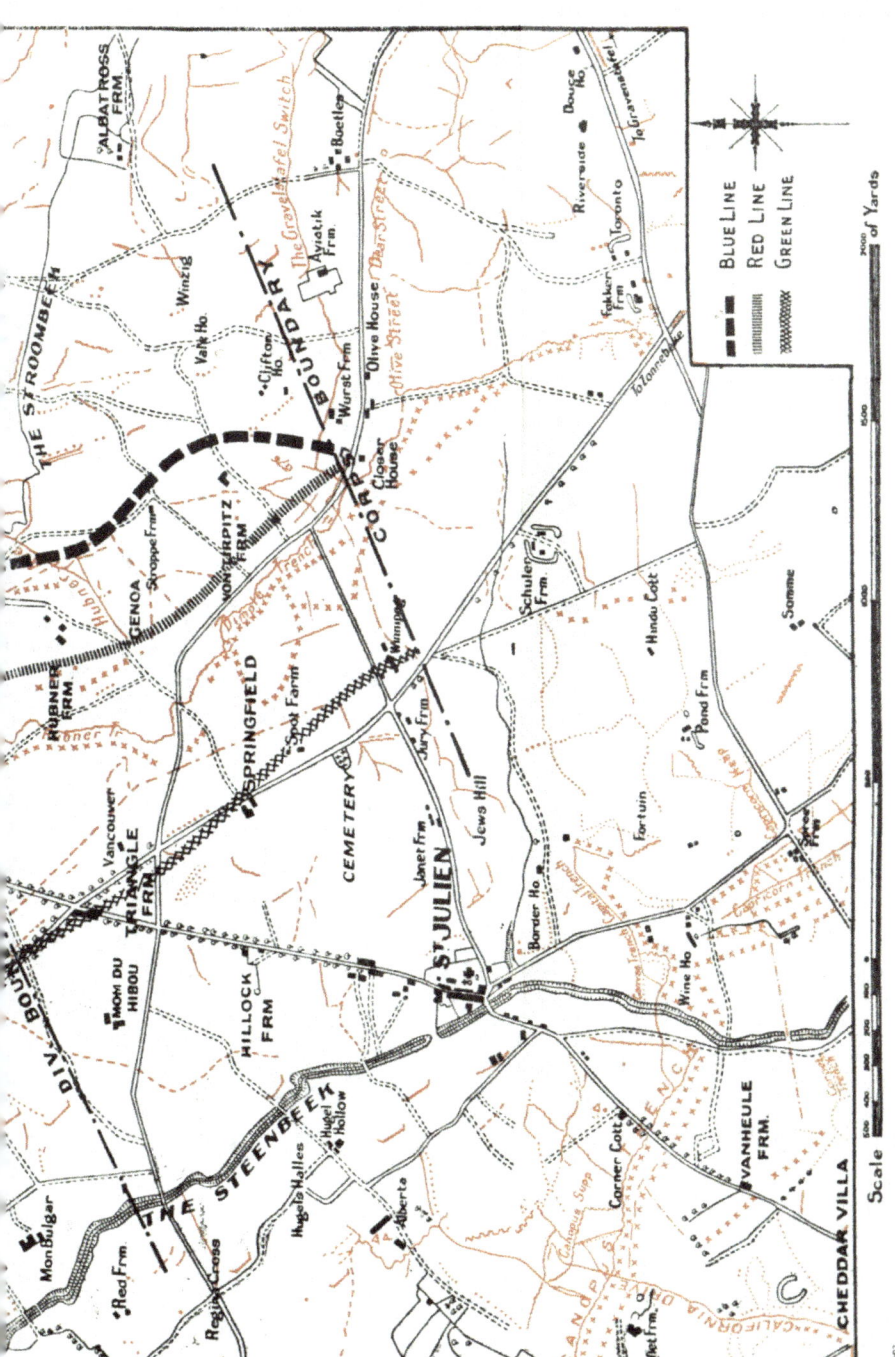

THE THIRD BATTLE OF YPRES 81

was concerned, the 1/4th Royal Berks and 1/4th Oxford and Bucks Light Infantry were to leave the canal bank at zero, move across country to assembly positions about the green line, and be ready to carry out the attack on the dotted blue line at zero plus five hours. The 1/5th Gloucesters and the Bucks Battalion were to leave the canal bank at zero plus three hours, and move to the assembly positions vacated by the other two battalions.

Zero was fixed for 1.55 p.m. August 27, 1917. At 4.55 p.m. the head of the Battalion, marching by platoons, passed the canal bank. There appeared to be every prospect of a thoroughly disagreeable march, as shells are never so plentiful as during the few hours succeeding an attack, but we were most fortunate, for the Steenbeek was reached with hardly a casualty. The ground, however, between that stream and the Triangle Farm–St. Julien road was being very heavily shelled. This caused us casualties, but they were few compared with the immense number of shells falling around us. This was largely due to the state of the ground, which, whilst so deep in mud as to make progress almost impossible for us, minimised the resistance to the bursting shells and so diminished the force of their explosion.

Heavy rain had fallen throughout the previous night, with the result that the battle area was nothing more or less than a sea of mud. Many who were wounded and fell got sucked in, and were not discovered till long afterwards, often when it was too late.

The situation on our arrival was most obscure, but it was evident that very little, if any, progress had been made by the two leading brigades. It had been a case of pulling one foot out of the mud and putting the other in, whilst the enemy took full advantage of the weary process and shot hard at good and slowly moving targets. Rifles, bombs and Lewis guns became coated with muddy slime, which quickly put them out of action. Apart from this, the way was perilous in the extreme. Under such conditions the task set was impossible of achievement, and further progress was out of the question. The only real gain was the capture of Springfield by the 1/8th Battalion Worcestershire Regiment.

The night, passed in the neighbourhood of Maison du Hibou, was intensely dark; the evacuation of wounded presented even greater difficulties than on the 16th, and at least eight men to a stretcher were found to be necessary.

The following day, August 28, the whole Division was relieved in the line, the Bucks Battalion handing over to the 2/7th Battalion London Regiment.

CHAPTER VIII

THE THIRD BATTLE OF YPRES—VIMY

September to Mid-November 1917

IN our joy to be rid of the Ypres area, we began at once to entertain hopes of never seeing it again. Vain hopes, for we were back again in under a month.

The first fortnight of our rest and preparations for future offensives was spent in camp close to St. Janster-Biezen. This was not sufficiently far behind the line to be entirely clear of the war, for enemy bombing planes paid us a most unwelcome visit every night that the weather was fine, and the Division suffered quite a number of casualties through them.

Leave reopened at once in a very fairly generous way, and everything that could be effected to make life more possible was done. Training was more important than anything, but this was completed in four and a half hours in the morning, and the afternoon and evening were given up to games. On one of these afternoons a number of officers and men of our 2nd line Battalion visited us, this being the first occasion on which the two Battalions had had any good opportunity of seeing each other since our second line came out.

Before we moved from this camp no fewer than thirteen officers had joined the Battalion as reinforcements, from the 1st Battalion Artists Rifles.

Our next move was carried out by train on September

16, the Battalion entraining at Abeele and detraining at Audruicq (north-west of St. Omer), whence a twelve-mile march brought us to Licques. Here the billets were excellent, as they had not been used as such before; and with the country and weather perfect, the rest promised to be all that one could desire. The training area included an excellent field-firing range, and in a company competition held throughout the Division C Company succeeded in gaining second place. A most successful Brigade horse show was also held on September 23, and the Battalion carried off more than its fair share of prizes.

The days in fact went all too quickly, and it was with feelings of genuine regret that we left the place at two o'clock on the morning of September 27, and, entraining at Audruicq, found ourselves at our old friend the canal bank on the same afternoon. Here we stayed for three days in reserve to the remainder of the Brigade, which had taken over the old divisional front close to St. Julien.

On our taking over the line from the 1/4th Battalion Oxford and Bucks Light Infantry on the night of September 30–October 1, it appeared that an appreciable though not very large advance had been made in our absence. The farms which we had seen so often on the map, but which wanted so much taking, namely, Hubner, Genoa, Von Tirpitz and the others, were at last ours, and the front line now ran along Cemetery Trench just in front of Quebec, and thence due south. The enemy shelling was as heavy as ever, especially at night, when the whole front area as far back as the Steenbeek became most "unhealthy." The ground at this time was not quite at its worst, but this was sure to be the case when no attack was in progress. It was only necessary for the 1/6th and 1/7th Battalions Royal Warwickshire Regiment to march up and relieve us,

THE THIRD BATTLE OF YPRES—VIMY

with a view to attacking the following morning, for the rain to come down in torrents. The Battalion was ordered to leave one company in the line to act as an outpost company during the forming up and first phase of the attack to be made by the Royal Warwicks, the remainder of the Battalion moving back to a camp about half a mile behind the canal bank.

The objectives of this attack were: 1st—Tweed House, York and Winchester Farms, and Albatross Farm; 2nd—County cross-roads, Vacher Farm and Burns House (Map No. 3).

Divisions on the right and left were co-operating, and zero was fixed for 6 a.m., October 4.

The whole of the first objective was gained by 8.30 a.m. The second objective, excepting Vacher Farm and Burns House, was captured by 10.30 a.m. Three officers and about 320 other ranks belonging to the 369th, 370th and 371st German Infantry Regiments were taken prisoners, and two anti-tank guns and numerous machine guns captured.

The attack in fact was successful, and, provided that we could be spared a little fine weather, there appeared reasonable prospects of our being able to make some substantial progress. On the 5th, however, it rained off and on all day; on the 6th it came down in torrents without ceasing; and on the 7th, when we were moved back to Dambre Camp, there were frequent heavy showers. We had not been two hours in this camp before we were warned to get ready to leave again for the line in relief of the 6th and 7th Royal Warwicks, who were dead-beat, soaked to the skin and plastered from head to foot in mud. Sorry as we were for those in the line, we were none too well pleased at the prospect of going in again ourselves, especially as we had been marching hard in the opposite direction within the last two hours. Our feelings, however, were distinctly

86 FIRST BUCKINGHAMSHIRE BATTALION

appeased on finding that we were to have a fleet of motor buses to take us up. These took us as far as Wieltje, where we debussed, proceeding by platoons up to the line via St. Julien. The relief was much complicated by the extreme darkness of the night and the indescribable condition of the forward area; in fact it was not until 2 a.m. that the relief was complete.

The Battalion dispositions then were (Map No. 3):

Battalion Headquarters—Hubner Farm.
C Company (front line)—Terrier Farm, County crossroads, Cemetery.
B Company (front line)—Cemetery, Trench 400 yards east of Winchester Farm.
D Company (support)—In front of Tweed House.
A Company (support)—By York Farm.

The 11th Division were on the left, and the 1/4th Royal Berks on the right.

Shelling throughout the night was heavy, and towards dawn the rain once again came down in great lumps. About 4 p.m. the Battalion received notice that it would be relieved during the evening by the 1/4th Battalion Gloucestershire Regiment on the left and the 1/6th Battalion of the same regiment on the right, and that these two battalions in conjunction with other Divisions on their flanks would attack at dawn. The relief of the right by the 1/6th Gloucesters was a comparatively easy matter, as trench boards had been laid almost up to the front. The relief of the left was a very different affair, and turned out to be a perfect nightmare. No trench boards had been laid in that direction from Hubner, and the road shown as leading past Quebec Farm and Tweed House had long ceased to exist and had become amalgamated with the general quagmire which swamped the whole area. Tweed and

Quebec existed as spots on the map, but were not there to be identified on the ground.

As we had only been in the area some twenty hours, during the greater part of which time it had been light and no movement had consequently been possible, guides who could really find their way without landmarks, in pitch darkness and with the rain teeming down, were very scarce. One had, however, been found for each platoon of the 1/4th Gloucesters, and some idea of the conditions will be obtained when it is said that this number proved wholly insufficient. It was impossible to walk twelve yards without either falling into a shell-hole or getting stuck fast in the mud, so that touch was constantly being lost between one man and the next. By 3 a.m. a few incomplete platoons of the 4th Gloucestershire Regiment had reached their assembly positions, many more were lost, and some had, after being lost, found their way back to Hubner and were wanting fresh guides. Nevertheless by zero we just succeeded in getting the majority of that Battalion to its positions, and this was largely due to the untiring efforts of two of our runners, by name L/Cpl. H. E. Collins and Pte. W. W. Cattell.

By zero the Battalion, with the exception of an outpost company (which had been left in the line to cover the forming up of the attacking Battalion), was concentrated round Cheddar Villa in divisional reserve. Zero was at 5.20 a.m., October 9. Although the rain ceased just before this time, the condition of the ground was such as to render the chances of a successful attack exceedingly small, if not quite impossible, but the progress actually made was considerably greater than expected, though casualties were heavy.

On the evening of October 10, the Division was relieved in the line by the 9th Division, and the Battalion left the Ypres battle area for good, being carried back to Dambre Camp from Wieltje in motor lorries. On leaving the Ypres sector the Divisional Commander received the following message from General Gough, commanding the Fifth Army :

" The 48th Division have taken part in much hard fighting during the past two months, including five general engagements. Their spirit and determination on all occasions have been admirable, and temporary setbacks have in no way affected their *moral*. I am very sorry to bid good-bye to such a dependable division and feel sure that the future holds many further successes for them."

After a twenty-four hours' halt at Dambre Camp and forth-eight hours at St. Jans-ter-Biezen, the Battalion entrained at Hopoutre on the evening of October 14, and proceeded by rail to Ligny-St. Flochiel, just east of St. Pol. Breakfasts were eaten here before we started on a long march to Mesnil-Bouché ; after three days there we moved to Villers-au-Bois, where the remainder of the month was spent.

The Division had now come under the orders of the Vth Corps, taking the place of the 2nd Canadian Division. As usual on our arrival in a new area, statements of impending operations were prevalent, and it was now freely rumoured that the corps was to take Lens before Christmas.

Nothing tangible, however, pointed to any such offensive, and when, on November 1, the Battalion went into the line in front of Vimy, it became clear that we had taken over some very good and reasonably quiet trenches. Our chief occupation in this part of the line was preparing trenches for the coming winter. That we were successful in this respect is proved by the following message, received by the Division after its withdrawal from the line in the middle of November, on relief again by the 2nd Canadian Division :

" On my own behalf and on behalf of the troops under my command, I would be glad if you would cause to be conveyed to the G.O.C. 48th Division, an appreciation of the excellent work carried out in this area by the troops under his command during the period between 18th October and 18th November. The erection of the four Battalion camps in Neuville-St. Vaast has been so exceptionally well carried out that the G.O.C. 2nd Canadian Division reports that his troops have never been housed in greater comfort. The amount of work in the forward area, and the thoroughness with which it has been carried out, bear testimony to the unremitting labour and zeal of all concerned.

" (Sd.) A. W. CURRIE, *Lieutenant-General*
"*Cdg. Canadian Corps.*"

When the 48th Division took over the Vimy sector, everything seemed to point to our settling down there for the winter; consequently, it was with considerable surprise, not unmixed with regret, that we heard we were to be withdrawn.

Speculation of the wildest sort was rife as to our destination. Every sphere of operations, from Russia to German East Africa, was suggested. But the bulk of opinion, fully conscious of the gravity of the situation in Italy, inclined to consider this as our probable destination, although a good many believed a move to the Cambrai area more probable, as whispers of an impending offensive in that neighbourhood were beginning to reach us.

The situation, however, did not remain doubtful very long. When the Division reached the Aubigny area (November 14), where we were given a fortnight to refit, the fact that we were intended for Italy had become fairly common knowledge. The news, on the whole, was welcomed. That life on the Western front was thoroughly unpleasant and precarious we knew; but Italy, despite the long months' disasters, only seemed to call up visions of sunshine, blue skies, and a general atmosphere of *dolce far niente*.

CHAPTER IX

ITALY

Mid-November 1917 *to April* 1918

It was in excellent spirits therefore that the move was begun, in spite of the obscurity of the military situation in Italy, and the prospects of immediate fighting of the unpleasant rearguard type. Our cheerfulness was amply justified, and the journey itself proved to be one of the most magnificent holidays the Battalion ever had. It was accomplished in two trains, which followed each other at about twelve hours' interval: the first containing half Battalion Headquarters (Commanding Officer, Adjutant and Transport Officer), Transport, and A and C Companies; the second containing the other half of Headquarters (second in Command, Assistant Adjutant, Medical Officer and Intelligence Officer), and B and D Companies.

The first half of the Battalion marched out of Tinques at 9 p.m. on November 23, 1917, and entrained at Savy, leaving about midnight. The second half left Tinques at 6 a.m. the next day, and pulled out of Savy about 9 a.m.

The route followed by both trains on the journey was the same, and the following names will indicate the line taken: Arras, Achiet-le-Grand, Albert, Amiens, Dijon, Pierrelatte, Avignon, Marseilles, Nice, Voghera, Piacenza, Bologna, and thence north to the Mantua and Este line.

The total time spent on the journey was six days. The experiences were very much the same in both trains, which ran most of the time within a very few hours of each other; the account of one train's week will therefore suffice to cover the history of both.

On November 24 the train passed, in bright sunny weather, through the Ancre Valley and Albert, which we had last seen on our way out of the hideous Le Sars sector about a year previously. Thence through Amiens, and on south towards Paris, round which we skirted at dusk.

The train was unusually commodious, there being enough of the usual cattle-trucks for the men to allow of something narrowly approaching comfort, while the officers were three to a compartment, so that if one slept on the floor, all of them could get a comfortable night's rest. In addition, there were a certain number of flats, which were not needed for our transport vehicles, but which afforded superb observation on sunny days. Comfort became almost a fine art. Every time the train stopped the men seemed to have a meal, as not only did the cooks achieve marvels on the cookers, which were at full blast all the day long, but also there were numerous *halte-repas*, at which hot water was always available, and, often enough, tea or coffee. As for the officers, they lived in that luxury which is only achieved by mess cooks when there is no facility for it. Adequate supplies had, of course, been laid in before we started, and the chances of buying eggs and other things on the journey were frequent. The nights were cold, but the cold was kept out as far as possible by braziers standing on tins in the trucks, and a carefully distributed rum ration.

The second day broke dull and raining, and this continued until evening, but a brisk, cold, sunny morning found us at Pierrelatte in the Rhone valley, and a

ITALY

glorious day followed of fine open country round the Rhone, with sudden sharp cliffs, offshoots of the Maritime Alps, and far-away views of blue-grey mountains, shutting in the rich plain which forms the delta of that great river. And so we passed through a charming landscape, made the more charming by the very friendly faces and the waving handkerchiefs of the inhabitants, to Avignon, with its castle glittering in the sunlight.

It was here that trains began to lose men, as from now onwards stops were always of somewhat doubtful duration. We came into Marseilles that evening, with the streets and harbour glowing with lights below us.

Early next morning (27th) we reached Les Arcques, where the men had breakfast. Then followed the best day of the whole journey. The weather was absolutely perfect, and sitting out on the open flats we rattled along the glorious coast of the French Riviera. Everywhere the people waved to us, cheered and threw us oranges, a compliment which we returned by throwing cigarettes to the French colonial sentries, who grinned and flashed at us their rows of perfect teeth.

By the afternoon we had crossed the frontier, where at Vintimiglia we detrained the men, and took them for a short, sharp march through the town and along the sea-front.

The journey from now onwards became far less interesting. There were interminable stops at out-of-the-way stations; and signs of the disorder in Italy, the result of the Caporetto disaster, became more frequent. At Bologna, where all the officers were very kindly provided with lunch-baskets by the Italian Comando di Tappa, refugees crowded the station, and that most pitiful spectacle was presented of strings of Italian deserters, chained together. It was clear that firmness was to be the order of the day.

From Bologna we went northwards, crossing the

river Po, and the two trains reached their respective destinations. The first arrived at Bevilacqua at 7 p.m. on November 29. Here the most hopeless confusion reigned, owing to the entire absence of any R.T.O. or orders of any sort. Endless interviews with the magnificent station-master took place, but as he could understand neither English nor French, and we were none of us able to speak Italian, the interviews were entirely fruitless. Eventually, however, having dispatched an officer to the R.T.O. at the previous station, we received orders to billet in Bevilacqua for the night, and were presented with an Italian interpreter.

The second train reached Este at 8 a.m. on November 30, where the remainder of the day and that night were spent. Orders were received to march next day to Agugliaro, where the two halves of the Battalion joined hands. For the next four days we marched every day and all day, billeting during the nights in the villages of Bosco di Nanto, Villafranca and Marsango, and eventually reaching Villa del' Conte on December 8. Lorry transport was very scarce during these marches, and the greatest difficulties were experienced in moving our 1,800 blankets from place to place. Our troubles in this respect were increased by having to move an unusually large number of valises, as we were at this time in possession of no less than forty-three officers. Twelve of these officers, however, were now dispatched to the base, and this relieved the congestion considerably.

Our arrival in Italy had been of a very different character from the one we had pictured. There was no dramatic deployment from the train to stem the Austrian onrush; as, indeed, there appeared at this time to be very little onrush to stem. The Italians were evidently making a firm stand on the Piave, a stand which became all the firmer as the knowledge grew that elements of the French and British Armies were at their backs in case of need.

Throughout the week spent in Villa del' Conte the Battalion was at two hours' notice to move to support the Italian army; but in spite of expecting hourly to receive such orders, nothing momentous occurred until the 14th, when we were moved some twelve miles to the village of S. Croce Bigolina, which lies about six miles west of Cittadella.

That this village rivalled in popularity the much-beloved village of Beauval in France, is astonishing and almost unaccountable. The billets were bad, crowded and scattered. There were no shops. Footballs were scarce, and grounds still scarcer. On the other hand, the inhabitants were most friendly, if not entirely honest, and the weather was perfect. It must surely have been those heavenly blue skies which entered into our souls and made us think so well of S. Croce.

The Division now formed part of the XIXth Corps, which was in reserve to the Italian Army, holding the line astride the Brenta valley in front of Valstagna.

Here a formidable attack by the enemy was confidently expected, as although the original onrush was being successfully stemmed by the Italian forces and those portions of the French and our own which were now in the line, it was thought very probable that the enemy, by using the remainder of the reserves collected from the Russian front, might try to increase the weight of their attack and break through from the mountains into the plains. In the event of this attack being delivered, the Division had orders to hold a reserve line in the mountains, which lay about Conco, Rubbio and Campolungo.

Thorough reconnaissances of this line were therefore most necessary, and some of us were sent on almost daily excursions in a F.I.A.T. lorry to that coldest of all bleak spots, Rubbio. The journey occupied some two and a half hours, along one of the most amazingly constructed roads in the country. Hewn for the most part out of solid rock, the road climbed 1,800 feet from our billets to Rubbio, zigzagging up the mountain, with a cliff on one side and a sheer drop of about 100 feet on the other.

The difference in the atmosphere between S. Croce and Rubbio was almost paralysing, and few of us will forget the frigid sensation and biting wind that assailed us on getting out of the lorry at the last-named village.

The line consisted of a rock-hewn fire-trench, sited on the forward slopes of a succession of hills or, rather, mountains. Communication with this line would have been most difficult, had we occupied it, for mule-tracks were rare, and none too good when found. To our relief, however, no enemy attack developed, and we were left in peace at S. Croce, where the Battalion spent its third Christmas away from home. In spite of these continual visits to Rubbio and constant hard field training, we had not allowed the time to slip by without a thought for Christmas festivities, and when the day arrived every man was able to eat turkey and plum pudding to his tummy's content, helping it down with more than sufficient *vino*.

This latter, nasty as it really was, had become a most popular tipple, and orderly room had for some time past been much troubled by its existence. It was not so much that it was a potent beverage, as that the men were unaccustomed to it, and thought that it could be treated in the same manner as the French wine. Only when a number of men found themselves in the throes of no less than twenty-eight days' field punishment No. 1 was *vino* shown the respect to which it had proved itself entitled.

With the exception of some snow falling at the

beginning of January, the weather continued perfect, and we considered our Italian campaign one of the better things in life, to which the only drawbacks were no E.F.C., a most irregular mail, and a succession of the very coldest church parades in a field at Villa Jonoch.

Unfortunately, all good things come to an end at some time, and this particular one ended on January 24, 1918, when the Battalion took an affectionate farewell of the natives of S. Croce and marched off towards the Piave, though it was not until a month later that we arrived there.

The billeting area in which we found ourselves, after two days' marching, was really far better than the one we had just left, though the general atmosphere was perhaps not quite so friendly. D Company, at first, revelled in being the sole British occupants of the village of Casacorba, while Battalion Headquarters and the remaining three companies had to content themselves with the rather inferior billets of Albaredo. Later, however, sufficient accommodation was found in Casacorba and the adjoining village of Viciliese to house the whole Battalion, and Albaredo was evacuated.

Our stay here was chiefly notable for a most virulent attack of " outposts " which seized the higher command, and the question whether it is better to fight the post or the piquet line was more than thoroughly debated. Suitable antidotes were soon found in the shape of plenty of football for the men, and a very limited allotment of Rome leave for the officers.

A further move was made on February 14 to Paese, which lies some six miles west of Treviso. This area had been very much troubled by constant bombing raids, carried out by the Austrian and German airmen at night; in fact, the hospital in our village had been hit a few days prior to our arrival, but during our occupation of Paese no further bombing of the village took place, although Treviso continued an almost nightly target, with the result that large numbers of civilians were evacuating it, and the place was becoming a town of ruins.

The knowledge that we were to take over the line on the Piave had now become common property, and on February 27 the Battalion relieved the 21st Battalion Manchester Regiment, 91st Brigade, 7th Division, in support positions on the Montello.

A few days later (March 3) we took over the front line, which for the most part consisted of a series of trench-posts, situated at intervals of 40 or 50 yards along the banks of the river. Our right included the village of Nervesa, and the posts here were dug out of the asphalt promenade on which the fashion of Italy besported itself in times of peace. The breadth of the Piave in front of us was at least half a mile, and consisted of numerous channels, dotted with islands, some of which, lying about 50 yards from our bank, we occupied, but the flimsy character of the bridges leading on to them made their occupation uncertain.

The current of the river varied according to the channels. In the main channel it ran at a rate of at least ten miles an hour in time of flood, and never dropped below three and a half miles an hour at summer level.

During our fortnight's stay here the river became one broad, rushing torrent, owing to the heavy rains, and any attempt on the part of a patrol to cross the river was generally out of the question; but on one night, after the river had gone down considerably, a patrol did succeed in getting across, though it should be described as a feat of endurance rather than a military accomplishment, as the men were so cold when they reached the other side that it is doubtful whether they

ITALY

could have used their arms had this been required of them.

The river, being unfordable at this time, deprived us of any means of getting at close quarters and really making our first acquaintance with a new enemy.

His shooting, so far as artillery was concerned, was decidedly good, and on more than one occasion he troubled us not a little with it. Nervesa was naturally his most popular target, and about the time of our departure he was rapidly demolishing it, chiefly by means of incendiary shells, with which he was most successful in setting the largest houses on fire.

We had not been in the sector a week before rumours of our being moved reached us. These rumours proved correct, and on March 14 the Division was relieved by the Italians. Preparations to ensure a really well-organised relief have no doubt been made by all units during the war, but whether any relief was ever prepared with such hyper-efficiency as this particular one may be doubted. Certainly "eyewash" never figured more prominently, or with so little effect; but our friends the Italians were not nearly so much impressed as had been intended, and our relief by the 163rd Italian regiment proved to be quite a normal proceeding, the greatest good-feeling existing on both sides.

The French, who had been on our left in the M. Tomba sector, were also withdrawn from the line about this time, and it became clear that both armies were intended to take over a new sector in the mountains in the neighbourhood of the Asiago plateau.

The march westward was commenced on the 15th, and after a series of long treks on exceedingly hot days, interspersed with a few days' rest at Piombino, Borgoricco, S. Georgio dell' Pertiche and Busiago Vecchia, we eventually reached S. Urbano on April 3. This village, charmingly situated amongst the foothills which lie between Vicenza and Verona, harboured us for just two weeks, while preparations were made for equipping ourselves suitably for mountain warfare.

Practice attacks were delivered on all the neighbouring hills, and several days were spent by officers in reconnoitring the line on the Asiago plateau.

Our transport was increased by the arrival of some twenty-five additional pack-mules, and although these threatened to displace all our heavy draught horses, G.S. waggons and cookers, we were eventually allowed to retain them all.

On April 17 the Battalion started on its move to the mountain line, halting for nights at Grumo, S. Maria (just east of Thiene) and Mare, which lies at the foot of the mountains that guard the Venetian plain from the North and rise from a series of low foothills, almost sheer, to a height of 4,000 feet. Military roads zigzagged their endless, wearisome way backwards and forwards, and hardly discoverable tracks led up in slippery, stony twists to the summit.

The day of our first journey to the top (April 23) gave us an excellent taste of the changed conditions before us. The ascent was made in single file up one of these mule-tracks, and occupied some four and a half hours; the system of progression adopted being twenty minutes' climbing and ten minutes' halting.

The actual climb to within a few hundred feet of the top was made in bright sunshine. Then abruptly came the change. The sun was clouded over, cold air seemed to come from nowhere, and a slight drizzle began to fall. In such conditions the climb was finished, and the road past Tattenham Corner, with a slight dip in the crest line, followed. A little farther on was a small level space, perhaps 600 yards long and half as many wide, between the masses of rough rock piled up on either side. In this space and round the edge of it

ITALY

nestled the hutment camp of Granezza. Here, and in offshoots of this little plateau, were concentrated two battalions of Infantry, Divisional Headquarters, Brigade Headquarters, a cinema, canteens, dumps, and all the other paraphernalia of a Division in the field.

A more depressing spot than this was when we arrived can hardly be imagined. The drizzle continued to fall, the road was a mass of mud, water dripped and oozed from the wooden huts, whose tarred-felt roofs were covered with dead branches as camouflage. Isolated fir trees, stripped of all their lower branches, stood here and there around the camp, gaunt and miserable, like sentries on a rainy night in the line. Dirty patches of unthawed snow lay among the rocks, and a motley collection of wet and muddy soldiers—English, French and Italian—flowed backwards and forwards along the grey, sticky road.

This, however, was Granezza in one of its worst moods. The next day, though different, was little better, for rain which was falling in the morning changed by mid-day to a full-dress snowstorm, accompanied by thunder and lightning. Snow fell for two or three more days, and all our time and energy were concentrated on clearing roads and tracks. But this was the last of the snow, and was succeeded by a period of bright sunshine, alternating with violent thunderstorms, which gradually changed to the glorious weather of August, September and October. During these months the sun shone all day, there was very little rain, and the heat was not sufficient to be uncomfortable by day nor the cold by night. The particular charm of this glorious weather lay in the fact that we had been assured that on the plateau there were only twenty-five fine days in the year, of which seventeen had already passed.

With the improvement in the weather came equally

a difference in the country, which had at first seemed so desolate. The area taken over by the British troops was divided by nature into two sectors, each of which was held by a Division. Two roughly parallel roads, about four kilometres apart, led to the front line, each feeding one Division's front. These roads were joined laterally by two other parallel roads, the one about two and a half, the other about six kilometres, behind the line. All intervening spaces were filled with rough rocky mountains, devoid of trees on the south side, but thickly wooded on the north side. The country gradually fell away towards the front line, which ran rather more than 1,000 feet below the level of Granezza. The line itself, cut partly in solid rock and partly in chalk, ran for the most part just inside the trees, which here stop short on the edge of the Asiago plateau. The plateau, about four kilometres wide, consists of undulating grassy land, treeless, but dotted here and there with farmhouses and tiny villages, all more or less damaged by shell-fire. About a kilometre off lay the Austrian front line, well out in the open, and away behind it the mountains rose up in a tremendous barrier 6,000 feet high, protecting the Val Sugana. To all of us it seemed a position that no troops in the world could capture, and we little guessed during the long months that we faced those mountains, that in the end we should ourselves successfully attack and overcome them.

CHAPTER X

THE AUSTRIAN ATTACK OF JUNE 15

May and June 1918

Reference map No. 4

ONE of the greatest problems when we lived in the mountains was the question of transport and supply. The Divisional ration-dump was made in the foothills, so it was obviously impossible for us to have all our transport with us in the mountains and send it to the ration-dump daily, as waggons would have been some ten hours on the roads. It was equally impossible to have all the transport living near the ration-dump and making daily pilgrimages up to the mountains. It was therefore decided to leave the 2nd echelon transport in the foothills at Fara, and to have the 1st echelon with us at Granezza. The former then brought the Battalion's rations each day as far as Tezze Sciessere, which lay half-way up the mountain by road, while the 1st echelon met it there and brought the supplies on to us.

Even this proved to be intensely hard on the horses, and it was afterwards arranged to do much of the work by a more generous use of Army motor lorries. There had been much discussion as to whether we should take up the cookers, and it was eventually decided to do so. One of these—namely, A Company's—was the victim of the only accident which befell us on our first journey up, as together with horses and driver it fell over the cliff from the roadside. By a miracle neither the driver nor the two horses were much hurt, in spite of their rolling with the vehicle for 50 feet down the mountain-side and taking a 10-feet drop at the end! As much cannot be said for the cooker, which was smashed beyond hope of repair.

Our first tour in a mountain sector, although interesting, was not eventful, and only lasted a month. This, however, was quite long enough in view of the climatic conditions at this time of year, for the weather had been vile, and one more often wore wet clothes than dry ones.

A complete change was experienced on arrival in the plains (May 19), for here the heat was intense. The villages of Grumo and Cereda, which had been allotted to us for billets, lay some thirty miles from Fara, our marches to these places being carried out at night to avoid the heat of the day. Khaki drill was now issued to replace the usual serge clothing, and this, with pith helmets for headgear, made a hot life possible. Training was carried out between six and ten o'clock in the morning, and again in the cool of the evening. During the other hours of daylight we lay and gasped.

We had been led to expect that the Division (less the 144th Brigade, who were still in the mountains) would be kept in billets in the plains for three weeks or a month, but this did not materialise, owing to receipt of rather sudden orders to relieve the 7th Division in the line. Two long marches, carried out in the early mornings, took us to Camisino, at the foot of the mountains, and on June 1 the Battalion negotiated the 3,000-feet climb, which occupied close on five hours. The rough and very steep mule-track, up which our path lay, seemed interminable, and in spite of making the start at 4.30 a.m., the heat during the last hour of the ascent proved very trying.

THE AUSTRIAN ATTACK OF JUNE 15

We were now in the left Divisional sector of the British front, whereas before we had been in the right. It was strange how very similar the two sectors were in the matter of roads, general formation of the country, and forestry. Our front line lay towards the foot of the northern slopes of M. Lemerle, and was sited well inside the wood, thus providing very bad observation for the enemy. His own front trenches, on the other hand, were right in the open, towards the other side of the plateau and distant from us some 1,400 yards. It was indeed for us a gunner's paradise. He had only to install himself in a carefully concealed observation post in one of the trees, and choose targets from the varied assortment which the trenches, villages and farms, provided for him.

The portion of line allotted to the Battalion lay on the extreme right of the Divisional line, and ran from a point about 700 yards due south of the village of Roncalto, where we joined with the 23rd Division, to the Ghelpac Fork (Map No. 4).

By night, outposts were pushed out well in front of this line, in many cases half-way across the broad "No Man's Land." These posts occupied all points of tactical importance, such as high ground on the plateau, and guarded the main approaches to our line.

In our case the Battalion outpost line ran from Pesaventi along the valley of the dried-up Ghelpac, with a standing patrol covering a hill known as 1002. Fighting patrols were sent out nightly in front of this outpost line, and reconnoitred the ground almost up to the enemy trenches. The enemy's style in "No Man's Land" was thus considerably cramped. He did, however, screw up his courage sufficiently to occupy at night two houses called Vaister, which were situated about 1,300 yards in front of our line and 500 yards in front of that of the enemy.

As we expected soon to undertake an offensive it was thought that his occupation of Vaister might prove an inconvenience to us, so it was consequently decided to turn him out of it. The scheme for this was to attack Vaister during the night (June 8/9) with two platoons, who were to be relieved by two fresh sections shortly before dawn. It was inadvisable to have a larger garrison there by day, as there was very little cover and they would become an easy target for the Austrian gunners, should they be spotted. Two platoons of B Company, under 2/Lieutenant R. W. Grace and 2/Lieutenant W. G. Butler, were detailed for this duty.

The artillery fired salvoes at the houses at half-hour intervals, starting at dusk, and at 1.15 a.m. the 18-pounders put down a one-minute barrage 150 yards north of the houses, in order to make the garrison keep their heads down. This barrage, which was the signal for the assault, was timed to lift 300 yards north of the houses after one minute, and to remain there for five minutes. The two platoons, who made a converging attack from south-east and south-west, got through the wire without much difficulty and reached the houses. They were empty. Rifle fire, however, came from some distance beyond, and it seemed pretty evident that our artillery fire had driven out the enemy, who had decided to take up a position on the spur behind.

At 1.45 a.m. the enemy suddenly assaulted the houses, but were driven off by our rifle and Lewis-gun fire, which caused them considerable loss. A flare, fired by our men, showed up the enemy as they retired, carrying their casualties, and a section was sent out to pursue them, but they only succeeded in catching one man, who stated that they had had twenty casualties.

Between 2.30 a.m. and 3 a.m. the enemy made two further attempts to assault from the direction of Canove, but each attempt was stopped by our fire.

THE AUSTRIAN ATTACK OF JUNE 15

At 3.30 a.m. two sections of D Company, under 2/Lieutenant F. J. Wilcox, relieved the two platoons of B Company, and established three posts covering the houses. They had not been there more than a very few minutes before the Austrians again attacked. Once more they were stopped, and our left section was pushed forward in the hope of catching the enemy retiring.

Later the enemy delivered a further assault from each side of the houses, and in this case succeeded in overrunning our right post. The position, however, was soon restored to us, and at 5.40 a.m. the section was ordered by Battalion Headquarters to withdraw to our lines.

During this tour in the trenches, the prevailing disease, a sort of very acute type of influenza, attacked the Battalion. Every company had some fifteen or twenty men affected and laid out by it, but as the effects, in the majority of cases, were felt for two or three days only, a comparatively small number of men were sent to hospital. There was good reason for conserving our man power as far as possible since orders were out for an offensive by the British Army in conjunction with the French on our right. These operations were to be undertaken with a view to driving the enemy off the actual plateau, and forcing him back on to the Winter Stellung, which was a trench system which he had constructed in front of M. Catz and M. Interrotto, some one and a half miles behind his present front line. Our positions in the event of the attack being successful would not be as favourable to us as they were at the present time, but it was hoped that the losses inflicted on the enemy would be great, and that we should be so much nearer to the key of all the Austrian positions —namely, M. Catz, M. Interrotto, and the mountains overlooking the Val d'Assa (Map No. 4).

Thus, from June 9 to the 14th our minds and plans

were concentrated on this prospective attack. Major P. A. Hall was now in command of the Battalion, owing to Lieutenant-Colonel Reynolds having assumed temporary command of the Brigade.

On the 9th we were relieved in the front line, moving back to Brigade support positions in the Lemerle Switch and Polderhoek Trench. On the evening of the 14th, at a conference at Brigade Headquarters, commanding officers were warned of a suspected attack by the enemy in the Brenta valley and on the Piave, which was thought likely to take place the following morning. It was not expected that the actual attack would affect the British, though it was probable that the enemy's bombardment might extend as far west, in order to mislead us as to the real point of attack. Plans and preparations for our own attack were to continue, zero day for which had been fixed for June 16.

Such were our information and ideas for the future on the night of the 14th. All were doomed to be frustrated by the enemy, and that within a very few hours.

At 3 a.m. the following morning the Austrians opened an intense bombardment, with guns of every calibre, on all our lines of defence. A large amount of gas shell was employed. The whole wood resounded with high-explosive shells bursting among the rocks. Ammunition dumps took fire, and became as dangerous as the enemy's shells. Trees crashed to the ground on all sides, and within a few minutes death was everywhere.

The Bucks Battalion immediately took up its battle stations in the Lemerle Switch and Polderhoek Trench, astride the Boscon road. The orders for the battalion holding these positions, in the event of the enemy breaking through the front line, were to hold on to the last man. This battalion was not to be used to reinforce forward positions. For the next four or five hours

THE AUSTRIAN ATTACK OF JUNE 15

shells rained down upon and around this line, the shooting of the enemy being exceedingly good. Although a break through of the front line was effected, the 1/4th Battalion Oxford & Bucks Light Infantry, who were in the front trenches, fought every yard of ground whilst giving way, and finally succeeded in definitely holding up the attack in the neighbourhood of Pelly Cross.

Thus the enemy never actually reached the line that the Bucks Battalion were holding, except on the extreme right, where he attempted to work round the Oxfords' flank; and the effects of the Austrian attack will be better understood if the attack is described from the Brigade point of view.

The 48th Division had two Brigades in the line: the 143rd in depth on a one-battalion front on the left, and the 145th on a two-battalion front on the right, the whole divisional frontage of four kilometres extending from Roncalto to Schulazzon. The 23rd British Division were on the right, and the 12th Italian Division on the left. Our 144th Brigade was in Divisional reserve, with three battalions in camps at Carriola and M. Brusabo, and one on the plains at the foot of the mountains.

The Divisional front trench line was of a very irregular trace, consisting of a series of acute salients and reentrants, making it impossible for most posts to see what was occurring on either side of them or to give each other mutual assistance. The dry bed of the Ghelpac ran in front of the left Brigade's line, the western part of it lying in a deep gorge. It was between this gorge and Cesuna Wood that the maximum weight of the Austrian onslaught fell, and this was the extreme western limit of the whole enemy attack.

At 3 a.m. the enemy's heavy bombardment opened. At 7 a.m. his infantry attack was launched, following

110 FIRST BUCKINGHAMSHIRE BATTALION

a concentrated bombardment of the front line. Owing to the trees and irregular features of the ground, it was in most cases impossible for our men to observe the advance, or bring effective fire to bear on the attacking columns, until they were actually on our wire. There was also a thick ground mist, which prevented observation from our look-out posts.

The first real break in the Divisional line occurred about the high ground near Perghele, where the enemy were seen advancing in large numbers about 7.50 a.m. From here they swept down the valley behind the 5th Gloucestershire Regiment, which held the centre of the Divisional line, and, taking this battalion in reverse, cut off all communication forward of the Battalion Headquarters. The support company took up a position astride the valley, but the enemy soon enveloped their left, and the company was gradually forced to retire on to the Cesuna-Canove road. This line they held for some time, until a heavy attack was delivered on their right, which forced them back astride the railway and severed their connection with the 1/4th Battalion Oxford & Bucks Light Infantry.

In the meantime, the Oxfords on the right had been putting up a very fine resistance. The enemy had, very early on, succeeded in driving a wedge between them and the Northumberland Fusiliers, who were holding the left of the 23rd Divisional line. The latter had been driven on to their switch line. The right flank of the Oxfords thus became exposed, and the enemy immediately began to work round it. This, however, was prevented by the extreme right of the Bucks Battalion in the Lemerle Switch.

By means of Bangalore torpedoes and flammenwerfers, the Austrians did succeed in forcing an entry about the centre of the Oxfords' line, and by 9 a.m. were in complete possession of the front line.

THE AUSTRIAN ATTACK OF JUNE 15

Throughout the morning, the Oxfords held up the attack in the most determined manner, never giving ground more than 200 yards behind the original line. By afternoon, however, the situation on their left became so serious that they were obliged to fall back on Pelly Cross Roads, where they linked up with the 1/4th Battalion Royal Berkshire Regiment, two of whose companies had been ordered forward in support of the Gloucesters.

Later in the day the enemy attack was further reinforced, and a swaying fight went on until night fell.

The enemy made little further ground, and at 6 p.m. the 145th Brigade front ran from the top of Hill 1021 to Pelly Cross Roads, and thence along Pine Avenue to the Cesuna Switch, where junction was made with the 143rd Brigade.

About 7 p.m. two battalions of the 144th Brigade commenced a counter-attack, from the Cesuna Switch in a north-easterly direction, with a view to clearing the "pocket" that the enemy had been held in. This made little headway, owing to the immense number of enemy machine guns, which were most difficult to dislodge from among the rocks and trees. Moreover, these battalions found it hard to keep direction, fighting through the middle of the wood, with no roads or paths to guide them. The attack, however, had the effect of reducing the pocket, and certainly impressed the enemy with the fact that he was firmly contained, as he made no further attempt to advance after this.

During the night arrangements were made for a general counter-attack to take place the next morning at 4.30. This attack was completely successful, meeting with what then appeared to be surprisingly little resistance. By 5.45 a.m. our original front line was entirely reoccupied and many prisoners were taken. A message was found on the body of a dead

Austrian officer, timed 2.50 a.m., ordering a complete withdrawal to their own original line. Thus the slight resistance met with in our counter-attack was accounted for, as the movement had by then been largely effected.

The enemy casualties in the attack had been very severe indeed, as was proved by the immense number of their dead, which lay strewn over the whole of the recaptured area. Of prisoners also we had a great number, and these included representatives of every unit of no fewer than two divisions, and of several units of two other divisions. A striking feature of the attack was the quantity and surprisingly good quality of the stores and equipment brought forward. Practically every man had evidently been issued with a new set of equipment previous to the attack. An enormous number of machine guns had been brought forward, many of which were left behind on retirement. Nearly all these were of the heavy type, and consequently most unsuited to a rapid advance over mountainous country on the scale which they had evidently anticipated, judging from the operation orders captured. These orders showed the enemy to have had the most far-reaching objectives, which, to those of us who knew the country, were almost impossible of attainment, even if resistance had been of the weakest, and Austrian infantry the finest soldiers in the world—which they most assuredly were not. Weight of numbers carried them so far as they got, and it may be considered partly due to their lack of push and enterprise that they failed to exploit a successful initial break through into and behind the line of the centre battalion.

Although the Bucks Battalion did not have a leading part to play in this battle, as the line it was holding was never attacked, it nevertheless did a great deal of important work.

C Company, on the right, stopped the enemy attempt

THE AUSTRIAN ATTACK OF JUNE 15

to envelop the 1/4th Oxfords' right. Several large officers' patrols were sent out to keep in touch with the two forward battalions, and on a few occasions they found themselves in a position to hold up parties of the enemy who had worked their way through. Much was done to maintain communication between the forward line and Brigade Headquarters, all the telephone lines having been broken shortly after the bombardment commenced.

Naturally, the Battalion did not suffer casualties to the same extent as other units in the Brigade:

Officers.—Wounded. 2/Lieut. H. R. Pigott.
2/Lieut. W. G. Butler.
2/Lieut. P. T. Herbert.
2/Lieut. F. J. Wilcox.
2/Lieut. E. T. C. Coxon.
Capt. H. Noke, C.F.

Other ranks.—Killed—8.
Wounded—42.

The days following the attack were fully occupied in mending our wire, burying the dead, and generally clearing the battle-field. The enemy himself, for the next three or four days, appeared to be in a state of confusion and suffering from lack of *moral*. Their men were to be seen walking about in daylight behind their trenches, having left lengths of their line unoccupied, while other parts were crowded. Two or three mountain guns, left out in " No Man's Land " after the enemy's withdrawal, were brought in by us in broad daylight. This state of affairs was exploited further by the 143rd and 144th Brigades, which were now holding the line, by sending out large patrols with the object of persuading the enemy to come back to our lines with them. This, however, was only partially successful, and their resistance soon stiffened again. It was evident, nevertheless, that the failure of the attack had left its mark on the Austrian troops opposite, and that their *moral* was thoroughly shaken by it.

On June 20, Major-General Sir Robert Fanshawe, K.C.B., gave up command of the Division. This was a very heavy blow, and was received with the greatest dismay throughout the Division. He had commanded it for three years, and during this time had won the unbounded confidence and affection of all ranks.

He was succeeded by Major-General Sir H. B. Walker, K.C.B., D.S.O.

CHAPTER XI

RAIDS

July to October 1918

Reference Map No. 4

VERY shortly after the Austrian attack the Division was relieved in the line by the 7th Division.

The 145th Brigade remained in the mountains for a week longer than the other two Brigades, acting as an additional reserve to the 7th Division in case the Austrians should venture to renew their attempt. But the situation soon became perfectly normal, and on June 30, at 12.30 in the morning, the Battalion marched to the Centrale district in the plains.

Two days later we moved again to billets at Grumo and Cereda. Here an intensely hot fortnight was passed, the heat during the day frequently reaching over 90° in the shade, and we were by no means displeased when we received orders to return to the mountains, and to relieve the 23rd Division in the right sector of the British front.

On July 19 the Battalion reached Granezza. This tour in the line proved to be one of exceptional activity, and ended with the astounding collapse of the Austro-Hungarian army.

Artillery action was considerable and constant on both sides. The Austrians, whatever their other failings may have been, were by no means to be despised as gunners, their shooting being extremely accurate.

116 FIRST BUCKINGHAMSHIRE BATTALION

Raids on the enemy's lines were of an almost nightly occurrence along the British and French fronts, the raiding parties usually consisting of one or more battalions. They met with a large amount of success on nearly every occasion, chiefly owing to the fact that the more often we raided, the more men did the enemy put into his front line, so increasing his casualties from our barrage and providing more prisoners for us to round up.

On August 8 and 9 raids were carried out on the enemy's trenches along practically the whole British and French fronts. These proved entirely successful and several hundreds of prisoners were taken, while but few casualties were incurred by the raiding troops.

Preparations and plans for these raids were organised with the very greatest care, and worked out to the smallest detail. This was in all cases the secret of success.

On the night August 26/27, the Battalion, in conjunction with the 1/4th Battalion Royal Berkshire Regiment, carried out one of these raids, for which the full orders are given in Appendix I c, with a view to showing the amount of detail to be dealt with. The object of the raid was to kill or capture the garrison of the Austrian trenches in the neighbourhood of Sec and Ave (Map No. 5). Owing to the absence of Lieutenant-Colonel L. L. C. Reynolds, D.S.O., on leave, the general plan of the raid was worked out by Major P. A. Hall, M.C., though the former returned in time to arrange the details.

The boundary between the 1/4th Royal Berkshire Regiment and the Bucks Battalion was the road running through the Austrian line midway between Sec and Ave, our Battalion's right boundary being the Clama-S. M. Maddalena road. We had the assistance of four 18-pounder batteries, 4·5 and 6-inch howitzers; and French ·77's also engaged selected targets.

MAP No. 5.

Area raided on night 26/27 Aug. 1918.

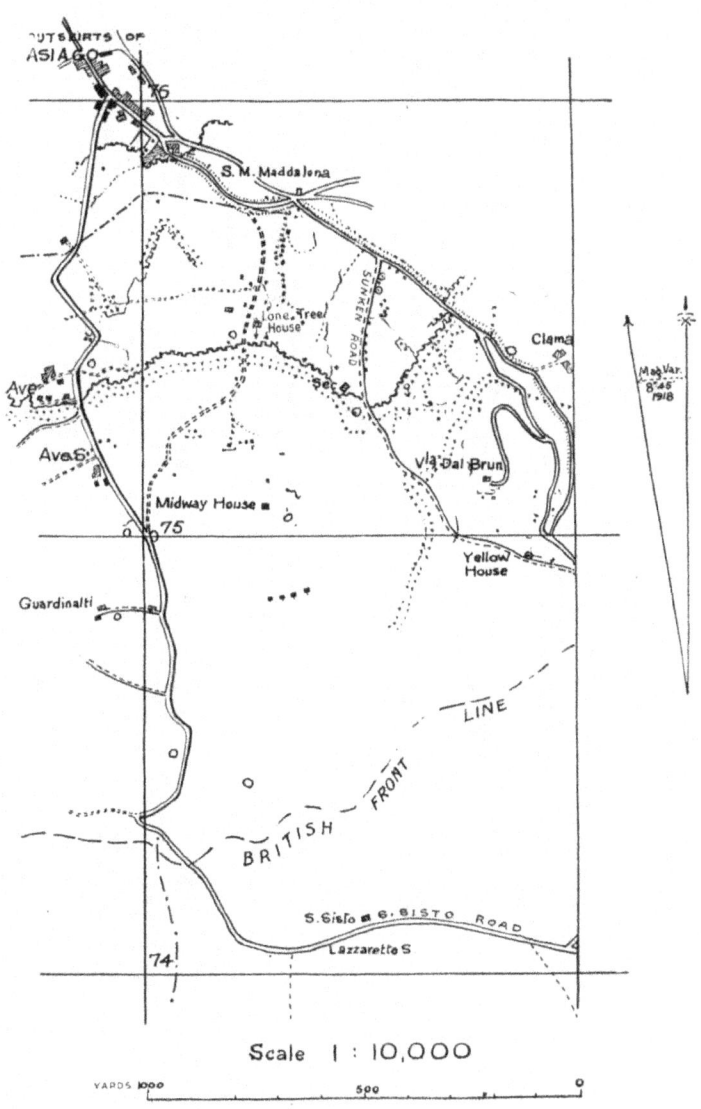

At zero (10.40 p.m., August 26) the 18-pounders put down a barrage on the enemy front line for five minutes. At zero plus five minutes the two right batteries lifted on to the sunken road for nine minutes, while the two left batteries first lifted for four minutes on to the group of dugouts north-east of Lone Tree House, and then on to the dugouts about S. M. Maddalena for five minutes, lifting again at zero plus 14 to form a protective barrage beyond.

The two right batteries at zero plus 14 lifted on to the portion of enemy front line facing south-east (between Sec and the Clama road) for eight minutes, when they, too, finally lifted off the area to form a protective barrage beyond.

The Battalion formed up behind the Midway House ridge. The point of entry for the whole Battalion was the trenches between Lone Tree House road and Sec, the enemy's front trenches to the right facing south-east being taken in reverse in the last phase.

Three platoons of A Company (Captain J. E. Firminger) were responsible for the front line between Sec and Lone Tree House, and the fourth platoon for the dugouts north-east of Lone Tree House.

Closely following the barrage D Company (Captain B. C. Rigden, M.C.) passed through A Company, two platoons dealing with the remainder of the dugouts north-east of Lone Tree House, the other two platoons those dugouts round S. M. Maddalena.

B Company (Lieutenant A. L. Brightman) and C Company (2/Lieutenant P. T. Herbert) had a more difficult task. C Company and two platoons of B Company passed through A Company, and moved along the west side of a communicator running north from Sec. Along this they formed up in two lines facing east. The first line took the dugouts in the sunken road, while the second line passed through the first, taking the front-line trench between Sec and the Clama road from behind. The other two platoons of B Company remained outside the front line until the barrage had lifted clear, when they entered the front line just left and right of the sunken road.

The whole attack went according to programme. The 18-pounder barrages were perfect on all lines. The timing of " lifts " could not have been better. The wire in front of the front-line trench proved a serious obstacle, and the leading company had a good many casualties in getting through it.

The front line was strongly held, the garrison putting up a good fight with rifle and machine-gun fire. When our leading platoons, however, closed with the bayonet, the enemy mostly surrendered.

At Sec, a machine gun was captured and the crew shot. A deep dugout, found about fifteen yards west of the sunken road, refused to divulge its occupants. A smoke bomb changed their ideas and no fewer than thirty eventually swarmed out, but as they brought their arms with them, the majority got killed.

The platoons that went to S. M. Maddalena found but few of the enemy there.

The attack on the sunken road and front line facing south-east went without a hitch. The former was found to be full of dugouts, and a large number of Austrians were killed or taken prisoner.

The signal to withdraw was given at 12.30 a.m. The withdrawal was carried out according to programme, and as far as could be then ascertained all our casualties had been brought in.

The enemy barrage was at no time very heavy, and the Austrian infantryman showed but little inclination to fight.

Prisoners taken amounted to about 165, while the number killed was estimated to be at least 150, and even

RAIDS

more if one was to judge from the number of men who returned with bloody bayonets.

Our casualties were :

Officers.—Wounded. Capt. J. E. Firminger.
                         Lieut. A. L. Brightman.
                         2/Lieut. L. W. G. Lorns.
                         2/Lieut. F. W. Blackmore.
                         2/Lieut. F. J. Wilcox.
                         2/Lieut. F. P. Bates.

Other ranks.—Killed—4.
              Wounded—75.
              Wounded and prisoner—1.
              Missing—4 (afterwards presumed killed).

The raid carried out by the 1/4th Royal Berks on our right was equally successful.

The Commander-in-Chief sent the following message :

" Please convey my hearty congratulations to men of Bucks Battalion and 1/4th Royal Berks, and to Brigadier-General Watt and staff, on their gallant, well-planned and successful raid. The results are of the greatest importance in ascertaining the enemy's intentions."

Several decorations were awarded to the Battalion for this operation, the Commander-in-Chief himself presenting the medal ribbons at Granezza.

During the next six weeks trench life, combined with a few days' periodical rest at Granezza, continued uninterruptedly.

On August 27, Brigadier-General D. M. Watt, D.S.O., handed over command of the 145th Brigade to Brigadier-General W. W. Pitt-Taylor, C.M.G., D.S.O., but the latter was shortly afterwards appointed B.G.G.S. of the XIVth Corps and Brigadier-General G. W. Howard, C.M.G., D.S.O., then assumed command of the Brigade.

About this time all brigades throughout the British Force in Italy were reduced to three battalions. The 1/5th Battalion Gloucestershire Regiment was consequently taken from the 145th Infantry Brigade and dispatched to France.

On October 8, Major P. A. Hall, M.C., was appointed to command the 1/7th Battalion Royal Warwickshire Regiment. He had, except for short intervals, been with the Battalion ever since mobilisation, and had rendered it invaluable service.

Captain P. L. Wright, M.C., was now promoted to fill his place as 2nd-in-command.

In connection with these changes on the Battalion Headquarters staff, it is worthy of record that no little success had been attained by the officers who originally embarked with the Battalion, or joined it very shortly afterwards. The original senior company commander, then Captain Reynolds, had assumed command of the Battalion early in 1916, and had commanded continuously ever since. Promotions to 2nd-in-command had invariably been made from officers within the Battalion. In addition, three of our officers had been appointed to command other battalions, and two others appointed as 2nds-in-command of other units, whilst four others had received staff appointments.

The 48th Division was now the only British Division holding the line, as the 23rd Division had shortly before been relieved on our left by troops of the 12th Italian Corps. It had been intended to send the 23rd and 7th Divisions to France, but the situation changed, and finally all three divisions remained in Italy.

At the beginning of October, the British Commander-in-Chief accepted the command of a mixed Italian-British Army, with a view to undertaking offensive

RESERVE BATTALION H.Q., KABERLABA N.

THE C.-IN-C. PRESENTING MEDALS TO THE BATTALION AT GRANEZZA,
AUGUST 1918.

RAIDS

operations on the Piave. The 7th and 23rd Divisions, being at this time in reserve, were to form part of this new Army, while the 48th Division, in order to make as little apparent change as possible, were to remain on the Asiago plateau, passing temporarily under the command of General Pennella, commanding XIIth Italian Corps.

When raids were not taking place, the sector, and more especially our headquarters at Kaberlaba North, was peaceful enough, but raids on the enemy lines now became more and more frequent, the French on our right being particularly successful.

The following figures show the number of prisoners captured during October by means of these raids:

October 3:
    6th Battalion R. Warwickshire Regiment   149
October 10:
    7th Battalion Worcestershire Regiment .   35
    French Battalion 300
    Italians 10
October 23:
    1/4th Battalion Gloucestershire Regiment 210
    3 Battalions French 700

On the night October 28/29, the Bucks Battalion raided the area Sec—S. M. Maddalena—Cassordar, full of hope, and anxious to beat all records in prisoners. The result was a disappointment. The whole area was found to have been completely evacuated by the enemy, who had that very night at dusk withdrawn to a line 3,000 yards in rear. This line was sited at the foot of the mountains which rose from the northern edge of the plateau. The enemy had been working on it for the past three months, and we had learned from prisoners that it was to be their position for the coming winter and was called the "Winter Stellung." One wretched Austrian had been left behind in the old line to loose off Verey lights, and he formed our only capture.

The discovery of the retirement was, however, most important. The following day, patrols sent out by the battalion holding the front line gained touch with the enemy at the Winter Stellung, the town of Asiago being occupied by the British.

The enemy's retirement, coupled with his diminishing *moral* and the fact that our attack had opened successfully on the Piave, made it clear that the time was now ripe for dealing him a decisive blow.

For this we now waited expectantly.

CHAPTER XII

THE AUSTRIAN DÉBÂCLE

November 1 to 4, 1918

Reference Map No. 4

THE sole orders for the initial attack leading up to the final operations of the war on the Italian front were received in the form of a brief telephone message. (Appendix I D.)

The 48th British Division, in conjunction with the 24th French Division on the right and the 20th Italian Division on the left, was to attack and capture the line Croce di S. Antonio—M. Mosciagh, the infantry attack to commence at 5.45 a.m. on November 1, 1918. The 48th Division was to attack with the 145th Brigade on the right, the 144th Brigade on the left, and the 143rd Brigade in reserve; the 145th Brigade to attack with the Bucks Battalion on the right, the 1/4th Battalion Royal Berkshire Regiment on the left, and the 1/4th Battalion Oxford & Bucks Light Infantry in reserve. The Bucks Battalion was to form up on a line Rendela—Ferragh, and to take as its right boundary the line Ferragh—west edge of Gallio Wood—road C. Giardini to Croce di S. Antonio. Our final objective was to be a line of, roughly, 800 yards of front due east of Croce di S. Antonio.

A glance at the map contours will give some idea of the mountainous nature of country to be advanced over.

The order to attack arrived when we were in Brigade reserve in rest-huts, just north of the Kaberlaba road. It was delivered on November 1 at the somewhat inconvenient hour of 1 a.m., when everyone, except telephone operators and sentries, was asleep. Companies were scattered, and it was consequently impossible for every man to be up and about for at least half an hour, and even more.

Zero was fixed for 5.50 a.m., at which hour we were to enter the first objective, the Winter Stellung, which lay some seven miles distant. Not a second must be wasted if the Battalion was to be formed up in time. Companies were to wear fighting order; water-bottles were to be full and haversack rations issued. Iron rations were, of course, included in fighting order. Packs and blankets had to be left in the huts we were vacating, and an officer with half a dozen men remained behind to arrange with the Quartermaster as to their removal.

The transport and quartermaster's stores being at Granezza, were too far away to be of any immediate assistance. Lewis gunners were consequently obliged to carry their guns and ammunition during the two-hour march to the forming-up positions.

Great efforts were made to provide tea for the men before setting out, but the time available was quite insufficient, and many had to start without it. Even so, when finally the whole Battalion had been got on the road and started off, it was evident that only if we were favoured with good going could we arrive to time.

The road, which ran over the old " No Man's Land " and through Asiago, had been fairly well repaired during the last day or two, and the going was not too bad.

It was not until the Battalion (Lieutenant-Colonel L. L. C. Reynolds, D.S.O.) reached the northern outskirts of Asiago that we encountered enemy shelling.

THE AUSTRIAN DÉBÂCLE 125

From here onwards to Rendela progress became most uncomfortable, although our casualties were wonderfully few.

The river-bed of the Ghelpac runs here between Rendela and Ferragh, on its way from the hills above Gallio. The enemy was paying much attention to this valley, by putting down a brisk barrage on it. It was decided, consequently, to form up on the line of the road Rendela—Gallio, with the Battalion's left on Rendela, and occupying a frontage of 600 yards.

A Company (Captain N. S. Flint) formed on the left, B Company (Lieutenant E. C. J. Allday) on the right, each on a two-platoon frontage.

C Company (Captain G. W. Higlett, M.C.) and D Company (Lieutenant H. A. Beaver) formed behind in depth in artillery formation.

It was 5.80 a.m. exactly when the forming-up was completed. Our hurried departure from rest-huts had been none too much hurried, and no slower pace could have been afforded on the road. We were just in time, with nothing to spare.

With the opening of our very thin barrage the enemy's barrage quickened, and as the advance proceeded, shells whistled their way in both directions just over our heads. Soon, sufficient daylight appeared for the enemy to see the attack, and rifle and machine-gun fire were quickly directed on us from Reutte, Costa, Straite and M. Catz.

The leading wave met with little difficulty in occupying the Winter Stellung from Villa Rossi to Reutte, but, on attempting to advance from it, met with heavy enfilade fire from Costa and M. Catz.

There was no sign of the attack on the left, from which direction this enemy fire came.

It was obviously impossible for our men to make progress without first silencing the enemy's machine guns on M. Catz. A Company therefore attacked Costa, and C and D Companies assaulted Straite and Rigoni di Sotto, where four machine guns were captured. A Company succeeded in rushing Costa, but then got temporarily held up by two machine guns on the southern slopes of M. Catz. Finally, one of these was put out of action by one of our Lewis guns, and the other was outflanked and its crew killed.

Meanwhile, C and D Companies continued their advance, working up the eastern side of M. Catz and assaulting the crest, where four more machine guns were taken. By 7 a.m. M. Catz was ours, and the whole garrison had either been killed or taken prisoner.

The enemy's heavy gunners were not long in spotting the khaki figures hurrying about the top of M. Catz, like ants on a mole-hill. They directed their fire accordingly, and soon covered the hill in a black pall of smoke, given off by the bursting of 5·9's. The hill, however, was ours, and it was our job to get on beyond it.

On the right, B Company had made excellent progress, but were now held up by fire from some trenches halfway up the western side of Gallio Wood. There were but few signs of the French blue uniforms, but it was thought possible that they had been attracted to their right, just as we had been forced to bear to the left on account of M. Catz. Moreover, so long as they were working through Gallio Wood it was difficult for us to see their progress.

It had now become necessary to send help to B Company. D Company were therefore dispatched to the spur north of Rigoni di Sopra. This made it too hot for the enemy holding up B Company, and they decided to go.

C Company continued their advance, and made good Roccolo N.E.

THE AUSTRIAN DÉBÂCLE 127

At 7.30 a.m. a company of the Royal Berkshires had come up to the trenches on the southern slopes of M. Catz. Their arrival enabled us to straighten out our line, preparatory to a further advance.

The enemy had now been decisively beaten, and even his heels were nowhere to be seen. Some isolated posts and refugees from the Winter Stellung were encountered here and there, but they soon surrendered, several of them with machine guns.

By 10.30 a.m. the Battalion had reached a line corresponding approximately with the 1,400 metre contour line just south-west of Croce di S. Antonio. We were again out of touch with both the French and the Royal Berkshires.

Companies were reorganised on their final objective, which had now been attained, while patrols were pushed forward and to both flanks.

No sign of the enemy could be found, except a few stragglers who were brought in. The French left was found on the east side of the Valle di Nos, and a company of the Royal Berkshires came up on our left a little later.

We had known, to our cost, for many months, that the enemy had gun positions in the Valle di Nos. Reconnoitring parties were accordingly sent out to see what could be found there. A number of guns of various calibres were found. Some had been firing until their ammunition supply was exhausted. Others had evidently been fired until we were almost up to them, when their breech-blocks had been removed and the crew had taken to their heels. Efforts had been made to get some of the guns away, but they had all eventually been abandoned.

In all, the Battalion captured on this day some hundreds of prisoners and a large quantity of material, including at least twenty-one guns of all calibres, fifteen machine guns and three motor lorries, besides a number of waggons.

Our casualties had so far been extraordinarily slight :

Officers.—Wounded. 2/Lieut. J. W. C. Read.

Other ranks.—Killed— 8.
Wounded—30.
Missing—1.

On the left of the Divisional attack little progress had been made. The 144th Brigade were held up in front of Camporovere, and the 20th Italian Division had been unable to get forward at all. Thus it seemed that, whatever he was to lose elsewhere, the enemy was determined to keep his hold on the Val d'Assa. To lose this would assuredly mean losing all.

But our progress on the right, together with that of the French, had been so great, that even our present positions threatened the rear of the enemy force who were holding up the 144th Brigade. The following day was to see this put to still better advantage.

The Battalion remained on the line it had reached at midday on November 1 throughout the afternoon and night. Very great care was taken to select the best defensive positions, in view of the possible re-appearance of the enemy in force to counter-attack the ground he had lost. Officers and men were tired out, and lack of a cup of tea began to make itself felt. The marching, fighting and general excitement of the whole day, which had begun at 1 a.m., made us all thankful for even a few hours' halt, but there was little enough rest, especially for the officers, who had to reconnoitre the ground all round them before nightfall. Being in the middle of a wood on the top of a mountain, as we now were, made this all the more difficult and all the more necessary.

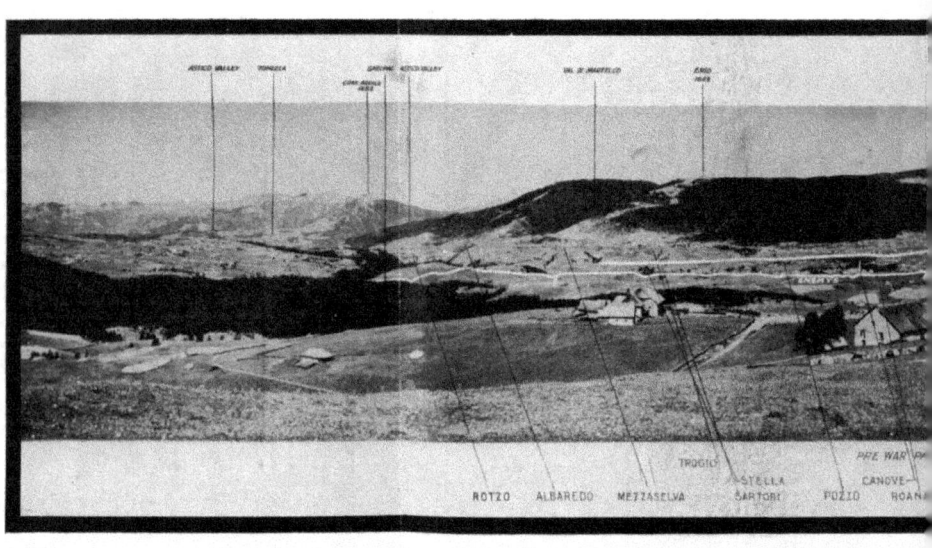

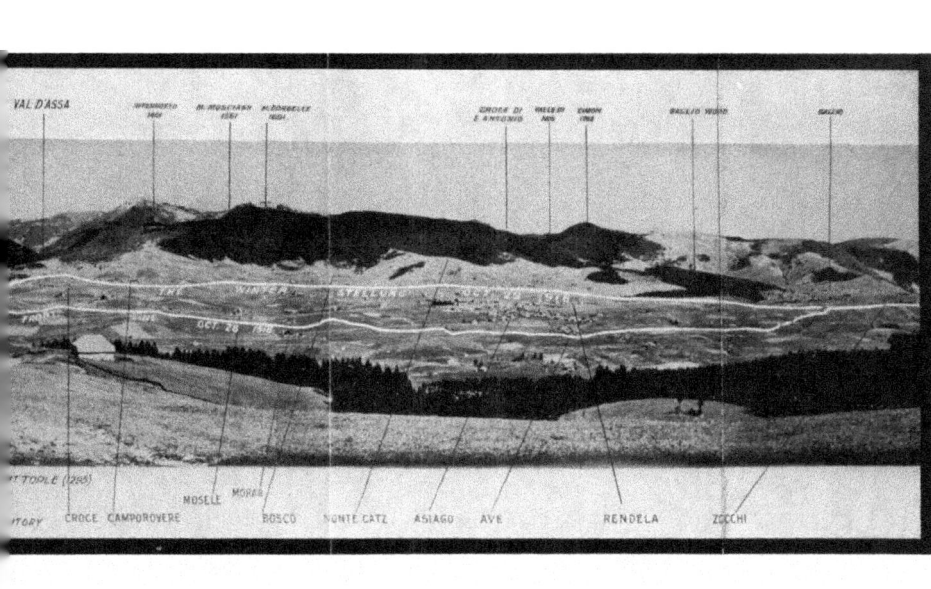

THE AUSTRIAN DÉBÂCLE

The getting forward of our rations caused us much anxiety. We had not been in touch with the Quartermaster at Granezza since the evening before our orders to attack arrived. He had, however, been instructed to bring our rations up the road past Reutte. Guides were to be sent there to bring him on. Unfortunately, but not unnaturally, in an absolutely strange country, much of which was wooded, these guides lost their way without finding him, and remained out all night. The darkness amongst the woods was intense. Of mule-tracks leading down the mountain there were several, though only one right one; when found, it was no easy matter to keep to it. The 2nd-in-command finally set forth in an endeavour to gain touch with the transport column. He also lost himself for some three hours, before he eventually found the longed-for rations towards dawn. Without further mishap, they were taken forward, but only to reach the Battalion's positions a good half-hour after the Battalion had moved off. A party had been left behind to manhandle the rations after them.

Thus, for the second day we set out without tea, and this time we were also without water or rations.

At dawn, the 1/7th Battalion Worcestershire Regiment, who had been concentrated during the night at Roccolo N.E., attacked and captured M. Mosciagh from the east. This made untenable the enemy positions on M. Interrotto, which had given so much trouble to the 144th Brigade the previous day.

The 1/4th Battalion Oxford & Bucks Light Infantry were at once moved against M. Meatta, where they disposed of the enemy garrison with little difficulty.

This turning movement on the part of the Worcesters and Oxfords threatened the main, and indeed only, line of Austrian retirement—along the Val d'Assa. The enemy holding out at the entrance to the valley beat a hurried retreat, and when the 143rd Brigade (which had been in reserve the previous day) attacked Camporovere at 10 a.m., they met with little resistance and advanced very rapidly up the Val d'Assa. By dusk they were in touch with the enemy, who were in prepared positions on the line Bosson—Vezzena—Marcia di Sotto. Here the Austrians were in considerable strength.

At 7 a.m. on the 2nd, the Bucks Battalion turned due west, and after making good M. Dorbelle, scaled M. Mosciagh, relieving the 7th Battalion Worcestershire Regiment there. Here, at 2 p.m., our long-lost rations and water reached us. We were getting done up for want of them, and never, never did tea taste so good. Even so, we had to be most careful with both the water and the food, as at our present rate of progression and most uncertain direction, it might be a long while before further supplies reached us.

On M. Mosciagh were Austrian guns of all calibres; stores and equipment left behind in all the huts testified to the hurried retreat of the enemy, and souvenirs lay on all sides.

At 3 p.m. we received orders to move down into the Valle di Portule, where the whole Brigade, less one company of the 1/4th Oxfords who remained on M. Meatta, bivouacked for the night. We found a large number of enemy huts here, but not sufficient to shelter the whole Brigade. Many of us were consequently obliged to spend another freezing cold night in the open, with no greatcoats and no blankets. These huts, which the Austrians had made themselves, were well fitted up. There was no lack of stoves, which worked well and gave out a good amount of heat. Tables, chairs and wire beds were quite numerous, all of them having been obviously made by the enemy on the spot. Packs, greatcoats and small articles of

THE AUSTRIAN DÉBÂCLE 131

equipment, together with papers, magazines, books and orders, were strewn over the whole encampment. The clothing for the most part was infested with vermin, which was natural, seeing the general state of filth which had been allowed to accumulate everywhere. A fairly well-stocked canteen was also found and promptly raided. In an adjoining hut a cask of brandy was unearthed, but the finders gave vent to such a shout of joy that the Adjutant took steps to ascertain the cause, and, on learning it, decided to place a strong guard over the cask.

Evidence abounded of the extreme haste of the enemy to get clear of the place. Judging from appearances, the flight had been considerably hampered by our shelling. Transport waggons, motor lorries and guns had become ditched by the roadside and so left. Horses, still harnessed to their carts, lay across the road, dead or dying; while their drivers had, in many instances, suffered a like fate.

It was the novelty of these sights, and the general feeling that we were really getting on with the war, which kept us all going, tired as we were.

At 8 a.m. the following day (November 8) the whole Division resumed the advance.

At 4.80 a.m. the Advanced Guard (148rd Brigade, with a Brigade of Field Artillery) commenced its attack on the Vezzena position. Considering the strength of the enemy on this line, a very feeble resistance was offered, and by 8 a.m. a large force, consisting of some fourteen battalions, was surrounded and captured.

The IIIrd Austrian Corps commander and three divisional commanders, with their staffs, were amongst the prisoners taken.

Vezzena had been their corps headquarters. The huts, of which there were a large number, contained food and fodder sufficient to last a corps for very many weeks. One huge hut contained nothing but flour, another dried vegetables, another hay and straw, and so on, embracing everything which an army in the field requires. The tale of shortage of food in the Austrian army appeared an unlikely one when we saw a sight of this kind, and yet shortage there must have been, or their men would not have looked so thin and badly nourished as they did.

The march of the main body, headed by the Battalion, proved to be a most memorable one. Abandoned guns, waggon parks, ammunition dumps, lay by the side of the whole route; the roads were littered with articles of Austrian equipment. In their anxiety to travel as fast and as lightly as possible, the enemy had cast away all that encumbered him. Gas masks, helmets, packs, haversacks, and, finally, rifles lay scattered along the road, down which but a few hours before the routed army had passed in their helpless, panic-stricken flight. One's dream of the typical army rout of history days had come true, and indeed surpassed all imagination.

As we neared Vezzena, we met whole battalions of the enemy marching to the rear, under the escort of a handful of British soldiers. In many cases an Austrian battalion commander led back his battalion complete, while in front of him walked a man with the white flag. Generals were permitted to ride, at footpace.

It was a pathetic sight to see these thousands of men trudging their weary way to our rear. Their spirit was broken, and tragedy was written plain on every officer's face.

Our Divisional commander had sent forward a car to pick up and bring back the Austrian corps commander, doubtless with the idea of eliciting full information from him as speedily as possible.

Just short of Vezzena we halted for a meal. We bad been on the road for seven hours, and had begun

THE AUSTRIAN DÉBÂCLE

to feel the effects. Excitement had kept every man going, and even the most sore-footed and weary held on, hoping that round the next corner he would see the Emperor Charles, with his hands up and shouting " Kamerad ! "

On passing Vezzena, on the road towards M. Rovere, the same strange sights continued to present themselves. As we advanced along the valley, a party of the enemy 500 or 600 strong were seen wending their way towards us down the side of the hill. Curiosity developed into astonishment when it was noticed that every man of them was armed with a rifle, while machine guns could be seen on the backs of mules which brought up their rear. This party seemed to think little of an enemy division marching in column of route through their country, while the idea that a few bursts from their machine guns, fired from the commanding position they held, would wipe us off the road, had not apparently struck them, as it had certainly struck us. So far as we were concerned there was no time, and apparently no necessity, to discontinue our march. The whole situation was so entirely favourable to us, that delay even now might mar the full fruits of what should be the most gigantic victory. So only one officer with a platoon was fallen out to deal with the enemy column. This officer, by means of an interpreter, ordered the column to halt, and requested the officer in charge to come down to him. The lieutenant-colonel who complied with this request appeared surprised when told that his battalion must march past, and every man lay down his arms as he did so. He was apparently under the impression that an armistice existed. However, on our further explanation that the rest of his corps had already performed the trifling ceremony that was required of him, and that his corps commander was in our hands, he decided to comply with the demand.

Advancing down the precipitous slopes of M. Rovere into the Val Sugana, the Battalion occupied Caldonazzo at 3.30 p.m. This town turned out to be either an Army or Corps railhead, and a large quantity of rolling-stock lay in the station and sidings. One complete train, loaded with 200 field-guns, had failed to get away, presumably owing to shortage of engines. Quantities of munitions, equipment and stores lay there ready for loading, while in an adjoining field was a large park of guns of all calibres, including one 17-inch howitzer.

On this afternoon, November 3, 1918, the G.S.O.I. of the division proceeded to Trent, the headquarters of the Third Austro-Hungarian Army, demanding the surrender of Trent and Pergine, with all hostile troops in the area. This demand was complied with.

The 144th and 145th Brigades billeted for the night November 3/4 in Caldonazzo. There was again little enough rest on that night, as some 10,000 prisoners had been collected here and guards had to be furnished over them.

The Battalion had on this day been fourteen hours on the move, and covered twenty-five miles. With little sleep and often short of water, the test had been severe, and one wondered how much longer it was to continue. Our astonishing experiences, and the knowledge that the 48th Division was the first British Division to enter an enemy's country on the Western front, had done wonders towards helping us along.

It was with little surprise that, about 7 a.m. the next day, November 4, 1918, we received this message :

" Armistice with Austria-Hungary has been signed 3rd November.—Armistice will come into effect from 15.00 hours (3 p.m.), 4th November.—Moves ordered

THE AUSTRIAN DÉBÂCLE

for 4th Nov. will take place, but all troops will halt on the line gained at 15.00 hours exactly.—All Austrians within the line gained this hour will be considered prisoners-of-war.—Austrians not within this line will at 15.00 hours retire for a distance of at least three kilometres.—The utmost care will be taken to see that these instructions are carried out.—The contents of this wire will be immediately passed to all units who are in touch, in case they should not receive them by other methods.—Acknowledge."

The Battalion took the news quietly. We were too weary to be jubilant; besides which, our rations for the day had not arrived, and there is never cause for joy under those conditions. Nor would these rations have turned up before we moved, had it not been for the strenuous efforts of the Quartermaster, Captain E. Nichol.

At 10 a.m. the Brigade (less 1/4th Battalion Oxford & Bucks Light Infantry, who remained in charge of the prisoners) once more took to the roads, and, after marching sixteen miles, reached by 3 p.m. the little village of Madrano, just east of Pergine. The towns and villages through which we passed were filthy in the extreme. Dead horses lay at intervals along the road, while the villagers were getting to work cutting rump-steaks off them.

Except for a few stragglers, no further signs of the enemy were seen.

The captures made by the Division since November 1 amounted to some 22,000 prisoners, 165 howitzers, 263 guns, besides uncountable small arms, machine guns, and material of all kinds. In addition, there were large numbers of abandoned guns in the neighbourhood of Vezzena and along the Val d'Assa, of which no count could be made.

On the evening of November 4, the Divisional Commander issued the following Order of the Day:

" OFFICERS, N.C.O.'S AND MEN OF THE 48TH DIVISION,

" Your achievement during the last few days of the most profound military events deserves unstinted praise. After fourteen weeks of trench warfare and arduous work, chiefly at night, combined with frequent raids of the most difficult though successful nature, you have undertaken an attack on a front originally allotted to two divisions, against what ought to have been impregnable mountain positions; you have swept away the enemy rearguards, and, acting as the vanguard of the Sixth Italian Army, you have advanced so rapidly and with such resolution, that the retiring enemy have had no time to reform and have left over 20,000 prisoners, hundreds of guns and immeasurable booty in the hands of the Division.

" The mere performance of the march in the time, and under the conditions you endured, would have been, even without opposition, considered a creditable feat. You can justly claim that the favourable situation of the Italian Armies on this front at 15.00 hours to-day, when one of the most memorable armistices in history was signed, is largely due to your exertions and resolution.

" As your Divisional Commander I cordially thank you.

" (Sd.) H. B. WALKER, *Major General,*
" *Cdg. 48th Division.*"

A few days later the Divisional Commander received the following message from General F. R. Earl of Cavan, K.P., K.C.B., M.V.O., Commanding-in-Chief British Force in Italy :

THE AUSTRIAN DÉBÂCLE

"I have been waiting to hear from Sixth Army Commander outlines of your great victory. I have also been waiting for the definite order for your concentration with the XIVth Corps. To-day I have received both, and I hasten to send all ranks my intense appreciation of their great service, and my sincere thanks to you personally for the drive and determination with which you conducted your arduous operations.

"The C.I.G.S. sent his special congratulations to the 48th Division to-day by King's Messenger. British troops may well be proud of their actions in mountains and in plains, but the pride I feel in them exceeds all."

And this, incredible as it seemed, was really the end of the war for the Bucks Battalion.

How little had we guessed, when we left that cold dark camp by the Kaberlaba road four days before, that we were setting out on an attack which would so swiftly complete an overwhelming disaster to Austrian arms and Austrian Empire, greater and more fatal than Austerlitz or Sadowa!

CHAPTER XIII

AFTER THE ARMISTICE—THE END

November 1918 to March 1919

ALTHOUGH we had good reason to hope that, for us, the Great War was over, there still remained the possibility that we might be called upon for an attack on Germany through Austria, and rumour, always busy when hopes were high, was inclined to send us back to the Western front, despite the news that operations were going wondrously well there without us. Our fate was decided, at any rate temporarily, on November 6, by receipt of orders to march back to Caldonazzo on the following morning. This proved to be the first of a six days' march, covering in all some eighty miles. Other nights were spent at our old haunts Vezzena, Val Portule, Granezza, Thiene, and on November 13 we reached the rest-billets allotted to the Battalion in the villages of Maglio and Novale.

Before the start on this march from Madrano, the Battalion had collected a motley assortment of additional transport which we had captured during the advance. It included five Austrian waggons with their horses, all of an indifferent stamp, underfed and ill-cared for, and a cooker drawn by two white ponies, rather bigger than mice. These must have been the favourites of the Austrians, and they were the delight of our own Transport section, every man clamouring to be detailed as their driver.

AFTER THE ARMISTICE—THE END

The various Austrian dumps provided more than sufficient material wherewith to fill our extra waggons, while at Vezzena it became most difficult to determine what should be taken and what left; for, as has been previously mentioned, this place had formed the dump of an Austrian Corps.

It was decided that flour, oats and hay would best repay their carriage, so our loads were made up largely of these.

To every company was allotted a sack of the captured flour, from which each man could make his own pudding. One man, however, thought stolen flour, like stolen kisses, the sweetest, and preferred to disregard orders and loot his portion; but he broke into the wrong hut, and was found later endeavouring to make his pudding out of cement.

At Granezza we received the great news that an armistice had been signed with Germany. We knew, of course, that this meant complete victory, but already we had lived ten crowded days of glorious life: hard fighting and hard marching, the utter rout of the whole Austrian Army, captures of prisoners, guns and material beyond our wildest dreams, the surrender of Trent, an armistice at our dictation, the daily rising flood of good news from France, bearing on its crest the certainty of speedy triumph. Enthusiasm could hardly mount higher.

It would be difficult to explain why so many of us were sorry to bid a last farewell to Granezza, for there was remarkably little attractive about it. But there had been so many occasions when, during a long turn in the trenches, we had looked forward intensely to a rest here, that no doubt it had come to frame itself in our minds as a pleasant spot. We had thought of Granezza when pleasant spots were rare, and our ideas of pleasure and comfort easily satisfied. But with visions of home in England, there was really little sense in our regrets at leaving.

The march down the hill and on south to Thiene was a long one of some twenty-two miles. The men, as usual, marched exceedingly well, in spite of having been on the road throughout the four previous days.

At Thiene we were ordered to hand over to the Italian authorities the whole of our captured transport, including even the two white ponies, which the Transport section dearly loved and longed to retain.

The following day's march of eighteen miles carried us to the villages of Maglio and Novale. It had been hinted that these were to be our final billets, so that we were most anxious that they should be comfortable or, at any rate, prove capable of being made so. Demobilisation was an uncertain quantity, and no man knew how much longer it would be necessary for him to remain in Italy. Though of one thing, every officer, N.C.O. and man was quite convinced—that when demobilisation did start he himself should be the very first man to be released.

On the whole, the billets did prove good, and were soon made still better.

" Spit and polish " at once became the order of the day. Discipline, so far from being relaxed, became stricter. On the other hand, the hours of training were considerably reduced, and sports and games organised and encouraged to fill the hours of leisure. Competitions of every description, organised by every unit and formation, became almost bewildering.

Of the Brigade events the Battalion won the cross-country race, and the inter-battalion and inter-company football competitions. C Company, who always seemed to shelter at least a dozen first-class players, were responsible for winning the Battalion competition, and represented the Brigade in the Divisional competition,

THE LAST QUARTER GUARD, ITALY, 1919.

AFTER THE ARMISTICE—THE END 141

where they reached the final before being beaten by a company of the 1/7th Battalion Worcestershire Regiment.

Training became largely a matter of drill, though difficulty was experienced even in this, as the size of the biggest field was only just large enough to allow of battalion drill being carried out on it.

All the necessaries were obtained to enable every man to turn himself out as smartly as possible, and at the end of a few weeks the Battalion probably looked smarter than it had ever done since the day it left Chelmsford on March 30, 1915.

The results showed themselves in inspections carried out by the Divisional and Brigade Commanders, and by a French Divisional Commander, by all of whom the Battalion was congratulated on its turn-out, smartness and march past.

Christmas was anticipated by the purchase in November of three large pigs, and a pig " board," which was specially appointed to superintend their welfare and organise their rations, became the target of no little humour—and this in spite of its members' efficiency.

In the past we had always been rather proud of being able to secure sufficient turkeys for the Battalion, but this year the home-fed pig was even more popular, and Christmas dinners of pork, vegetables, plum pudding, oranges, nuts and beer, were voted a huge success.

Demobilisation, which at first proceeded slowly, quickened up about the middle of January, and gradually increased throughout February, when men were dispersed at the rate of over fifty a week.

Those men who had enlisted during and after 1916, and who were consequently retained in the Service, were given the choice of two battalions to which they could transfer, the 1/5th Battalion Royal Warwickshire Regiment and the 1/6th Battalion Gloucestershire Regiment, these being the two which had been detailed to represent the Division in the Army of Occupation. The Royal Warwicks were to remain in Italy, while the Gloucesters were to be moved to Scutari.

The large majority of our men voted for the 5th Royal Warwicks, partly on account of their destination, but chiefly because they were now commanded by Lieutenant-Colonel P. A. Hall, D.S.O., M.C., a Bucks officer.

To those of us who were left with the Battalion, this form of demobilisation became a most melancholy proceeding. To watch the Battalion, of which we were all so proud, being gradually reduced to nothing, was depressing in the extreme. One longed that the end could have come with a last and final dismissal of the full Battalion on a parade ground in England.

By the middle of March we were reduced to a cadre of five officers and fifty other ranks, which was the most that any infantry unit was allowed to retain in order to bring home the Regimental stores.

On March 23 the cadre left Novale, reaching Aylesbury on the 31st. Here these remnants, under Lieutenant-Colonel L. L. C. Reynolds, D.S.O., paraded once again on that Square in front of the Town Hall where, more than four and a half years ago, the whole Battalion had paraded on mobilisation.

And so ended for us those wonderful years, in our brief record of which no claim is made of greater deeds than were achieved by others; enough that the Battalion never failed to uphold the great traditions of the British Army. Throughout those long, hard years, trying to the utmost the patience, the resolution, the courage

THE CADRE, 1919.

and the endurance of all ranks, every officer, N.C.O. and man did his duty cheerfully.

In many a Midland home, for generations to come, names shall be held in honour, and question shall be asked, " What did they do ? " Let the answer be : " In the Great War they served with The First Bucks Battalion."

APPENDIX I

OPERATION ORDERS

Secret.   O.O./2.

A

1st Bucks Battalion

TOMBOIS FARM

April 1917

1. *48th Division* will continue its advance to-night. Bucks Battalion will capture Tombois Farm, with a second objective the ridge due E. of the farm. 4th R. Berks Regiment will capture Gillemont Farm. 143rd Infantry Brigade will capture Catalet Copse and Le Petit Priel Farm.

2. *Zero hour*—11.30 p.m.
Zero hour for 143rd Infantry Brigade will be—10 p.m.

3. Bucks Battalion will attack with three Companies,— C Company right, B Company left, D Company will be in echelon behind C Company, and will go through to second objective.
A Company will take over outpost line as early as possible after dusk. One Company 1/5th Gloucester Regiment, with half-section machine-gun company, will be in support about F.16.b.1.9.

4. *Formation.*—Attacking companies will be deployed (by zero — 80 minutes) on a two-platoon frontage of 150 yards, each platoon in two lines, 25 yards' distance between lines.

Each of the attacking companies will have one Bombing Section equipped as such.

5. *Forming-up positions:*

Right Company	. . .	W. of Sart Farm.
Left Company	. . .	About F.10.d.5.7.
Third Company	. . .	About F.16.b.7.6.

6. *Objectives:*

(a) *Right Company* will direct its attack S. and E. of Tombois Farm.

(b) *Left Company* on W. and N. of Tombois Farm.

Each of the above companies will arrange to leave one section at point where its outer flank crosses enemy trench, to protect its flank against possible counter-attack up trench.

(c) *Third Company* will follow Right Company, and occupy enemy trench F.11.b.3.1. to F.11.d.5.9., and remain on line until satisfied that leading companies have attained their objectives, retaining its formation (i.e. rear lines not closing up), when it will go through and occupy ridge E. of Tombois Farm, approximately E. of road running N. and S. through F.12.a.

7. *Consolidation:*

(a) *Right Company*, on attaining its objective, will establish itself from road F.11.b.3.5. (exclusive) to F.12.c., with support about trench F.11.c.0.5.

(b) *Left Company* will establish itself from road F.11.b.3.5. (inclusive) to F.3.c., gaining touch with 143rd Brigade (1/5th R. Warwick Regiment), with support about F.10.b.

(c) *Third Company* will establish itself on ridge, extending S. to gain touch with 1/4th R. Berks Regiment, in F.12.c., with support dug in on our side of slope.

8. *Artillery Barrage* as communicated to companies this afternoon.

9. Attacking companies will carry S.O.S. signal lights, Very lights and pistols, aeroplane flares. Every man will carry one extra bandolier S.A.A. All available wire-cutters will also be taken forward.

10. *Dump for S.A.A.* will be formed about road junction in F.15.b., under Regimental Sergeant-Major.

11. *Dump of Tools* will be formed at road junction F.16.a.9.7. Support Company will be prepared to take these forward without delay.

12. *Dividing Line* between the Battalion and 1/4th R. Berks Regiment, during attack and after capture of objectives, will be line F.17.c.0.0.—A.7.b.0.0.

13. *Covering Parties* will be pushed forward during the work of consolidation.

14. *Countersign* to be made known to all concerned. This has been communicated to 143rd Infantry Brigade.

15. One section Royal Engineers and one platoon R. Sussex Regiment will be available to help with work of consolidation.

16. *Contact Aeroplane* will fly over at about 6.30 a.m., or, if misty, one hour after mist lifts. Advanced troops will be careful to answer the call for flares.

17. *Battalion Headquarters*—F.15.d.9.7. (present C Company Headquarters).

18. *Report Centre*—F.16.a.9.8.

19. *Dressing Station*—F.15.b.4.0.

(*Sd.*) P. L. WRIGHT,
Captain and Adjutant, 1st Bucks Battalion.

16.4.17.

Copies to :
  1–4 Companies.
  5 Support Company.
  6–7 Battalion Headquarters.
  8 1/5th Gloucester Regiment.
  9 File.
  10–11 War diary.

Secret.　　　　　　　　　　　　　　　　　　0.0.25., *Copy* 6.

B

1ST BUCKS BATTALION

STEENBEEK AND ST. JULIEN

August 1917

1. Fifth Army will attack on "Z" day.

2. The Battalion will capture two objectives and push out an outpost line in front of second objective.

OPERATION ORDERS

3. Objectives and boundaries as in plan issued herewith.

4. 1/5th Gloucesters will attack on right, and 1/4th Oxfords on left of this Battalion. 1/4th R. Berks are in Brigade Reserve.

5. The Battalion will attack on a two-company frontage and in four waves. Each company on a two-platoon front. A Company on left and B Company on right, will form the first and second waves. C Company on left and D Company on right, will form third and fourth waves.

6. Deployment will be covered by troops of 143rd Infantry Brigade, located 150 yards E. of Steenbeek.

(This did not take place, as Warwicks were unable to get their outposts across the stream, the enemy being too close.)

7. The two leading companies will deploy E. of the Steenbeek, with 15 yards between lines and 30 yards between waves. The two rear companies will be in Artillery formation between the Steenbeek and a line 350 yards W. of it, and will advance in this formation to deploy 350 yards behind the Green Line, unless rifle or machine-gun fire is encountered, when they will deploy any time after crossing Steenbeek.

7a. The initial deployment is close to avoid enemy barrage. When advance begins, waves will open out to obtain a distance of 350 yards.

8. First wave will halt on and consolidate a line running through Hillock Farm and the line of gun-pits to its right. Each platoon will be followed by a mopping-up party of one bombing section, which will deal with the enemy strong point in its line of advance, and will hold this until further orders are received.

9. Second wave at zero + 35 minutes will capture, mop up and consolidate the Green Line (Spot Farm—Springfield —Langemarck Road). Each platoon will be followed by a mopping-up party of one bombing section, which will deal with any enemy strong points or trenches which may be met with after passing through first wave.

10. Third wave will be ready to cross Green Line at zero + 55 minutes, and follow barrage.

Right Company third wave, at zero + 1.30, will capture,

mop up and consolidate the Red Line from Bend to South. Consolidation will be carried out W. of old enemy wire. This company will immediately put out a temporary outpost line from D.7.b.0.8., where it will link up with Gloucesters, through the houses at D.7.a.8.9. to 1.9.

Left Company third wave, at same hour, will double-block the Red Line at the Bend, and put out a temporary outpost line from this point to our junction with the Oxfords, on the Green Line facing N.

At zero + 8 hours, this third wave will capture, mop up and consolidate the remainder of the Red Line, having swung to the right with the barrage from zero + 2.85.

11. Fourth wave at zero + 8 hours will capture and consolidate the Blue Line.

Right Company: Stroppe Farm, and link up with Left Company.

Left Company: Genoa and Hubner Farm.

Posts will be thrown out in front of these points to cover consolidation.

12. Gloucesters will capture their portion of Red and Blue Lines at zero + 1.80.

Oxfords will capture their Red and Blue Lines at zero + three hours.

13. In each case, before advance of barrage begins, it will quicken up for the preceding five minutes.

14. Machine-gun barrages will conform to Artillery.

15. During pause on Green Line there will be a smoke barrage.

(*Sd.*) L. L. C. REYNOLDS,
Lieutenant-Colonel,
Comdg. 1st Bucks Battalion.

12.8.17.

Copies to:
    1–4—Companies.
    5—Headquarters.
    6—File.
    7-8—War Diary.

OPERATION ORDERS

Secret. *Copy No.* 6

1st Bucks Battalion

Amendment No. 1 to 1st Bucks Battalion O.O.25.

1. Paragraph 11, delete lines 1 and 2, and substitute :
" Fourth wave at zero + 3 hours will pass through third wave, after the latter has assaulted and captured the remainder of the Red Line, and will follow the barrage to assault, capture and consolidate their objectives on the Blue Line."

2. Each wave, having captured its objective, will at once reorganise, and be prepared to assist the next wave in the capture of its objective if required.

(Sd.) L. L. C. REYNOLDS,
Lieutenant-Colonel,
Comdg. 1st Bucks Battalion.

13.8.17.

Copies to all recipients of O.O.25.

Secret. *Copy No.* 6

1st Bucks Battalion

Amendment No. 2 to 1st Bucks Battalion O.O.25

Reference paragraph 7, the two leading companies will deploy W. of Steenbeek, and will start to cross it at zero—7 minutes, reforming on E. side before advancing.

(Sd.) L. L. C. REYNOLDS,
Lieutenant-Colonel,
Comdg. 1st Bucks Battalion.

14.8.17.

Copies to all recipients of O.O.25.

Secret. O.O.26., *Copy* 6

1st Bucks Battalion

Reference O.O.25.

ARTILLERY BARRAGES.

1. The Artillery Barrage will commence at zero, 300 yards E. of Steenbeek, and creep forward at the rate of 100 yards

every five minutes, to lift off the Green Line at zero + 85 minutes, i.e. second wave has 85 minutes to go 900 yards—nearly four minutes for every 100 yards.

2. Barrage halts 200 yards in front of Green Line, from zero + 50 to zero + 1.10. It will slow down, but will quicken up at zero + 1.5, i.e. five minutes before again moving forward; this will be the signal for the next (third) wave to get up to it.

3. At zero + 1.10, barrage will again move forward, at same rate on the right flank but slower on the left, to lift off the Red Line from the Bend to the S. at zero + 1.20.

4. Barrage halts 150 yards in front of Dotted Green and Blue Lines, from zero + 1.40 to zero + 2.35. It will slow down to quicken up again five minutes before moving on.

5. At zero + 2.35, that part of the barrage W. of Red Line will roll back to lift off remainder of Red Line, i.e. that part N. of the Bend, at zero + 3.0.

6. The barrage will continue to roll back from zero + 3.0 to zero + 3.35, when it will be about 200 yards E. of the Blue Line, and will continue here until zero + 5.35, when it will cease.

(Sd.) L. L. C. REYNOLDS,
Lieutenant-Colonel,
Comdg. 1st Bucks Battalion.

12.8.17.

Copies to:
    1–4—Companies.
    5—Headquarters.
    6—File.
    7–8—War Diary.

Secret.   *Copy No.* 6

1st BUCKS BATTALION

Instructions Reference 1st Bucks Battalion 0.0.25.

1. **Battalion Headquarters** at zero will be at C.12.c.0.3.—House. It will probably move forward after capture of Green Line to about C.12.c.5.9.

OPERATION ORDERS

2. *Brigade Headquarters* will be at Cheddar Villa. Brigade Forward Station from zero − 2 hours will be at C.12.a.0.7. After zero it will move forward to Hillock Farm, C.12.a.5.5., as soon as situation permits.

3. *Dressing Station* will be at Battalion Headquarters at C.12.c.0.8.

4. Reports of completion of assembly will be sent to Battalion Headquarters.

5. Each post will have a plan of action ready to meet a counter-attack. This must be explained to all.

6. Troops will keep close to barrage and conform with it.

7. The word "Retire" will not be used. Any one heard to say it will be shot immediately.

8. Compass-bearings will be required to march on. Compasses will be carried by all officers and sergeants.

9. German counter-attacks are now often led by low-flying aeroplanes. These will be fired on by Lewis guns and rifles. Care will be taken to aim well in front of the aeroplanes. Look-out will be kept to avoid shooting any of our own machines which may dive on the enemy planes.

10. All troops will be warned not to bunch behind tanks, as these draw enemy fire.

11. *Tanks.* All ranks will be warned to look out for tank signals. Officers and as many N.C.O.'s as possible will carry "Tank Coloured Disc and Light Code."

12. A derelict tank may be used to form a strong point.

13. Mopping up will be done carefully, as enemy may hide in cellars or ditches, etc., some distance from his fighting positions. Search will be thorough.

14. All ranks will be warned that prisoners are only required to give name and regiment, and that any further information given to the enemy means loss of their comrades' lives.

15. *Contact Aeroplanes:*

(a) Markings—Two black rectangular flags, 2′ × 1′ 8″, attached to and projecting from lower plane on either side of fuselage.

APPENDIX I

(b) Contact aeroplanes will be flying at approximately:

Zero + 1 hour.
Zero + 1 hour 45 minutes.
Zero + 3 hours 15 minutes.
Zero + 4 hours 15 minutes.

At these hours Infantry will be particularly on the look-out for a call to light flares, although calls may come at other times as well.

(c) Leading line *only* to show flares, which will be lighted in groups of three when actually called for.

(d) A protection aeroplane will work all day "Z" day to warn Artillery of any enemy counter-attacks.

16. Use of dummy trenches to distract enemy's fire should be remembered.

17. The greatest care will be taken over synchronisation of watches.

18. No barrage maps, orders or notes of operations will be carried into action.

19. The following maps only will be taken:
Poelcappelle, 1/10,000, Edn. 1 (Paper Map), and the Message Maps issued.

20. *Distinguishing Marks.* Third and fourth waves will wear white patch on back. The same will be worn by the leading Battalion of 143rd and 144th Infantry Brigades. Arm-bands, as issued, will be worn by signallers, runners, etc.

21. C Company's left platoon on the Red Line will dig a strong point about C.6.d.7.8., which will be named Bucks Fort.

22. Visual Signalling stations will be established at Mouse Trap Farm, Cheddar Villa and Hillock Farm.

23. *Prisoners of War.* Companies will escort prisoners back as far as the Steenbeek, where they will be taken over by escort detailed by 143rd Infantry Brigade at St. Julien Road Bridge, and by 144th Infantry Brigade at C.11.b.6.4., just N.E. Hugel Hollow. All documents and other belongings of prisoners will be sent with the prisoners as far

as Divisional Headquarters. This is most important, and must be made known to all ranks.

(*Sd.*) P. L. WRIGHT,
Lieutenant and Adjutant, 1st Bucks Battalion.

14.8.17.

Copies to all recipients of O.O.25.

Secret. *Copy No.* 9

C

BUCKS BATTALION ORDER No. 282

RAID ON AUSTRIAN TRENCHES

Reference Map: Camporovere 1/10,000

1. The Bucks Battalion (on right) and 1/4th Battalion R. Berks Regiment (on left) will raid area of Austrian trenches shown on attached tracing, on " X " day, at a time to be notified later, and capture or kill the garrison.

2. The Battalion will mop up the whole of the area shown from Centre Road (inclusive) to the right.

Objectives as given on map issued to companies yesterday.

3. The Battalion will be formed up ready to attack by zero — 15 minutes, according to plan issued to companies yesterday.

4. The forming-up positions will be 50 yards S. of track Ave—Midway House, and immediately to west of latter point.

5. Two platoons of B Company will cover the front and right flank of Battalion while forming up. Should any enemy be in a position to interfere with the forming-up, they will be rushed silently with the bayonet.

As soon as the forming up is complete, these platoons will withdraw silently to their allotted position on the right flank, and be responsible for that flank until the time arrives for them to proceed to their own objective.

6. Point of entry into enemy lines, except for two flank

platoons of B Company, will be from *E* in S*E*C on right to Battalion left boundary. The two flank platoons of B Company will move at zero to a position south of Sec, and will rush their objective from there as barrage lifts at zero + 22 minutes.

7. *The Attack.* All platoons, except two platoons of B Company mentioned above, will advance to the attack in the order of forming-up:

A Company will move direct to its objective;

D Company will pass through A Company direct to its objectives, as artillery barrage permits;

C Company and leading two platoons of B Company will take disused trench running north from *E* in S*E*C as a guide. They will move up close to west side of this trench until opposite their objectives, when they will turn to the right.

The right platoons will gain a position to rush their objectives in Sunken Road, when artillery barrage lifts at zero + 14 minutes.

The left platoons will pass through the right platoons, and rush their objectives on enemy front line facing S.E., when Royal Artillery barrage lifts at zero + 22 minutes. At this same time the two flank platoons of B Company will rush their objective in enemy front line, and will be prepared to help their platoon in Sunken Road if necessary.

8. Platoons will be prepared to remain in their objectives until zero + 90 minutes.

9. *Withdrawal.* The withdrawal will not commence until the party of the R. Berks at the farthest objective have completed their task. A liaison-post with the R. Berks will be established at H.728.559. D Company will detail a section under a sergeant for this duty, who will receive special instructions.

The signal for withdrawing will be Gas Rattles.

When withdrawal commences it will be from the farthest objectives first. Platoons will remain in their objectives until those in front of them are reported all clear, A and B Companies' platoons in the front line being the last to withdraw.

10. The Artillery action will consist of five phases. 18-pounder barrages, as shown on attached tracing.

6-inch howitzers, 4·5 howitzers and French Artillery will engage special targets.

11. The Battalion will move to forming-up position by San Sisto—Ave road, and thence through gap which will be made in piquet-line wire about H.725.483. Road allotted to this Battalion from 9.30 p.m. to 10 p.m., by which time it will be clear for the R. Berks.

12. The withdrawal will be by the same route.

13. A " Checking-in " Post will be established at the gap in piquet-line wire, to which all parties will report on withdrawal.

14. On morning of zero day the Battalion will move into support position in Right Brigade Sector, and will be relieved there on zero + one day.

15. " Special Instructions " are issued separately.

16. Battalion Command Post will be at western end of Gun-pit Post, H.730.485.

17. Aid Post position will be notified later.

(Sd.) L. L. C. REYNOLDS,
Lieutenant-Colonel,
Comdg. Bucks Battalion.

23.8.18.

Copies to :
    1–4—Companies.
    5—1/4th Battalion R. Berks Regiment.
    6—145th Infantry Brigade.
    7—File.
    8-9—War Diary.

Secret.

Amendment No. 1 to Bucks Battalion Order No. 232

1. Paragraph 16 cancelled, substitute : Battalion Command Post until zero will be Midway House; after zero it will move forward to Lone Tree House, H.726.548.

2. Reference tracing of R. Artillery barrages, the barrage at zero will come down 100 yards in front of enemy front

line. At zero + 1 it will lift to front line, where it will remain until zero + 5, as before arranged.

8. Reference paragraph 17.

R.A.P. will be off S. Sisto road at H.718.423, a dugout usually used by machine-gun Battalion. There will be a guide on road to show any wounded the place.

(Sd.) L. L. C. REYNOLDS,
Lieutenant-Colonel,
Comdg. Bucks Battalion.

25.8.18.

Secret.

Special Instructions for Raid on " X " Day, to accompany Bucks Battalion Order No. 232

1. All officers will wear camouflage dress and carry rifles. Sticks are forbidden.

2. Other ranks will wear drill order.

3. All will wear a white band, 6 inches wide, on each upper arm.

4. Distinctive marks for parties detailed for separate objectives will not be worn.

5. All will blacken their faces.

6. An inspection will be held to ensure that no papers, maps or identity discs, or other marks, are carried.

7. Rifle grenades will be taken.

8. Each man will carry two bombs in bandoliers or special bags. Adjutant will arrange.

9. P. bombs (forty per Battalion) will be taken.

10. S.A.A. only 50 rounds per man. Reserve will be obtained from Piquet Line if required.

11. Wire-cutters (thirty-two per Battalion) will be taken.

12. Torches (fifty per Battalion) will be taken.

13. One T.M. will be attached to each battalion. Thirty rounds per gun will be carried. Reserve of twenty per gun will be placed in Piquet Line. Pack transport will be used.

14. Battalion Command Post will have two separate telephones, placed so that one shell will not destroy both. Wires also will be well separated.

OPERATION ORDERS

15. Sufficient runners and visual signalling will be arranged.

16. Each battalion provides a Liaison Officer with two runners for the other, and the two battalion command posts will be connected by a special wire and telephones.

17. The Second-in-Command will be responsible for all assembly arrangements, including forming up tapes, tapes from Front Line through Piquet Line, wire to Deployment positions, and a supply of tapes to take forward to enemy front line.

18. 144th Infantry Brigade will arrange to:
    (1) Take over all prisoners at Piquet Line. Escorts from Front, on handing over, will form a Battalion Reserve.
    (2) Provide extra stretcher-bearers.
    (3) Cover the flanks if required.
    (4) Keep all routes clear.

19. One R.A. officer will be at Brigade Command Post, and one at each Battalion Command Post, with separate telephone and wire.

20. Red flares will be the signal for the protective barrage to re-open for ten minutes on each call.

21. All ranks will be shown all available photos and plans.

22. Every officer and sergeant will read S.S. 602 on $X-1$ day.

23. All will be warned that if wounded (unless seriously) it is their duty to fight on, unless permission to fall out is obtained from a senior officer.

24. Wounded will, if at all capable, bring back their arms and equipment.

25. Moppers-up will be detailed fully.

26. Each Battalion will establish one block on the outer flank.

27. Every dugout will be bombed.

28. All will be cautioned to shoot at once anyone saying " Retire."

29. Every man cutting wire will be covered by a comrade.

30. Countersign will be notified later.

APPENDIX I

31. Watches will be checked at Battalion Command Post at an hour to be notified.

32. Battalions will be reported ready in position by code word LION.

33. Signal for retire will be Gas Rattles.

34. Instructions, reference routes, etc., for move to front and withdrawal through Front Line will be issued later.

35. (*a*) A Company's right platoon in enemy front line will detail a Lewis gun and bombers to stop in trench between *E* in S*E*C and house until B Company's platoon join them.

(*b*) C Company's northern platoon in enemy front line will detail a similar party to block trench where it crosses road and stop any attempt of enemy to counter-attack from N. and N.E.

(*c*) C Company's platoons in Sunken Road, and D Company's platoons at S. M. Maddalena, will each post two Lewis guns to stop any enemy interference from N.

(*Sd.*) L. L. C. REYNOLDS,
Lieutenant-Colonel,
Comdg. Bucks Battalion.

24.8.18.

Secret.

Special Instructions No. 2 for Raid on " X " Day, to accompany Bucks Battalion Order No. 282

In order to mystify and mislead the enemy, the following arrangements will be made :

I. (1) Each platoon detailed to occupy the front line will tell off a selected lance/corporal and two men, whose duty will be to fire Very lights from the Austrian front line *towards the British line.*

(2) Each party will take a Very pistol and such ammunition as can be arranged—Austrian, if available—and if not, twelve rounds British.

(3) They will be instructed to fire only from parts of the

trench where enemy posts are found, or show signs of such occupation.

(4) They will also be provided with torches and will search for stores of white Austrian Very lights. Only white ones must be fired.

(5) Care will be taken that no coloured lights are fired by these parties.

II. (1) Each Battalion Headquarters will be provided with red and green Very lights.

(2) These will be used by order of the C.O. only.

(3) Special and reliable men will be told off for these and provided with Very pistols.

(4) Close observation will be made, and if it is seen that red lights bring down the Austrian barrage, green will be fired.

(5) If green lights bring down the enemy's barrage, then red will be fired.

(Sd.) L. L. C. REYNOLDS,
Lieutenant-Colonel,
Comdg. Bucks Battalion.

25.8.18.

Prisoners will be taken over by the 144th Infantry Brigade at Yellow House.

Secret.

Special Instructions No. 3. for Raid on " X " Day, to accompany Bucks Battalion Order No. 232

1. " Checking-in " Post will be established at gap in piquet-line wire immediately W. of Gun-pit Post, consisting of :

> R.S.M.,
> Provost Sergeant,
> Police,
> Pioneers.

2. Prisoners will be sent to " Checking-in " Post, where they will be taken over by Provost Sergeant, who will send

them back to junction of S. Sisto Road with Front Line, where they will be handed over to 144th Brigade and a receipt obtained.

Escorts from front will return to their platoons after handing over to Provost Sergeant.

Previous order concerning prisoners is cancelled.

3. Only officers will carry Gas Rattles.

4. Platoons of B and C Companies in enemy front line will watch right flank, especially during the withdrawal, in case enemy should attempt to counter-attack from direction of Clama.

5. All Lewis guns will be taken into action.

6. All ranks will be cautioned of the importance of silence while advancing to forming-up position and while forming up, to move quietly and prevent arms rattling.

7. Leading platoons in the advance must be prepared to cut rapidly any wire which causes obstruction.

8. Platoons will be warned of the importance of keeping locked up close during the advance to forming-up position. The Platoon Commander will lead his platoon, and the next senior will march in rear to see that those in front are closed up.

9. Advance guard platoons of B Company will report to Major Hall, at junction of S. Sisto Road and Front Line, at 9 p.m.

10. Companies will move up in the following order, passing point on road opposite present Battalion Headquarters at times stated, maintaining 100 yards between platoons; formation—file :

Battalion Headquarters	. . .	9.00 p.m.
A Company	. . . . .	9.02 p.m.
C ,,	. . . .	9.06 p.m.
B ,, (less two platoons)	. .	9.10 p.m.
D ,,	. . . .	9.12 p.m.

On reaching gap in front-line wire single file will be formed and maintained until Assembly position is reached, when units will re-form file.

The leading platoon, after passing front line, will move

at a very slow pace to enable platoons in rear to close up to twenty paces' interval, which will be strictly maintained.

11. Watches will be synchronised at Battalion Headquarters at 5 p.m.

One officer per company, with two reliable watches, will report at that time.

(Sd.) L. L. C. REYNOLDS,
Lieutenant-Colonel,
Comdg. Bucks Battalion.

26.8.18.

D
ATTACK OF NOVEMBER 1, 1918
[COPY OF WIRE]

Words, 160.	Received. From : H.R.Q. By : L/Cpl. Witney.	
SERVICE INSTRUCTIONS : H.R.Q. Urgent Priority.		
TO	Rush.	
Sender's Number BM 157	Day of Month 1	In reply to Number —	AAA

Divn. will capture line Croce San Antonio—Mosciagh to-day aaa French are attacking M. Longara aaa Right bdy. west edge of Gallio Wood along C. Giardini—S. Antonio road inclusive aaa Left boundary of Bde. Capitello Mulche—Bosco—C. Sichestal Mosciagh road inclusive aaa Inter-battn. boundary L of RENDELA—first E of EBENE—300 yards E. of Z in M. CATZ to grid line at 70 and north to 71 aaa Arty. bombardment commencing 0500 hours on back area aaa Barrage on Winter Stellung 0545 to 0550 aaa M. Catz and grid line 69.79.89 0550 to 0635 aaa Grid line 60.70.80 0635 to 0735 aaa Grid line 61.71.81 0735 to 0935 aaa Objectives to be captured at last-named hours in each case aaa Rush right Roar left Run reserve aaa Rapid will not move aaa Other arrangements as fixed by telephone aaa ref. map C. Dodici and Asiago 1/25000.

FROM	Race.

APPENDIX II

ROLLS OF OFFICERS WHO TOOK PART IN THE MAIN ACTIONS OF 1916—1917—1918

ROLL OF OFFICERS WHO TOOK PART IN THE ATTACK ON THE GERMAN TRENCHES BETWEEN OVILLERS AND POZIÈRES, ON THE NIGHT JULY 20/21, 1916.

Battalion Headquarters
Lieut.-Col. L. L. C. Reynolds (commanding Battalion).
Lieut. P. L. Wright (Adjutant).
2/Lieut. J. B. Hales (Intelligence Officer).
Capt. L. E. Hughes, R.A.M.C. (Medical Officer).

A Company (attacking Company)
Capt. N. S. Reid, M.C.
2/Lieut. B. C. Rigden (wounded).
2/Lieut. C. G. Abery (killed).
2/Lieut. H. E. Molloy.

B Company (attacking Company)
Capt. L. W. Crouch (killed).
Lieut. R. Gregson-Ellis.
Lieut. R. E. M. Young.
2/Lieut. H. C. E. Mason (wounded).

C Company (attacking Company)
Capt. G. G. Jackson (wounded and prisoner).
2/Lieut. H. M. Shepherd (wounded).
2/Lieut. A. P. Godfrey (wounded).
2/Lieut. J. P. Chapman (killed).
2/Lieut. C. W. Trimmer (killed).

D Company (Company in reserve)
Capt. E. V. Birchall.
2/Lieut. F. D. Earle.
2/Lieut. F. H. Rover.
2/Lieut. J. F. Arnott.

ROLL OF OFFICERS WHO TOOK PART IN THE ATTACK ON THE GERMAN TRENCHES AT 6.30 A.M. ON JULY 23, 1916.

Battalion Headquarters
Lieut.-Col. L. L. C. Reynolds (commanding Battalion).
Lieut. P. L. Wright (Adjutant).
2/Lieut. J. B. Hales (Intelligence Officer).
Capt. L. E. Hughes, R.A.M.C. (Medical Officer).

A Company (Company in support)
Capt. N. S. Reid, M.C.
2/Lieut. H. E. Molloy.

B Company (attacking Company)
Capt. O. V. Viney (wounded).
Lieut. E. N. C. Woollerton (wounded).
2/Lieut. E. R. Hillman.
2/Lieut. F. Niall (wounded).

C Company (Company in reserve)
Capt. P. A. Hall.
2/Lieut. E. G. H. Bates.

D Company (attacking Company)
Capt. E. V. Birchall (wounded, died of wounds).
2/Lieut. F. D. Earle.
2/Lieut. F. H. Rover.
2/Lieut. J. F. Arnott.

ROLLS OF OFFICERS

ROLL OF OFFICERS WHO TOOK PART IN THE ATTACK ON SKYLINE TRENCH ON AUGUST 14 AND 15, 1916

Battalion Headquarters
Lieut.-Col. L. L. C. Reynolds (commanding Battalion).
Lieut. P. L. Wright (Adjutant).
2/Lieut. J. B. Hales (Intelligence Officer).
Capt. L. E. Hughes, R.A.M.C. (Medical Officer).

A Company
Capt. N. S. Reid, D.S.O., M.C.
Capt. V. C. Heathcote-Hacker (wounded).
2/Lieut. W. R. Heath.

B Company
Capt. G. R. Crouch.
Lieut. R. Gregson-Ellis.
2/Lieut. E. R. Hillman.

C Company
Capt. P. A. Hall.
2/Lieut. E. G. H. Bates.
2/Lieut. D. Fallon (wounded).
2/Lieut. H. M. Breton.

D Company
Lieut. F. D. Earle (wounded).
2/Lieut. J. F. Arnott.
2/Lieut. F. C. Dixon (wounded).

ROLL OF OFFICERS WHO TOOK PART IN THE ATTACK ON THE GERMAN TRENCHES BETWEEN OVILLERS AND POZIÈRES ON AUGUST 23, 1916.

Battalion Headquarters
Lieut.-Col. L. L. C. Reynolds (commanding Battalion).
Lieut. P. L. Wright (Adjutant).
2/Lieut. J. B. Hales (Intelligence Officer).
Capt. L. E. Hughes, R.A.M.C. (Medical Officer).

A Company (*attacking Company*)

Capt. N. S. Reid, D.S.O., M.C.
Lieut. M. Bowen (wounded).
2/Lieut. W. R. Heath (killed).

B Company

Capt. G. R. Crouch.
Lieut. R. E. M. Young.

C Company (*attacking Company*)

Capt. P. A. Hall.
2/Lieut. E. G. H. Bates (killed).
2/Lieut. H. M. Breton (wounded).

D Company

Capt. R. Gregson-Ellis.
2/Lieut. J. F. Arnott.
2/Lieut. F. H. Rover.

ROLL OF OFFICERS WHO TOOK PART IN THE OPERATION OF TOMBOIS FARM ON NIGHT APRIL 16/17, 1917.

Battalion Headquarters

Lieut.-Col. L. L. C. Reynolds, D.S.O. (commanding Battalion).
Major A. B. Lloyd-Baker (2nd-in-Command of Battalion).
Capt. P. L. Wright, M.C. (Adjutant).
Lieut. H. J. Pullman (Intelligence Officer).
Capt. L. E. Hughes, R.A.M.C. (Medical Officer).

A Company

Capt. N. S. Reid, D.S.O., M.C.
2/Lieut. P. A. Coates.

B Company

Lieut. M. Bowen.
2/Lieut. G. A. Johnston.
2/Lieut. R. F. Chatham.
2/Lieut. E. H. Fawcitt.

C Company

Lieut. J. B. Hales.
Lieut. G. R. F. Knight.
Lieut. F. D. Ollard.

D Company

Capt. R. Gregson-Ellis (wounded, died of wounds).
2/Lieut. J. Jack (wounded).
2/Lieut. B. C. C. Olivier (wounded).
2/Lieut. N. S. Flint (wounded).

Roll of Officers Who took Part in the Attack on German Positions N.W. of St. Julien, on August 16, 1917.

Battalion Headquarters

Lieut.-Col. L. L. C. Reynolds, D.S.O. (commanding Battalion).
Capt. M. Bowen (asst. 2nd-in-Command of Battalion).
Capt. P. L. Wright, M.C. (Adjutant).
Lieut. J. E. Firminger (Signal Officer).
2/Lieut. G. A. Johnston (Intelligence Officer) (wounded).
Capt. L. E. Hughes, R.A.M.C. (Medical Officer).
Capt. H. Noke (Chaplain).

A Company

Capt. G. R. F. Knight (killed).
2/Lieut. F. M. Passmore (wounded).
2/Lieut. F. C. Marshall (wounded).

APPENDIX II

B Company

2/Lieut. E. H. Fawcitt (wounded).
2/Lieut. F. G. Vaughan.
2/Lieut. R. E. Norman (wounded).

C Company

Capt. G. V. Neave (killed).
Lieut. F. D. Ollard (wounded).
2/Lieut. W. O'B. Rigden.
2/Lieut. A. T. Moyle (wounded).

D Company

Lieut. H. J. Pullman.
2/Lieut. C. G. Reeves.

ROLL OF OFFICERS PRESENT WITH THE BATTALION IN THE LINE DURING THE AUSTRIAN ATTACK ON OUR TRENCHES ON THE ASIAGO PLATEAU, ON JUNE 15, 1918.

Battalion Headquarters

Major P. A. Hall, M.C. (commanding Battalion).
Capt. G. R. Crouch (2nd-in-Command of Battalion).
Capt. C. G. Reeves, M.C. (Adjutant).
2/Lieut. F. P. Bates (Intelligence Officer).
2/Lieut. F. J. A. Corfield (Signal Officer).
Capt. H. S. Thomas, R.A.M.C. (Medical Officer).
Capt. H. Noke, C.F. (Chaplain).

A Company

Capt. J. E. Firminger.
Capt. G. L. Troutbeck.
Lieut. N. S. Flint.
2/Lieut. H. R. Pigott (wounded).
2/Lieut. L. W. G. Lorns.

ROLLS OF OFFICERS

B Company
Capt. A. P. Darby.
Lieut. A. L. Brightman.
2/Lieut. W. G. Butler (wounded).

C Company
Lieut. G. W. Higlett.
2/Lieut. P. T. Herbert (wounded).

D Company
Capt. B. C. Rigden, M.C.
2/Lieut. G. B. Baker.
2/Lieut. E. T. C. Coxon (wounded).
2/Lieut. F. J. Wilcox (wounded).
2/Lieut. J. R. Pike.

Roll of Officers Who took Part in the Raid on the Austrian Trenches on the Asiago Plateau on August 26, 1918.

Battalion Headquarters
Lieut.-Col. L. L. C. Reynolds, D.S.O. (commanding Battalion).
Major P. A. Hall, M.C. (2nd-in-Command of Battalion).
Capt. C. G. Reeves, M.C. (Adjutant).
2/Lieut. L. McCracken (Intelligence Officer).
2/Lieut. F. J. A. Corfield (Signal Officer).
Capt. H. S. Thomas, R.A.M.C. (Medical Officer).

A Company
Capt. J. E. Firminger (wounded).
2/Lieut. L. W. G. Lorns (wounded).
2/Lieut. M. W. Butlin.

B Company
Lieut. A. L. Brightman (wounded).
2/Lieut. F. W. Blackmore (wounded).
2/Lieut. A. H. Herbert,

C Company

2/Lieut. P. T. Herbert, M.C.
2/Lieut. F. B. Bates (wounded).
2/Lieut. L. R. Curram (wounded).

D Company

Capt. B. C. Rigden, M.C.
2/Lieut. G. B. Baker.
2/Lieut. F. J. Wilcox.

Roll of Officers Who took Part in the Attack on the Austrian Positions on the Asiago Plateau, on November 1, 1918, and the Subsequent Advance into the Trentino.

Battalion Headquarters

Lieut.-Col. L. L. C. Reynolds, D.S.O. (commanding Battalion).
Major P. L. Wright, M.C. (2nd-in-Command of Battalion).
Capt. C. G. Reeves, M.C. (Adjutant).
2/Lieut. F. J. A. Corfield (Signal Officer).
2/Lieut. A. H. Herbert (Intelligence Officer).
Capt. H. S. Thomas, R.A.M.C. (Medical Officer).

A Company

Capt. N. S. Flint.
2/Lieut. G. B. Baker.
Lieut. F. H. Rover (advance only).
2/Lieut. D. Cullinan (advance only).

B Company

Lieut. E. C. J. Allday.
2/Lieut. W. G. Butler.
2/Lieut. R. W. Grace.

C Company

Capt. G. W. Higlett, M.C.
2/Lieut. P. T. Herbert, M.C.

D Company

Lieut. H. A. Beaver.
2/Lieut. J. W. C. Read (wounded).
2/Lieut. J. R. Pike.
2/Lieut. C. B. Ellwood.

APPENDIX III

HONOURS AND DECORATIONS GAINED BY OFFICERS OF THE 1ST BUCKS BATTALION

C.M.G.

Lieut.-Col. F. O. Wethered, attached 6th Battalion Royal Warwickshire Regiment.

BAR TO D.S.O.

Lieut.-Col. L. L. C. Reynolds.
Lieut.-Col. A. J. N. Bartlett, attached 1/4th Battalion Oxford & Bucks Light Infantry.

D.S.O.

Gained while serving with the Battalion

Lieut.-Col. C. P. Doig, Seaforth Highlanders (attached).
Lieut.-Col. L. L. C. Reynolds.
Major P. A. Hall.
Major P. L. Wright.
Capt. E. V. D. Birchall.
Capt. N. S. Reid.

Gained while serving with other Units

Lieut.-Col. A. B. Lloyd-Baker, attached 1/4th Battalion Royal Berkshire Regiment.
Lieut.-Col. A. J. N. Bartlett, attached 1/4th Battalion Oxford & Bucks Light Infantry.
Major C. J. Mitchell, G.S.O.3, 48th Division.
Major H. V. Combs, 23rd Battalion Machine Gun Corps.

HONOURS AND DECORATIONS

BAR TO MILITARY CROSS
Gained while serving with the Battalion

Capt. B. C. Rigden.

MILITARY CROSS
Gained while serving with the Battalion

Capt. N. S. Reid.
,, H. V. Combs.
,, P. A. Hall.
,, P. L. Wright.
,, E. Nichol.
,, J. E. Firminger.
,, H. J. Pullman.
,, A. P. Darby (Essex Regiment, attached).
,, L. E. Hughes (R.A.M.C., attached).
,, N. S. Flint.
Lieut. M. Bowen.
,, A. D. B. Brown.
,, G. W. Higlett.
2/Lieut. B. C. Rigden.
,, J. F. Arnott (Wiltshire Regiment, attached).
,, G. A. Johnston.
,, C. G. Reeves.
,, D. Fallon.
,, G. B. Baker.
,, F. P. Bates.
,, F. W. Blackmore.
,, W. G. Butler.
,, C. B. Ellwood.
,, P. T. Herbert.
,, F. J. Wilcox.
Capt. H. Noke, C.F.

Gained while serving with other Units

Major G. R. Crouch, attached 1/5th Gloucestershire Regiment.
Capt. G. E. W. Bowyer, attached 61st Division.
,, B. Green, attached Machine Gun Corps.
,, F. L. Wright, attached 11th Division, G.S.O.3.

APPENDIX III

Capt. J. B. Hill, attached 144th Infantry Brigade (Staff Captain).
,, J. B. Hales, attached 48th Division, G.S.O.3.
2/Lieut. F. M. Passmore, attached 2/1st Bucks Battalion.
,, C. E. Clothier, attached 145th Trench Mortar Battery.

Order of the British Empire

Capt. J. B. Hill, attached 144th Infantry Brigade (Staff Captain).

Mentioned in Dispatches
While serving with the Battalion

Lieut.-Col. C. P. Doig (Seaforth Highlanders, attached).
,, L. L. C. Reynolds (five times).
Major A. B. Lloyd-Baker (twice).
,, P. A. Hall.
,, P. L. Wright (twice).
Capt. E. V. D. Birchall.
,, N. S. Reid.
,, H. V. Combs.
,, G. R. Crouch.
,, R. Gregson-Ellis.
,, J. E. Firminger.
,, B. Green.
,, G. L. Troutbeck.
,, J. B. Hales.
,, C. G. Reeves.
,, L. E. Hughes (R.A.M.C., attached).
,, H. S. Thomas (R.A.M.C., attached).
,, A. P. Darby (Essex Regiment, attached).
Lieut. W. Maggs.
,, L. McCracken.
,, G. V. Neave.
,, E. Nichol.
2/Lieut. F. J. A. Corfield.
,, F. M. Passmore.

HONOURS AND DECORATIONS

While serving with other Units

Lieut.-Col. A. B. Lloyd-Baker, attached 1/4th Battalion Royal Berkshire Regiment.
Lieut.-Col. P. A. Hall, attached 1/7th Battalion Royal Warwickshire Regiment.
Major C. J. Mitchell, attached 48th Division, G.S.O.3.
Major H. V. Combs (twice), attached 23rd Battalion Machine Gun Corps.
Capt. E. L. Wright (twice), attached VIIth Corps, G.S.O.3., and 2nd Division, Brigade Major 6th Infantry Brigade.
Capt. J. B. Hill (twice), attached 144th Infantry Brigade (Staff Captain).

FOREIGN DECORATIONS

FRENCH CROIX DE GUERRE AVEC PALME

Lieut.-Col. L. L. C. Reynolds.

ITALIAN SILVER MEDAL FOR VALOUR

Lieut.-Col. L. L. C. Reynolds.
Capt. J. E. Firminger.
2/Lieut. L. W. G. Lorns.

ITALIAN BRONZE MEDAL FOR VALOUR

Capt. N. S. Flint.
2/Lieut. L. R. Curram.

Gained while serving with other Units

Lieut.-Col. P. A. Hall, attached 1/7th Battalion Royal Warwickshire Regiment.

ITALIAN CROCE DI GUERRA

Gained while serving with other Units

Lieut.-Col. A. B. Lloyd-Baker, attached 1/4th Battalion Royal Berkshire Regiment.
Capt. J. B. Hill, attached 144th Infantry Brigade (Staff Captain).

APPENDIX IV

HONOURS AND DECORATIONS GAINED BY WARRANT OFFICERS, N.C.O.'s, AND MEN OF THE 1ST BUCKS BATTALION WHILE SERVING WITH THE BATTALION

MILITARY CROSS

Regtl. No.	Rank.	Name.	Regtl. No.	Rank.	Name.
265001	C.S.M.	Sirett, A. G.	52414	R.S.M.	Vincent, H.
212	,,	Smith, F.	265039	C.S.M.	Watts, H.

DISTINGUISHED CONDUCT MEDAL

Regtl. No.	Rank.	Name.	Regtl. No.	Rank.	Name.
2403	Corpl.	Atkins, T. W.	2582	Sergt.	Jennings, P.
2405	Sergt.	Baker, H. C.	265052	C.S.M.	Loveday, C.
1855	,,	Baldwin, W. J.	2710	Pte.	Nolan, M.
2244	Corpl.	Barnwell, W. G.	200212	L/Cpl.	Merriman, H.
265078	C.S.M.	Bishop, S. G.	265046	C.S.M.	Richardson, G. A.
265791	Sergt.	Bowery, G.	265146	Sergt.	Saunders, W. G.
266100	,,	Bridges, E.	2238	Bugler	Scragg, J. E.
266447	Corpl.	Buckland, W.	266343	Sergt.	Smith, W.
1208	L/Cpl.	Gostelow, G.	265698	Pte.	Stevens, E. J.
265094	Sergt.	Golding, T.	266851	Corpl.	Yeo, A. C.
265610	,,	Hopcraft, T. P.			

MILITARY MEDAL

Regtl. No.	Rank.	Name.	Regtl. No.	Rank.	Name.
265114	Sergt.	Allaway, C. W.	267670	Pte.	Cohen, M.
3566	L/Cpl.	Auger, C.	265473	,,	Cripps, F. T.
2031	Corpl.	Baldwin, C.	265296	,,	Cross, H. E.
1935	Sergt.	Baldwin, J. W.	266058	,,	Cutter, F.
2244	Corpl.	Barnwell, W. G.	266352	,,	Dickens, W.
265791	L/Sgt.	Bowery, G.	285002	Sergt.	Dixon, G. H.
33905	L/Cpl.	Brolley, J.	33569	L/Cpl.	Evans, J.
2875	Pte.	Busby, C. C.	265135	Sergt.	Fountain, A. G.
201335	,,	Bushnell, C.	2973	L/Cpl.	Garrett, F. R.
33818	,,	Carey, A. A.	34033	Pte.	Getting, J. T.
265657	,,	Cattell, W. W.	1908	L/Cpl.	Goldswain, J.
202073	,,	Clark, J.	266452	Corpl.	Guise, W. F.

HONOURS AND DECORATIONS 177

Regtl. No.	Rank	Name
33496	Corpl.	Guise, T. H.
265036	Sergt.	Hart, A. J.
1805	L/Cpl.	Haynes, J. G.
266461	Pte.	Herbert, A.
2072	L/Cpl.	Hicks, F. A.
265803	Corpl.	Hines, W.
265119	,,	Hollyoake, A. G.
2582	L/Cpl.	Jennings, P.
265498	Pte.	Lambourne, W.
265712	Sergt.	Lovell, S.
285074	Pte.	Moore, F.
33999	,,	Murphy, J.
265478	Sergt.	Niblett, T. W.
265670	Pte.	Piddington, F.
265642	Corpl.	Plumridge, P.
265107	,,	Porterfield, V. E.
33940	L/Cpl.	Pounteney, T. F.
1392	,,	Odell, G. H.
265046	Sergt.	Richardson, G. A.
266371	L/Cpl.	Robbins, W. G.
265923	Sergt.	Rogers, S. G.
2299	Corpl.	Rogers, F. L.
201637	Corpl.	Salcombe, G.
33689	Pte.	Saunders, J.
267533	L/Cpl.*	Seward, F. G.
266286	Pte.	Seymour, A. E.

Regtl. No.	Rank	Name
1246	L/Cpl.	Shaw, F. T.
266469	Corpl.	Shillingford, J.
33947	L/Cpl.	Shepperd, W.
265974	Sergt.	Sinclair, F. J.
278	Corpl.	Smewin, G.
266266	Pte.	Smith, F.
285065	,,	Smith, S.
265105	Sergt.	Stokes, A.
266733	Corpl.	Stone, S.
2097	L/Cpl.	Timson, F. W.
266528	L/Cpl.	Tipping, T.
265279	Pte.	Twitchen, G.
267535	L/Cpl.	Underwood, W.
33874	,,	Vigurs, W.
2217	,,	Vincent, T. W.
265622	,,	Way, H. J. P.
265292	Sergt.*	Wallington, G.
266899	Corpl.	Waters, T. H.
33584	Pte.	Wellington, R.
266045	Corpl.	West, J.
266275	L/Cpl.	Windsor, R.
265405	Sergt.	Woodham, S. T. H.
267542	Pte.	Worling, A.
34011	,,	Wright, H.
266078	L/Cpl.	Young, A. E.

MERITORIOUS SERVICE MEDAL

265095	R.Q.M.S.	Benning, W. J.
265054	C.Q.M.S.	Jolliffe, B.
265021	Q.M.S.	McBright, S.
265038	Sergt.	Newton, S. W.
265128	L/Cpl.	Read, J.
265334	C.Q.M.S.	Sawyer, H.
265358	Sergt.	Steptoe, F. J.

MENTIONED IN DISPATCHES

265095	R.Q.M.S.	Benning, W. J.
265615	Sergt.	Canvin, H. A.
265641	,,	Carter, H.
265921	Private	Crook, E. H.
265098	C.Q.M.S.	How, W. E.
265655	L/Cpl.	Hyde, E. V.
265054	C.Q.M.S.	Jolliffe, B.
265038	Sergt.	Newton, S. W.
265478	,,	Niblett, T. W.
265066	,,	Nicholson, S. R.
265260	,,	Orchard, R.
265046	C.S.M.	Richardson, G. A. (twice)
265375	Sergt.	Rivers, G.
265923	,,	Rogers, S. G.
265334	C.Q.M.S.	Sawyer, H.
265974	Sergt.	Sinclair, F. J.
265358	,,	Steptoe, F. J.
265105	,,	Stokes, A.
265602	Sergt.	Taberner, T. M.
265651	L/Cpl.	Witney, F.

FOREIGN DECORATIONS

CROIX DE GUERRE

265078 C.S.M. Bishop, S. G.

* Denotes award of Bars.

APPENDIX IV

(BELGIAN) CROIX DE GUERRE
33548 Corpl. Collins, H. E.

ITALIAN CROCE DI GUERRA

265114 Sergt. Allaway, C. W.	266343 Sergt. Smith, W.
200212 Pte. Merriman, H.	265046 C.S.M. Richardson, G. A.
265140 L/Cpl. Odell, G. H.	267548 Pte. Worraker, A.

MEDAL OF ST. GEORGE (2ND CLASS)
2244 Corpl. Barnwell, W. G.

(ITALIAN) MEDAGLIO DI BRONZO

33900 Pte. Campbell, A.	265974 Sergt. Sinclair, F. J.

BELGIAN ORDER DE LEOPOLD II CHEVALIER
265260 Sergt. Orchard, R.

APPENDIX V

ROLL OF OFFICERS WHO SERVED WITH THE 1ST BUCKS BATTALION DURING THE PERIOD MARCH 1915—DECEMBER 1918

NOTES

1. Where no dates are shown against decorations, these decorations have been gained when the officer concerned was serving away from the Battalion.
2. Several dates of gazettes of decorations are not available; when this is the case the date of the action for which these decorations were awarded has been given.
3. "Mentions" gained while serving with other units are *not* given.

Name.	Date of Joining.	Rank on Joining.	Promotion.	Decorations.	Mentions in Dispatches.	Casualty.	Date of Casualty.	Remarks.
Doig, Claude Prendergast (Seaforth Highlanders)		T/Lt.-Col.	—	D.S.O. 11.1.16	11.1.16	Accident while riding	27.1.16	Embarked with Battn. as C.O.
Hawkins, Lionel Comber	Pre-War		T/Major 1.9.14 Major 9.3.16 T/Lt.-Col. 27.2.16	—	—	Accident while riding	2.6.16	Embarked with Battn. 31.3.15 as 2nd-in-C. Commanded Battn. from 27.1.16 to 2.6.16.

APPENDIX V—continued

Name.	Date of Joining.	Rank on Joining.	Promotion.	Decorations.	Mentions in Dispatches.	Casualty.	Date of Casualty.	Remarks.
Reynolds, Lewis Leslie Clayton	Pre-War		Capt. 18.7.03 T/Major 26.2.15 Major 1.6.16 T/Lt.-Col. 3.6.16 Bt/Lt.-Col. 3.8.18 Lt.-Col. 3.6.16	D.S.O. 1.10.16 Bar to D.S.O. 6.9.17 Italian Silver Medal for Valour 26.8.18 French Croix de Guerre 9.12.18	1.1.17 21.12.17 30.5.18 6.1.19 3.6.19	Wounded Rejoined	6.5.15 27.7.15	Embarked with Battn. as O.C. A Coy. 2nd-in-C. of Battn. from 27.1.16 to 2.6.16. Commanded Battn. from 2.6.16 until cessation of hostilities. Took part in all main actions undertaken by Battn. in Belgium, France and Italy.
Crouch, Lionel William	Pre-War		Capt. 19.6.12	—	—	Killed	21.7.16	Embarked with Battn. as O.C. B Coy.
Birchall, Edward Vivian Dearman	Pre-War		Capt. 5.10.13	D.S.O. 23.7.16	1.1.17	Wounded Died of Wounds	23.7.16 10.8.16	Embarked with Battn. as O.C. D Coy.
Bowyer, George Edward Wentworth	Pre-War		Capt. 1.9.14	M.C.	—	Wounded	6.5.15	Embarked with Battn. as O.C. C Coy. Joined 61st Div. after being wounded.
Crouch, Guy Robert	Pre-War		T/Capt. 1.9.14 Capt. 1.6.16	M.C.	—	Hospital Rejoined Wounded Rejoined	21.4.15 7.8.16 28.2.17 24.5.17	Embarked with Battn. as 2nd-in-C. of B Coy. Commanded B Coy. latter half of 1916 and beginning of 1917. Appointed 2nd-in-C. of 1/5th Gloucester Regt. 26.7.18.

Name		Rank			Remarks
Hall, Philip Ashley	Pre-War	T/Capt. 1.9.14 Capt. 1.6.16 A/Major 29.7.17	M.C. 1.1.17 D.S.O. 1.1.19 Italian Bronze Medal for Valour	6.1.19 12.1.20	—	Embarked with Battn. as 2nd-in-C. of D Coy. Commanded C Coy. for greater part of two years. Appointed 2nd-in-C. of Battn. in July 1917. Appointed to command 1/7th R. Warwick Regt. in Oct. 1918. Took part in Somme battles, Peronne advance, and actions on Asiago plateau.
Jackson, Gerald Goddard	Pre-War	T/Capt. 1.9.14 Capt. 1.6.16	—	—	Wounded and Prisoner of War	21.7.16	Embarked with Battn. as 2nd-in-C. of C Coy. Was commanding C Coy. in action of 21.7.16 on the Somme.
Reid, Noel Spencer	Pre-War	T/Capt. 12.9.14 Capt. 1.6.16	M.C. 11.1.16 D.S.O. 25.8.16	4.1.17	Wounded	16.8.17	Embarked with Battn. as 2nd-in-C. of A Coy. Commanded A Coy. for greater part of 1916 and first 5 months of 1917. Attached to 145th Inf. Bde. to learn Staff work from May 1917 to Aug. 1917. Took part in Somme battles, Peronne advance, and 3rd battle of Ypres.
Combe, Hugh Vivian	Pre-War	T/Capt. 21.5.15 Capt. 1.6.16	M.C. 16.5.16 D.S.O.	15.6.16	—	—	Embarked with Battn. as Machine Gun Officer. Proceeded to England on 22.6.16 for transfer to M.G.C. Afterwards served with 23rd Div.
Vernon, Arthur Stanley	Pre-War	Lieut. 5.8.14 T/Capt. 6.6.15 Capt. 1.6.16	—	—	—	Embarked with Battn. as platoon comdr. in A Coy. Proceeded to England on 22.6.16 for transfer to M.G.C.

APPENDIX V—continued

Name.	Date of Joining.	Rank on Joining.	Promotion.	Decorations.	Mentions in Dispatches.	Casualty.	Date of Casualty.	Remarks.
Viney, Oscar Vaughan	Pre-War		Lieut. 1.9.14 T/Capt. 6.8.15 Capt. 1.6.18	—	—	Wounded Rejoined To hospital	23.7.16 21.2.17 12.3.17	Embarked with Battn. as Scout and Intelligence Officer. Was commanding B Coy. in action of 23.7.16 on the Somme.
Green, Bernard	Pre-War		T/Lieut. 1.9.14 Lieut. 20.10.15 Capt. 17.6.17	M.C.	—	Wounded Rejoined	6.5.15 27.7.15	Embarked with Battn. as platoon comdr. in A Coy. Seconded for duty with 145th M.G. Coy.—11.1.16.
Backhouse, John William	1.9.14	2/Lieut.	T/Lieut. 1.9.14 T/Capt. 10.6.15	—	—	Killed	10.2.16	Embarked with Battn. as platoon comdr. in C Coy.
Wright, Egerton Lowndes	3.9.14	2/Lieut.	T/Lieut. 3.9.14 Lieut. 27.9.16 T/Capt. 10.6.15 Capt. 10.8.16	M.C.	—	Killed (while serving with 6th Inf. Bde.)	11.5.18	Embarked with Battn. as platoon comdr. in C Coy. Attached 145th Inf. Bde. for Staff duty in June 1915. Afterwards appointed G.S.O.3 VII Corps, and then G.S.O.3 11th Div. Appointed Bde. Major 6th Bde. in Dec. 1916.
Bartlett, Alfred James Napier	52nd Light Infty.		—	D.S.O. Bar to D.S.O.	1.1.16	—	—	Embarked with Battn. as Adjt. Proceeded to 3rd Army Inf. School as Instructor on 10.11.15. Afterwards appointed to command 1/4th Oxford & Bucks L.I.

Name	Pre-War			D.S.O.			Remarks
Lloyd-Baker, Artur B.			Capt. 19.6.12 A/Major 3.8.16 Major 1.6.16	7.1.17	—	—	Embarked as Staff Capt. 145th Inf. Bde. Rejoined Battn. for duty on 16.2.16. Commanded C Coy. for 2 months. Appointed 2nd-in-C. of Battn. 2.6.16. Attached to 1/4th Oxford & Bucks L.I. on 14.7.17 as 2nd-in-C. Afterwards appointed to command of 1/4th R. Berks Regt.
Hill, John Burrow	10.9.14	2/Lieut.	T/Lieut. 10.9.14 Lieut. 1.6.16 T/Capt. 22.6.16 Capt. 17.6.17	M.C. 4.8.17 Italian Croce di Guerra O.B.E.	—	—	Embarked with Battn. as Transport Officer. Attached to 145th Inf. Bde. for Staff duty. Appointed Staff Capt. 144th Inf. Bde. on 27.7.17.
Kennish, Alan Charles Edward Forbes	10.9.14	2/Lieut.	T/Lieut. 28.2.15 Lieut. 20.10.15	—	—	—	Embarked with Battn. as platoon cmdr. in B Coy. Seconded for duty with 90th T.M.B., and transferred to England sick in 1916.
Reynolds, Francis Godfrey Baylie	1.9.14	2/Lieut.	T/Lieut. 21.4.15 Lieut. 20.10.15 Capt. 1.6.16	—	—	—	Embarked with Battn. as platoon comdr. in A Coy. Transferred to R.F.C. 21.6.16.
Brown, Alexander Denis Burnett	2.9.14	2/Lieut.	T/Lieut. 6.5.15 Lieut. 21.7.16 Capt. 1.6.16	M.C. 11.1.16	—	Wounded Rejoined Wounded	12.7.15 10.1.16 13.6.16	Embarked with Battn. as platoon comdr. in D Coy.

APPENDIX V—continued

Name.	Date of Joining.	Rank on Joining.	Promotion.	Decorations.	Mentions in Dispatches.	Casualty.	Date of Casualty.	Remarks.
Woollerton, Edwin Norman Collet	2.9.14	2/Lieut.	T/Lieut. 6.5.15 Lieut. 10.8.16 T/Capt. 22.6.16 Capt. 21.7.16	—	—	Wounded Rejoined Hospital Rejoined Hospital	23.7.16 12.3.17 23.3.17 13.10.17 21.12.17	Embarked with Battn. as platoon comdr. in B Coy. Took part in the Somme fighting and part of the Peronne advance.
Earle, Francis Douglas	2.9.14	2/Lieut.	T/Lieut. 1.7.15 Lieut. 27.9.16 T/Capt. 22.7.16 Capt. 10.8.16	—	—	Wounded	15.8.16	Embarked with Battn. as platoon comdr. in D Coy. Took part in Somme fighting.
Hobart-Hampden, Geo. Miles Awdry	2.9.14	2/Lieut.	T/Lieut. 6.5.15 Lieut. 20.9.16	—	—	Wounded Rejoined	1.6.15 5.9.16	Embarked with Battn. as platoon comdr. in D Coy. Transferred to R.F.C. in Dec. 1916, and was afterwards killed while flying.
Gregson-Ellis, Rex	21.9.14	2/Lieut.	T/Lieut. 10.6.15 T/Capt. 22.7.16	—	25.5.17	Wounded Died of wounds	16.4.17 17.4.17	Embarked with Battn. as platoon cmdr. in B Coy. Attached to No. 1 Entrenching Battn. at the Base for 11 months during 1915 and 1916. Commanded D Coy. for 8 months. Took part in Somme battles and advance from Peronne.

Name	Date	Rank		Honours	Date		Remarks
Wright, Philip Lowndes	2.1.15	2/Lieut.	T/Lieut. 10.6.15 Lieut. 1.6.16 A/Capt. 11.8.16 Capt. 4.8.17 A/Major 24.9.18	M.C. 1.1.17 D.S.O. 3.6.19	30.5.18 3.6.19	—	Embarked with Battn. as platoon comdr. in C Coy. Adjt. to the Battn. throughout 1916 and 1917. Acted as Bde. Major 144th Inf. Bde. from 24.5.18 to 25.7.18. Appointed 2nd-in-C. of Battn. Oct. 1918. Took part in all main actions undertaken by Battn. in Belgium, France and Italy.
Neave, Gerald V.	20.2.15	2/Lieut.	T/Lieut. 11.2.16 Lieut. 1.6.16 A/Capt. 23.1.17	—	4.1.17	Killed	16.8.17	Embarked with Battn. as platoon cmdr. in A Coy. Acted as Bde. Bombing Instructor for 14 months during 1915 and 1916. Commanded C Coy. during 1917. Took part in Somme battles, advance from Peronne, and 3rd battle of Ypres.
Nichol, Edward	Pre-War		Lieut. 17.2.15 Capt. 14.3.18	M.C. 1.1.19	21.12.17	—	—	Embarked with Battn. as Quartermaster. Present with Battn. throughout its period on active service.
Williamson, Norman Bruce	20.2.15	2/Lieut.	—	—	—	Wounded Rejoined	4.4.15 11.1.16	Embarked with Battn. as platoon cmdr. in A Coy. Transferred to 145th Bde. M.G. Coy. immediately after rejoining on 11.1.16.
Norwood, Robert Cecil	24.5.15	2/Lieut.	Lieut. 11.1.16	—	—	Killed	18.7.16	Platoon cmdr. in D Coy.
Hales, John Baseley	27.6.15	2/Lieut.	Lieut. 1.6.16 T/Capt. 15.4.18	M.C. 1.1.19	4.1.17 30.5.18	—	—	Platoon cmdr. in D Coy. for nearly 12 months on joining. Afterwards Battn. Intelligence Officer. Commanded C and D Coys. during 1917. Attached to Bde. and Div. during later part of 1917 to learn Staff duties. Appointed G.S.O.3 48th Div. 15.4.18. Took part in Somme battles, advance from Peronne, and 3rd battle of Ypres.

APPENDIX V—continued

Name.	Date of Joining.	Rank on Joining.	Promotion.	Decorations.	Mentions in Dispatches.	Casualty.	Date of Casualty.	Remarks.
Pullman, Harold John	27.6.15	2/Lieut.	Lieut. 20.9.16 A/Capt. 1.9.17	M.C. 18.10.17	—	—	—	Platoon cmdr. in C Coy. for 9 months. In hospital greater part of 1916. Commanded D Coy. for several months during 1917. Afterwards commanded C Coy. for nearly 12 months in France and Italy. Transferred to England June 18 for duty with 52nd R. Warwick Regt. Took part in advance from Peronne and 3rd battle of Ypres.
Young, Ralph Ernest Markham	27.7.15	2/Lieut.	Lieut. 5.2.16 Capt. 1.6.16	—	—	Wounded Rejoined	23.7.16 22.8.16	Platoon cmdr. in B Coy. Took part in battle of Somme. Attached to Bde. during greater part of 1917.
Newbery, Basil James	2.8.15	2/Lieut.	Lieut. 10.8.16	—	—	—	—	To hospital sick in Jan. 1916. Afterwards served with 61st Div.
Godfrey, Arthur Poole	5.12.15	2/Lieut.	—	—	—	Wounded	21.7.16	Platoon cmdr. in C Coy. Afterwards served with Household Batvn. and was killed in action.
Hall, Charles	12.12.15	2/Lieut.	—	—	—	Wounded Died of Wounds	17.7.16	Platoon cmdr. in A Coy.
Furley, Robert Basil	11.1.16	2/Lieut.	—	—	—	Killed	13.8.16	Platoon cmdr. in B Coy.
Rigden, Brian Cawes	13.1.16	2/Lieut.	Lieut. 1.7.17 A/Capt. 18.10.17	M.C. 18.8.16 Bar to M.C. 24.9.18	—	Wounded Rejoined	25.1.16 21.7.16 30.8.17	Platoon cmdr. in A Coy. Commanded D Coy. for about 8 months during 1918. Proceeded to England 11.11.18 for transfer to Indian Army.

Name					Remarks
Jones, Cecil Ynyr (13th Battn. London Regt.)	5.3.16	2/Lieut.	—	—	Hospital	30.5.16	Battn. Signal Officer for 2 months. Rejoined his own Regt. on leaving hospital.
Rolleston, John Marcus	12.3.16	2/Lieut.	Lieut. 1.6.16	—	Wounded	16.8.16	Platoon cmdr. in B Coy. Afterwards served with 61st Div.
Chapman, John Percy	18.3.16	2/Lieut.	—	—	Killed	21.7.16	Platoon cmdr. in C Coy.
Bates, Eric George Henry	18.3.16	2/Lieut.	T/Lieut. 20.7.16	—	Killed	23.8.16	Platoon cmdr. in C Coy.
Abrey, C. G.	21.3.16	2/Lieut.	—	—	Killed	21.7.16	Platoon cmdr. in A Coy.
Aitken, Robert	25.3.16	2/Lieut.	—	—	Wounded	9.4.16	Platoon cmdr. in B Coy. Afterwards served with 61st Div.
Rover, Fredk. Harold	7.5.16	2/Lieut.	Lieut. 1.7.17	—	Wounded Rejoined	17.2.17 8.11.17	Platoon cmdr. in D Coy. Instructing at Base from Sept. 16 to Feb. 17, when wounded in bombing accident. Served with Battn. throughout 1918. Took part in Somme fighting.
Trimmer, Charles William	5.6.16	2/Lieut.	—	—	Killed	21.7.16	Platoon cmdr. in C Coy.
Mason, H. C. E.	23.6.16	2/Lieut.	—	—	Wounded Rejoined Wounded	21.7.16 24.5.17 6.8.17	Platoon cmdr. in B Coy. in 1916 and in D Coy. 1917. Took part in action of 21.7.16 on Somme.
Shepherd, Hugh Vincent (Middlesex Regt.)	1.7.16	2/Lieut.	—	—	Wounded	21.7.16	Platoon cmdr. in C Coy. Took part in Somme battle.
Hillman, Eric Rodman (Middlesex Regt.)	1.7.16	2/Lieut.	—	—	—	—	Platoon cmdr. in B Coy. Took part in Somme battles. Transferred to Special Works' Park, R.E., in March 1917.
Niall, Francis (Wilts. Regt.)	1.7.16	2/Lieut.	—	—	Wounded (bombing accident)	8.8.16	Platoon cmdr. in B Coy. Took part in Somme battle.
Arnott, John Frederick (Wilts. Regt.)	3.7.16	2/Lieut.	—	M.C. 28.9.16	—	—	Platoon cmdr. in D Coy. Took part in Somme battles. To hospital sick, Sept. 1916.

APPENDIX V—continued

Name.	Date of Joining.	Rank on Joining.	Promotion.	Decorations.	Mentions in Dispatches.	Casualty.	Date of Casualty.	Remarks.
Molloy, Henry Edmund	10.7.16	2/Lieut.	—	—	—	Wounded (bombing accident)	8.8.16	Platoon cmdr. in A Coy. Afterwards killed in action with 61st Div.
Fallon, David	31.7.16	2/Lieut.	—	M.C. 1.1.17	—	Wounded Rejoined Wounded	15.8.16 4.9.16 16.11.16	Platoon cmdr. in C Coy. Took part in Somme battles.
Heathcote-Hacker, Victor Clare (Manchester Regt.)	7.8.16	T/Capt.	—	—	—	Wounded	15.8.16	2nd-in-C. of A Coy.
Breton, Harold Moyle (Manchester Regt.)	7.8.16	2/Lieut.	—	—	—	Wounded	23.8.16	Platoon cmdr. in C Coy.
Dixon, Frank Charles (Manchester Regt.)	7.8.16	2/Lieut.	—	—	—	Wounded	15.8.16	Platoon cmdr. in D Coy.
Heath, Walter Rowland	12.8.16	2/Lieut.	—	M.C. 15.6.17	—	Killed	23.8.16	Platoon cmdr. in A Coy.
Bowen, Martin	20.8.16	2/Lieut.	Lieut. 11.1.16 Capt. 1.6.16	—	—	Wounded Rejoined Wounded Died of wounds	23.8.16 10.9.16 3.10.17	Embarked with 48th Divl. Cyclists. Posted to B Coy. on joining Battn. Afterwards commanded that company. Took part in Somme battles and 3rd battle of Ypres.
Alloway, William Victor (Army Cyclist Corps)	27.8.16	2/Lieut.	—	—	—	—	7.10.17	Platoon comdr. in C Coy. To hospital sick 19.9.16.
Vaughan, Francis Gerald	28.8.16	2/Lieut.	Lieut. 1.7.17	—	—	—	—	Platoon cmdr. B Coy. Took part in the advance from Peronne and 3rd battle of Ypres. In hospital for several weeks during 1917. Finally to hospital 13.10.17.

Name		Rank			30.5.16			Remarks
Firminger, John Egerton	5.9.16	Lieut.	Lieut. 1.6.16 Capt. 9.7.17	M.C. 26.8.18 Italian Silver Medal for Valour 26.8.18	—	Wounded	26.8.18	Battn. Signal Officer 25.9.16 to 3.1.17. Afterwards commanded A Coy. for nearly 12 months. Took part in 3rd battle of Ypres, part of the Peronne advance, and some actions on Asiago plateau.
Warwick, John Douglas Barford (Hunts Cyclist Battn.)	10.9.16	Capt.	—	—	—	Killed	10.3.17	Commanded A Coy. for 3 months.
Fordham, Reginald Fredk. (Essex Regt.)	10.9.16	2/Lieut.	—	—	—	Killed (with T.M.B.)	30.10.17	Served with 145th T.M.B. from Oct. 1916 to date of death.
Pether, Wilfred Guy (Essex Regt.)	12.9.16	2/Lieut.	—	—	—	—	—	To hospital very soon after joining.
Wiseman, Stanley (Essex Regt.)	12.9.16	2/Lieut.	—	—	—	Killed	10.3.17	Platoon cmdr. in A Coy.
Knight, Gerald Robert Frank (Essex Regt.)	14.9.16	Lieut.	—	—	—	Killed	16.8.17	Platoon cmdr. in C Coy. Commanded A Coy. in July and Aug. 1917.
Maggs, William	14.9.16	2/Lieut.	Lieut. 1.7.17 A/Capt. 8.9.18	—	30.5.18 3.6.19	—	—	Platoon cmdr. in B Coy. Battn. Transport Officer for over 12 months. Afterwards Bde. Transport Officer.
Johnston, George Adam	14.9.16	2/Lieut.	Lieut. 7.5.17	M.C. 16.8.17	—	Wounded	16.8.17	Platoon cmdr. B Coy. for 3 months. Attached 4th Army Musketry Camp, Dec. 1916 to March 1917, as instructor. Appointed Assist. Adjt. 1.5.17. Took part in advance from Peronne and 3rd battle of Ypres.
Tucker, James Millard (Essex Regt.)	14.9.16	2/Lieut.	—	—	—	Hospital	6.3.17	Platoon cmdr. in C Coy.

APPENDIX V—continued

Name.	Date of Joining.	Rank on Joining.	Promotion.	Decorations.	Mentions in Dispatches.	Casualty.	Date of Casualty.	Remarks.
Darby, Alexander Pierre (Essex Regt.)	14.9.16	2/Lieut.	Lieut. 1.7.17 A/Capt. 5.1.18	M.C. 3.6.19	6.1.19	—	—	Platoon cmdr. in C Coy. for 12 months. Battn. Lewis Gun Officer. Commanded B Coy. for 12 months. Took part in advance from Peronne. Present with Battn. until cessation of hostilities.
Mann, Herbert Edmond (Essex Regt.)	14.9.16	2/Lieut.	—	—	—	—	—	Reposted to 2nd Oxford & Bucks L.I. on 24.11.16.
Cooper-Smith, Reginald Burston (Essex Regt.)	14.9.16	2/Lieut.	—	—	—	Killed	10.3.17	Platoon cmdr. in A Coy.
Clarke, John James (Essex Regt.)	14.9.16	2/Lieut.	—	—	—	—	—	Reposted to 2nd Battn. Oxford & Bucks L.I. on 24.11.16.
Sloan, Archibald (Essex Regt.)	14.9.16	2/Lieut.	—	—	—	—	—	To hospital sick one month after joining.
Coates, Philip Adrian (Essex Regt.)	14.9.16	2/Lieut.	—	—	—	Wounded	27.8.17	Platoon cmdr. in A Coy. Took part in advance from Peronne and 3rd battle of Ypres.
Jack, James (Essex Regt.)	15.9.16	2/Lieut.	—	—	—	Wounded	16.4.17	Platoon cmdr. in D Coy. Took part in advance from Peronne.
Bore, Thomas Edgar	5.10.16	2/Lieut.	—	—	—	—	—	To hospital sick 6 weeks after joining.
Piperno, Joseph Henry	19.10.16	2/Lieut.	—	—	—	—	—	Reposted to 2nd Battn. Oxford & Bucks L.I.—24.11.16.
Rydings, Douglas Gerald	20.10.16	2/Lieut.	—	—	—	—	—	Reposted to 2nd Battn. Oxford & Bucks L.I.—24.11.16.
Brettelle, Leonard Maurice Clifford	20.10.16	2/Lieut.	—	—	—	—	—	To hospital sick 6 weeks after joining.

Name	Date	Rank	Promotion	Honours	Date	Casualty	Date	Remarks
Olivier, Basil Coutts Carr	20.10.16	2/Lieut.	—	—	—	Wounded	16.4.17	Platoon cmdr. in D Coy. Took part in advance from Peronne.
Chatham, Robert Felton	20.10.16	2/Lieut.	—	—	—	Wounded (slightly)	16.4.17	Platoon comdr. in B Coy. Took part in advance from Peronne.
						Wounded	21.4.17	
Rigden, Walter O'Brien	26.1.17	2/Lieut.	Lieut. 26.3.18	—	—	—	—	Platoon cmdr. in C Coy. Took part in 3rd battle of Ypres. Transferred to R.A.F. June 1918.
Stephens, R. (43rd Light Infantry)	31.1.17	Capt.	—	—	—	—	—	Appointed to command 48th Divl. School very shortly after joining. Afterwards commanded 1/4th Batln. Oxford & Bucks L.I. for short period.
Flint, Norman Samuel	24.2.17	2/Lieut.	Lieut. 1.7.17 A/Capt. 9.10.18	M.C. 1.11.18 Italian Bronze Medal for Valour 1.11.18	—	Wounded Rejoined	16.4.17 6.1.18	Platoon cmdr. in several companies. Commanded A Coy. during last 3 months of 1918.
Ollard, Francis Douglas	12.3.17	Lieut.	—	—	—	Wounded	16.8.17	Platoon cmdr. in C Coy. Took part in 3rd battle of Ypres.
Passmore, Francis Marsland	12.3.17	2/Lieut.	—	M.C.	21.12.17	Wounded	16.8.17	Platoon cmdr. in A Coy. Took part in 3rd battle of Ypres.
Fawcitt, Edwin Henry	1.4.17	2/Lieut.	—	—	—	Wounded	16.8.17	Platoon cmdr. in B Coy. Took part in 3rd battle of Ypres.
Stevens, George Cecil	1.4.17	A/Capt.	—	—	—	—	—	To hospital sick few days after joining.
Reeves, Cecil Gilbert	2.5.17	2/Lieut.	Lieut. 11.12.17 A/Capt. 29.12.17	M.C. 18.10.17	6.1.19	—	—	Platoon cmdr. in D Coy. 3¾ months. Assist. Adjt. from Aug. 1917 to Dec. 1917. Adjt. from Dec. 1917 until cessation of hostilities. Took part in 3rd battle of Ypres and in all actions on Asiago plateau.

APPENDIX V—continued

Name.	Date of Joining.	Rank on Joining.	Promotion.	Decorations.	Mentions in Dispatches.	Casualty.	Date of Casualty.	Remarks.
Dipple, Thomas Denis	2.5.17	2/Lieut.	—	—	—	Wounded	5.8.17	Platoon cmdr. in B Coy. Took part in 3rd battle of Ypres
Marshall, Frederick Charles	8.5.17	2/Lieut.	—	—	—	Wounded	16.8.17	Platoon cmdr. in A Coy. Took part in 3rd battle of Ypres.
Troutbeck, George Lancelot	27.7.15	2/Lieut.	Lieut. 17.6.17 Capt. 17.6.17	—	3.6.19	—	—	(Attached H.Q. 3rd Army as R.S.O. from 5.8.15 to 6.7.17.) Platoon cmdr. in A Coy. Afterwards 2nd-in-C. of A Coy, commanded C and D Coys. at different periods.
Norman, Raymond Elder	18.5.17	2/Lieut.	—	—	—	Wounded	16.8.17	Platoon cmdr. in B Coy. Took part in 3rd battle of Ypres.
Moyle, Arthur Thomas	28.7.17	2/Lieut.	—	—	—	Wounded	16.8.17	Platoon cmdr. in C Coy. Took part in 3rd battle of Ypres.
Fleeming, William Henry	25.8.17	2/Lieut.	Lieut. 26.3.18 A/Capt. 9.10.18	—	—	Wounded Rejoined	27.8.17 12.10.17	Platoon cmdr. in D Coy. Commanded A, C, and D Coys. for short periods. Took part in 3rd battle of Ypres.
Newton, Henry James Hall (Hunts Cyclist Battn.)	30.8.17	Lieut.	—	—	—	—	—	Platoon cmdr. in D Coy. Employed away from Battn. for nearly 8 months. Finally to G.H.Q. Musketry School as instructor, 8.5.15. To hospital one week after joining.
McNish, John Archibald (Hunts Cyclist Battn.)	30.8.17	2/Lieut.	—	—	—	—	—	
Morfey, Percy Albert (Hunts Cyclist Battn.)	30.8.17	2/Lieut.	—	—	—	—	—	Reposted to 1/5th Battn. Gloucester Regt. on 18.10.17.
Fisher, George Alfred	30.8.17	2/Lieut.	—	—	—	—	—	Platoon cmdr. in A Coy. Assist. Transport Officer for 6 months. Battn. Transport Officer 6 months.

Name		Rank						Remarks
Browne, Sidney Noel	7.9.17	2/Lieut.	—	—	—	—	—	Platoon cmdr. in B Coy. Attached to G.H.Q. Italy for several months in 1918.
Caulfield, Robert Charles Fredk. (Essex Regt.)	7.9.17	2/Lieut.	Lieut. 23.11.18	—	—	—	—	Platoon cmdr. in C Coy. Attached to 145th T.M.B. for several months in 1918.
Smith, Charles Vivian Salisbury (Essex Regt.)	7.9.17	2/Lieut.	Lieut. 26.12.18	—	—	—	—	To 145th T.M.B. on 7.11.17, with whom he served until cessation of hostilities.
Seago, George William Edward (E. Kent Regt.)	9.9.17	2/Lieut.	—	—	—	—	—	Reposted to 1/5th Battn. Gloucester Regt. 18.10.17.
Sanders, Chas. Hayden George (E. Kent Regt.)	9.9.17	2/Lieut.	—	—	—	—	—	Reposted to 1/5th Battn. Gloucester Regt. 18.10.17.
Clothier, Clarence Edwin (Oxford & Bucks L.I. attd.)	9.9.17	2/Lieut.	—	M.C.	—	Wounded	28.9.17	Platoon cmdr. in A Coy. To 145th T.M.B. on 6.2.18, with whom he served until cessation of hostilities.
Stanway, Percy Anderton	10.9.17	2/Lieut.	—	—	—	—	—	To hospital 5 days after joining.
Cowlishaw, Vernon Clarke Paine	15.9.17	2/Lieut.	—	—	—	—	—	Platoon cmdr. in D Coy. Several months in hospital. Proceeded to England for Intelligence course. 4.10.18.
Bates, Frederick Percy	15.9.17	2/Lieut.	—	M.C. 2.12.18	—	Wounded	28.8.18	Platoon cmdr. in C Coy. Afterwards became Battn. Scout and Intelligence Officer.
Ellwood, Claude Bertram	15.9.17	2/Lieut.	—	M.C. 1.11.18	—	—	—	Platoon cmdr. in D Coy. With Battn. until cessation of hostilities.
Stokes, Wilfred Victor	15.9.17	2/Lieut.	—	—	—	Hospital	12.1.18	Platoon cmdr. in A Coy.
Corfield, Frederick John Arthur	25.9.17	2/Lieut.	—	—	3.6.19	—	—	Platoon cmdr. in B Coy. Afterwards became Battn. Signal Officer. With Battn. until cessation of hostilities.

APPENDIX V—continued

Name.	Date of Joining.	Rank on Joining.	Promotion.	Decorations.	Mentions in Dispatches.	Casualty.	Date of Casualty.	Remarks.
Lorne, Lionel William Goldhawk	22.9.17	2/Lieut.	—	Italian Bronze Medal for Valour 26.8.18	—	Wounded	26.8.18	Platoon cmdr. in A Coy.
Booking, Harry Charles	22.9.17	2/Lieut.	Lieut. 1.2.19	—	—	Wounded	24.8.18	Platoon cmdr. in B Coy.
McCracken, Leslie	22.9.17	2/Lieut.	Lieut. 1.2.19	—	3.6.19	—	—	Platoon cmdr. in D Coy. Assist. Adjt. from April 1918 until cessation of hostilities.
Baker, Gerald Broadbent (R. West Kent Regt.)	25.9.17	2/Lieut.	Lieut. 1.2.19	M.C. 2.12.18	—	—	—	Platoon cmdr. in D Coy. Afterwards commanded A Coy. on several occasions. Served with Battn. until cessation of hostilities.
Hayes, Gordon Stanley (R. West Kent Regt.)	25.9.17	2/Lieut.	—	—	—	—	—	Reposted 1/5th Battn. Gloucester Regt. 29.9.17.
Phinn, Charles Walter	25.9.17	2/Lieut.	—	—	—	—	—	Reposted 1/5th Battn. Gloucester Regt. 29.9.17.
Pigott, Henry Rudolph (Oxford & Bucks L.I. attd.)	12.10.17	2/Lieut.	—	—	—	Wounded	15.6.18	Platoon cmdr. in A Coy.
Higlett, George Willibert	12.10.17	2/Lieut.	Lieut. 31.12.17 A/Capt. 29.7.18	M.C. 19.10.18	—	—	—	Platoon cmdr. in C Coy. Afterwards commanded C Coy. Served with Battn. until cessation of hostilities.
Butler, William George	12.10.17	2/Lieut.	Lieut. 1.2.19	M.C. 1.11.18	—	Wounded Rejoined	15.6.18 25.8.18	Platoon cmdr. in B Coy. With Battn. until cessation of hostilities.
Cornish, Thomas Martin	12.10.17	2/Lieut.	—	—	—	—	—	Platoon cmdr. in C Coy. Transferred to R.A.F. 11.6.18.

Name	Date	Rank		Honours		Wounded	Date	Remarks
Grace, Reginald William	12.10.17	2/Lieut.	Lieut. 1.2.19	—	—	—	—	Platoon cmdr. in B Coy. Appointed Battn. Demobilisation Officer after cessation of hostilities.
Coxon, Edward Thomas Charles (R. West Kent Regt.)	12.10.17	2/Lieut.	—	—	—	—	—	Platoon cmdr. in C Coy. and later in D Coy. Transferred to R.A.F. 6.7.18.
Brightman, Arthur Lindrea	24.10.17	T/Lieut.	Lieut. 16.2.18	—	—	Wounded	26.8.18	2nd-in-C. of B Coy. Commanded that company on several occasions.
Wilcox, Francis John	25.10.17	2/Lieut.	—	M.C. 24.9.18	—	Wounded (slightly, at duty)	15.6.18	Platoon cmdr. in D Coy.
Herbert, Percy Thomas	25.10.17	2/Lieut.	—	M.C. 24.9.18	—	Wounded (slightly, at duty)	26.8.18 15.6.18	Platoon cmdr. in C Coy. Served with Battn. until cessation of hostilities.
Sherwin, George	25.10.17	2/Lieut.	—	—	—	Wounded	29.10.18	Platoon cmdr. in A Coy.
Blackmore, Frank William	8.11.17	2/Lieut.	—	M.C. 2.12.18	—	Wounded	26.8.18	Platoon cmdr. in B Coy.
Read, John William Charles	8.11.17	2/Lieut.	—	—	—	Wounded	1.11.18	Platoon cmdr. in D Coy.
Curram, Leslie Reginald	8.11.17	2/Lieut.	—	Italian Bronze Medal for Valour 26.8.18	—	Wounded (slightly, at duty) Wounded Rejoined	26.8.18 29.10.18 16.12.18	Platoon cmdr. in C Coy. Served with Battn. until cessation of hostilities.
Butlin, Max William	6.1.18	2/Lieut.	—	—	—	—	—	Platoon cmdr. in A Coy. Served with Battn. until cessation of hostilities.
Pike, John Robert	6.1.18	2/Lieut.	—	—	—	—	—	Platoon cmdr. in D Coy. Served with Battn. until cessation of hostilities.
Herbert, Albert Henry	6.1.18	2/Lieut.	—	—	—	—	—	Platoon cmdr. in B Coy. and afterwards with C Coy. Served with Battn. until cessation of hostilities.

APPENDIX V—continued

Name.	Date of Joining.	Rank on Joining.	Promotion.	Decorations.	Mentions in Dispatches.	Casualty.	Date of Casualty.	Remarks.
Beaver, Henry Allan (52nd L.I. attd.)	2.10.18	Lieut.	—	—	—	—	—	2nd-in-C. of D Coy. Commanded that company for several months after cessation of hostilities.
Allday, Edward Cyril James (52nd L.I. attd.)	2.10.18	Lieut.	—	—	—	—	—	2nd-in-C. of B Coy.
Cullinan, Daniel (R. Munster Fus. attd.)	7.10.18	2/Lieut.	—	—	—	—	—	Platoon cmdr. in A Coy.
Campbell, Harry Douglas Caulfield (52nd L.I. attd.)	19.11.18	Lieut.	—	—	—	—	—	Platoon cmdr. in C Coy.

MEDICAL OFFICERS AND CHAPLAINS ATTACHED TO BATTALION

Name.	Date of Joining.	Rank on Joining.	Promotion.	Decorations.	Mentions in Dispatches.	Casualty.	Date of Casualty.	Remarks.
Hughes, Leslie Edward (R.A.M.C. [T.])	Feb. 1915	Lieut.	Capt. 12.7.15	M.C. 1.1.18	1.1.17	Hospital	26.8.17	Medical Officer. Took part in Somme battles, advance from Peronne, and 3rd battle of Ypres.
Noke, Hubert (C.F.)	1.4.17	Capt.	—	M.C. 1.1.19	—	—	—	Chaplain. Took part in advance from Peronne, 3rd battle of Ypres, and several actions on Asiago plateau. With Battn. until cessation of hostilities.
Thomas, Harold Seburt (R.A.M.C.)	Sept. 1917	T/Lieut.	T/Capt. 14.3.18	—	1.1.19	—	—	Medical Officer. Took part in 3rd battle of Ypres and actions on Asiago plateau. With Battn. until cessation of hostilities.

APPENDIX VI

NOMINAL ROLL OF WARRANT OFFICERS, N.C.O.'S AND MEN WHO SERVED WITH THE BATTALION DURING THE PERIOD MARCH 1915—DECEMBER 1918

Abbey, H. E.
Abbott, A.
Abbott, G.
Abbott, S.
Abbott, W.
Abrahams, H.
Absolem, G. J. S.
Adams, A. E.
Adams, E.
Adams, F.
Adams, H.
Adams, H. R.
Adams, J.
Adamson, T.
Aitken, R. S.
Alcock, J.
Alcock, L. J.
Alderman, R. H.
Aldous, A.
Aldred, A.
Aldridge, G.
Alexander, A.
Allaway, C. W.
Allchurch, H.
Allen, A.
Allen, G. H.
Allen, H.
Allen, L. B.
Allen, R.
Allen, S.
Allport, S.
Allum, E. G.
Alworthy, A.
Anderson, A. M.
Anderson, J. A.
Andrews, W.
Annear, L. G.

Anstead, E.
Anstee, W. A.
Anstiss, F. W.
Appleby, J.
Arlick, H.
Arlick, R.
Armitage, C.
Armitage, H.
Armstrong, T.
Arnold, B.
Ashford, A.
Ashley, F. L.
Ashley, G. W.
Aston, D.
Aston, H. E.
Atkins, A.
Atkins, D.
Atkins, E.
Atkins, G.
Atkins, H.
Atkins, J.
Atkins, S. J.
Atkins, T. C.
Atkins, T. W.
Atkins, W. H.
Atkinson, J.
Attwood, T.
Auger, C.
Austin, A. G.
Austin, J.
Austin, T.
Avery, H.
Avery, T. W.
Axtell, A. E.
Axtell, A.
Ayres, R.

Bacon, T.
Badger, C.
Badrick, E.
Badrick, H.
Badrick, T. C.
Bailey, A.
Bailey, C.
Bailey, C. H.
Bailey, F.
Bailey, F.
Bailey, H. J.
Bailey, P. L
Bailey, V. G.
Baker, C. H.
Baker, F.
Baker, F.
Baker, G. C.
Baker, H. C.
Baker, J. T.
Baker, W. J.
Bakewell, R. T.
Balcombe, L.
Balding, A. J.
Balding, F.
Baldock, W. C.
Baldwin, A. E.
Baldwin, C.
Baldwin, J.
Baldwin, J. F.
Baldwin, J. W.
Baldwin, O.
Baldwin, R.
Baldwin, W. J.
Balkin, P.
Ball, A.
Ball, E. A.
Ball, G.

APPENDIX VI

Ball, G. J.
Ball, H.
Ball, H.
Ball, S.
Ball, W. H.
Ballard, C. W.
Bandy, F. J.
Banks, A.
Banks, C.
Barber, T.
Bardell, A.
Barlow, J.
Barmer, A. C.
Barnard, F.
Barnes, C.
Barnes, E.
Barnes, F.
Barnes, H.
Barnes, L.
Barnett, A.
Barnett, G.
Barnsley, F.
Barnwell, W. G.
Barrass, W. H.
Barratt, H.
Barrell, L. J.
Barrett, E. J.
Barrett, F.
Barrett, H. F.
Barrett, L. G.
Barrett, P.
Barrett, P.
Barrie, R.
Bartlett, P. J.
Bartlett, R.
Bartlett, S. W.
Barton, A.
Barton, T.
Baskerville, F. W.
Bass, F.
Batchelor, A.
Batchelor, C.
Batchelor, W.
Bateman, R. J.
Bateman, R. R.
Bates, A.
Bates, F.
Bath, T. H.
Batterson, W.
Baxter, A. E.
Baxter, H.
Baxter, P. E.
Beadle, G. W.
Beal, E. G.
Beales, H. W.
Beament, F.

Beasley, J.
Beck, R.
Beckett, A.
Beckett, F. E.
Beckett, G.
Beckett, L.
Beckley, F. P.
Bedford, H.
Bedwell, W.
Beechey, H.
Beedham, G. E.
Beer, J.
Beere, J.
Belcher, G.
Belgrove, F.
Bell, T.
Bennell, T. J.
Bennett, A. J.
Bennett, A. W.
Bennett, C.
Bennett, L.
Bennett, W. C.
Benney, J.
Benning, B.
Benning, W. J.
Bentley, H.
Bentley, W.
Bensusan, B.
Berg, I.
Bernstein, M.
Berrett, A. H.
Berridge, G.
Bibby, W. G.
Bierton, T.
Biggey, W.
Biggs, A. E.
Biggs, E. G.
Biggs, E. W.
Biggs, F. J.
Biggs, J. A.
Bignall, L.
Bignell, F.
Bignell, F.
Bignell, R.
Biles, R.
Binns, H.
Birch, E.
Birch, W.
Birchell, S. T.
Bird, C.
Bird, H. T.
Bird, J.
Bird, T. A.
Bishop, A.
Bishop, S. G.
Bishop, W. S.

Bissell, W.
Biswell, H.
Blackburn, J. M.
Blackwell, F. J.
Blackwell, W.
Blake, E.
Blake, H.
Blake, W. A.
Bland, A. R.
Blay, C. F. J.
Blick, C.
Bloomfield, W.
Bloomstein, M.
Boast, O.
Boast, W.
Boddy, G.
Bodsworth, P.
Bolland, G.
Bond, H. J.
Bond, R.
Bone, E.
Bone, F.
Bone, H.
Bonham, A. T.
Bonham, E.
Bonham, H.
Bonham, J. W.
Boon, A. E.
Boot, A. F.
Booth, C. H.
Booth, F.
Botley, C.
Botley, P.
Boughton, A. J.
Boughton, H.
Bowden, C.
Bowden, F.
Bowden, P. J.
Bowden, W.
Bowery, E. A.
Bowery, G.
Bowler, F. H.
Bowles, A. J. G.
Boyce, A. H.
Boyle, H. E.
Boyles, F.
Brack, J.
Brackley, A.
Bradbury, F.
Bradbury, F. J.
Bradbury, J.
Bradbury, J.
Bradley, W.
Braes, J.
Brain, H.
Brain, J.

ROLL OF WARRANT OFFICERS, ETC. 199

Brandon, H.
Brandon, J. C.
Bravington, F. H.
Bravington, V.
Bravington, W.
Brawn, A.
Brazier, J.
Brelly, F.
Brett, P. S.
Brewer, R. E.
Brewer, T.
Brice, W. G.
Bridges, E.
Bridges, J.
Bridges, N. C.
Bridgett, T. J.
Bright, H. G.
Brightman, E.
Brill, A.
Brinton, J. C.
Brion, C.
Brion, E. J.
Briscoe, H.
Bristow, A. G.
Bristow, A. T.
Bristow, L. W.
Bristow, V. F.
Bristow, W. E.
Bristowe, H. J.
Britton, S.
Brogden, C. J.
Brolly, J.
Brook, W. S. J.
Brooke, G. E.
Brooks, A.
Brooks, A. W.
Brooks, E. A.
Brooks, H. J.
Brooks, J.
Brooks, L.
Brooks, W. G.
Brown, A.
Brown, E.
Brown, E. H.
Brown, F.
Brown, G.
Brown, J.
Brown, J. B.
Brown, J. C.
Brown, J. W.
Brown, J. W.
Brown, T.
Brown, W.
Brownjohn, O. E.
Brownsell, J.
Bruce, A.

Bruce, A. E.
Bruce, W. H.
Bruton, G.
Bruton, W. C.
Bryant, A.
Bryant, G.
Bryant, G.
Buchanan, G.
Buckingham, A.
Buckland, E.
Buckland, F. C.
Buckland, W.
Bull, S.
Bull, W. H.
Bunby, A. E.
Bunce, C. W.
Bunce, G.
Bunyan, A.
Bunyan, W.
Burch, C.
Burden, J. R.
Burden, W. A.
Burgess, A. W.
Burgess, C.
Burgess, W.
Burnham, G.
Burnham, G.
Burnham, J.
Burnham, J.
Burnham, W. J.
Burns, H. H.
Burrell, C.
Burrows, F.
Burrows, J.
Burrows, T. G.
Burton, L. B.
Busby, C. C.
Bushnell, C. M.
Bushrod, P. J. T.
Buss, P. A.
Butcher, H.
Butcher, J.
Butler, G. G.
Butler, J. A.
Butler, R.
Button, G.
Byron, F.

Cadwallader, W. T.
Caldwell, A. E. C.
Callaway, C. G.
Campbell, A.
Campbell, C. S.
Cannell, A.
Cannon, A. A.
Canvin, H. A.

Capel, C.
Capt, E. E. H.
Careless, J. R.
Carey, A. A.
Carey, W.
Carney, W.
Carpenter, J.
Carpenter, R.
Carr, D.
Carr, R.
Carrick, W.
Carroll, S.
Carter, H.
Carter, W.
Cartwright, F.
Cartwright, W. G.
Cashmore, C. V.
Cassenbaum, J.
Casson, P. W.
Castle, H. P.
Castle, T.
Catchpole, H.
Cattell, W.
Cave, F. W.
Cave, W. E.
Chamberlain, J. E.
Chamberlain, W.
Chambers, A.
Chandler, E. S.
Chapman, A.
Chapman, A.
Chapman, C.
Chapman, F.
Chapman, H. G.
Chapman, W. H.
Chaplin, F. E.
Chappell, A. G.
Chappell, T.
Chappell, W. E.
Chenhalls, J.
Cherrett, W. A.
Cherry, A.
Cherry, J.
Cheshire, A. B.
Cheshire, J. H.
Childs, J.
Chilton, W. E.
Chimes, G. D.
Chinn, E. T.
Chirgwin, A.
Chown, C. A.
Christie, W.
Chubb, V. H.
Church, H.
Clarfelt, S.
Claridge, R.

APPENDIX VI

Clark, C.
Clark, S.
Clark, W.
Clark, W. W.
Clarke, C.
Clarke, G.
Clarke, J.
Clarke, J.
Clarke, J. C.
Clarke, S.
Clarke, T. F.
Clarke, W.
Clarke, W. C.
Clarke, W. H.
Claydon, W. J.
Cleaver, A. H.
Cleaver, L.
Clee, G. H.
Clegg, J. W.
Clements, A.
Clements, G. E.
Clewlow, A. E.
Clibbon, A.
Cliff, J.
Close, R.
Clutton, S.
Coates, J.
Coates, W. A.
Cock, W.
Cockburn, W. L.
Cockle, E.
Coggins, T.
Cohen, B.
Cohen, G.
Cohen, I.
Cohen, J.
Cohen, M.
Cohen, M.
Cohen, S.
Colbrook, R.
Cole, J. G. J.
Cole, P. C.
Colebourne, A. J.
Coleman, A.
Coleman, C.
Coleman, F. J.
Coleman, H.
Coleman, H.
Coleman, W.
Coles, A.
Coles, A. R.
Coles, E.
Coles, S.
Collard, G.
Collett, C. F.
Collett, H. G.

Collier, A. G.
Collings, R.
Collins, A.
Collins, B.
Collins, F. C.
Collins, F. S.
Collins, H. E.
Collins, H. W.
Collins, J.
Collins, J. S.
Collinson, E. A.
Colville, H.
Congdon, S.
Conn, L.
Connor, J. H.
Cook, A.
Cook, A
Cook, A.
Cook, C.
Cook, G.
Cook, H.
Cook, J.
Cook, J. H.
Cook, R. W.
Cook, R. W.
Cook, S.
Cook, W. A.
Cook, W. J.
Cookson, H. W.
Cooling, T.
Cooper, E. W.
Cooper, H. J.
Cooper, W. C.
Cooper, W. F.
Copcutt, G. D.
Coppock, A. T.
Corbin, V. M.
Corder, E. H.
Cordery, J.
Corke, S. C. W.
Cornish, O. B.
Cosby, T.
Cottrill, H.
Courtney, W.
Cousins, S.
Cousins, W.
Coward, E. W.
Cox, C. E.
Cox, F. G.
Cox, H. J.
Cox, H. S.
Cox, J. T.
Cox, R. T.
Cox, T.
Cox, W.
Cox, W. A.

Cox, W. H.
Coxhill, O. R.
Coy, L.
Crack, W.
Craker, R.
Crane, J.
Crawder, E.
Crawley, P.
Crawthorne, J. W.
Crego, M.
Cressey, P. T.
Cresswell, P. G.
Crew, W.
Cripps, C. P.
Cripps, E. G.
Cripps, F. A.
Cripps, F. T.
Cripps, R. C.
Crockett, G.
Croft, A.
Croker, R.
Cromey, J. F.
Crook, E. H.
Crook, R.
Cross, A. J.
Cross, F.
Cross, F.
Cross, F.
Cross, H. E.
Cross, W. C.
Cross, W. H.
Crouch, A.
Crouch, B. E.
Crouch, R. C.
Crowden, A.
Crowther, C. A.
Cruden, D. C. L.
Cruikshank, P. J.
Culley, A. E.
Culpeck, L. W.

Dafter, T. E.
Daggers, R.
Dagwall, F. L.
Daley, J.
Dancer, A.
Dancer, F. G.
Dancer, G.
Dancer, T.
Darbyshire, J. T.
Darch, W.
Darling, H. S.
Darling, W. J.
Dart, C.
Darville, H. G.
Daultry, E.

ROLL OF WARRANT OFFICERS, ETC. 201

Daultry, G.
Davess, G.
Davis, A. W.
Davenport, G. W.
Davey, C.
Davey, F.
Davey, P.
Davidson, G.
Davidson, J.
Davies, G.
Davies, G. A.
Davies, J.
Davies, J. E.
Davies, J. T.
Davies, S.
Davis, C. W.
Davis, G.
Davis, L. C.
Davis, R. W.
Davis, S.
Davis, V. J.
Daw, W. H.
Dawes, T.
Day, A.
Day, A. J.
Day, W. J.
Dealey, J.
Dean, A.
Dean, H. H.
Dean, S. F.
Dean, W.
Dearing, J.
Dearing, W.
Dearn, A.
Dearness, A.
Delaney, T.
Dell, M.
Dell, W. H.
Denenberg, P.
Dennis, A. J.
Dennis, W. C.
Denton, J. H.
Deswart, H.
Deverall, F.
Devening, S.
Devonshire, J.
Dibben, P. R.
Dickens, C.
Dickens, F.
Dickens, T. E.
Dickens, W.
Dickens, W.
Dickenson, W.
Dickinson, F.
Dickinson, W.
Dillow, T. J.

Dimmock, C.
Dimmock, S.
Diskett, A. E.
Dixon, A. W.
Dixon, C.
Dixon, C.
Dixon, D. M.
Dixon, G. H.
Dixon, J. G.
Dixon, W. T.
Dobbins, J.
Doble, H.
Dodds, R. W.
Dodds, W.
Dodson, C. J.
Dodwell, G.
Doel, A.
Dombey, W.
Doming, W. L.
Dormer, F.
Dormer, G.
Dorrell, H.
Dorsett, J. W.
Dowers, E. J.
Dowling, H.
Downing, C. T.
Dovey, W.
Drayton, W.
Dredge, J.
Dredge, S. E.
Drewitt, G.
Drewitt, H.
Drewitt, W. C.
Drury, G. F.
Dubbin, E.
Duckett, G. H.
Dudley, F. G.
Dudley, S.
Duffield, A. J.
Dumbleton, W.
Dunk, F.
Dunkley, E. W.
Dunkley, J. G.
Dunkley, L.
Dunstan, W. J.
Dunster, J.
Durdin, E. R. C.
Dutton, H. J.
Dwight, J.
Dwight, P.
Dyer, A.
Dyer, G. M.
Dyer, V. J.
Dyke, W. E.
Dymond, H. P.

Eames, C. H.
Earis, E. W.
Earl, F. K.
Earle, G.
Easeman, W.
East, F.
East, F. J.
Easton, J. H.
Eccles, J. B.
Eccleston, C. J.
Edgerley, E. G.
Edmans, W. J.
Edwards, A. W.
Edwards, H.
Edwards, J.
Edwards, J.
Edwards, P.
Eglington, F. S.
Elliott, A.
Elliott, C.
Elliott, D. C.
Elliott, J. H.
Elliott, R.
Ellis, A.
Ellis, W.
Ellis, W. G.
Evans, A. E.
Evans, C. H. H.
Evans, E.
Evans, H.
Evans, J.
Evans, M. H.
Evans, W. J.
Evans, W. S. C.
Everitt, E. A.
Eves, G.
Ewers, A.
Ewers, G.

Falconer, J. G.
Fall, W.
Fane, S.
Faraker, L. H.
Fargher, T. J.
Farmer, W. J.
Farrar, J.
Fasey, A.
Faulkner, G.
Faulkner, J.
Fell, C.
Fenn, S.
Ferguson, A. A.
Ferris, J.
Field, G.
Field, R.
Fielding, D. P.

APPENDIX VI

Fielding, F.
Fielding, F. H.
Figg, J.
Fimister, R.
Final, G.
Finch, L. G.
Finch, T.
Fincher, E. H.
Fincher, F. J. M.
Fineberg, H.
Fisher, E. J.
Fisher, G. W.
Fisher, J. T.
Fisher, T.
Fisher, W.
Fisher, W. B.
Fishwick, F.
Fitton, R.
Fitzer, A. H.
Fitzpatrick, F.
Flannigan, J.
Fleet, E.
Fletcher, A.
Fletcher, J.
Fletcher, J. G.
Fletcher, W. J.
Flint, A.
Flitney, F.
Flitney, S.
Foolkes, T. G.
Ford, B.
Ford, F. W.
Fordanski, J.
Foreman, F.
Forsdick, H.
Foulkes, C. T.
Fountain, A. G.
Fountain, J.
Fountaine, R.
Fowler, A. E.
Fowler, A. J.
Fowler, C.
Fowler, R. J.
Fowler, V. S. R.
Fowles, C.
Fox, W. H. J.
Francis, T.
Franklin, A.
Franklin, F. J.
Franklin, J.
Franklin, J. W.
Franklin, P.
Franks, F.
Freeman, A.
Freeman, A. C.
Freeman, M.

Freestone, A. W.
French, C. A.
French, G.
Fretwell, A.
Frith, W. H. J.
Frost, C.
Fry, W.
Fryer, C.
Fryer, F. R.
Fulcher, G. C.
Furlong, W.

Gale, F. R.
Game, F.
Gardener, W. C.
Gardner, A.
Gardner, F.
Gardner, F.
Gardner, F. T.
Gardner, W. T.
Garner, F.
Garratt, F. R.
Garratt, R. W.
Garrett, A. L.
Garrett, H.
Garrotty, V. B.
Gates, H.
Gay, W. G.
Gay, W. G.
Gaylor, C.
Geeson, P.
Gelder, J.
Gentles, J. R.
German, R.
Gerrish, J. G.
Gething, J. T.
Gibbard, A.
Gibbard, T.
Gibbard, W.
Gibbins, T.
Gibbons, M. P.
Gibbs, F.
Gibbs, G.
Gibbs, R.
Gibbs, W. E.
Gibson, W.
Gilbert, F. W.
Gilbert, G.
Gilbert, W.
Gill, P.
Gill, T. J.
Gill, W. J.
Gillions, C.
Gillott, W.
Gitsham, F. J. L.
Ghillyer, H.

Glaister, J.
Glanville, H.
Glass, W.
Glassman, M.
Glazier, A.
Glenister, W.
Glover, H. T. G.
Godber, A.
Goddard, S.
Godfrey, F.
Godfrey, F.
Godfrey, J.
Godfrey, W. T.
Goldberg, A.
Golding, T.
Goldsmith, L.
Goldstein, R.
Goldswain, J.
Goldwater, P. H.
Gomm, A.
Gomm, J. E.
Gomm, T.
Good, R.
Goodall, A. J.
Goodchild, C. J.
Goodey, F.
Goodfellow, C.
Gooding, J. A.
Goodman, E. W.
Goodman, H. F.
Goodman, L.
Goodman, S.
Goodridge, E. J. W.
Goodway, P. W.
Gordon, D. B.
Goss, T. A.
Gostilow, G.
Gostick, T. V.
Gough, F.
Gould, A. H.
Gould, C. T.
Goundry, J. G.
Govey, J.
Gower, G.
Goymer, J.
Grace, H.
Gracie, G. A.
Graham, W. W.
Grant, G.
Grant, G.
Grantham, W.
Gray, A.
Gray, E.
Gray, F.
Gray, J. G.

ROLL OF WARRANT OFFICERS, ETC. 203

Gray, W.
Gray, W. J.
Graydon, E.
Grayson, H.
Greaterex, J.
Green, A.
Green, A.
Green, A.
Green, A. J.
Green, A. S.
Green, C. E.
Green, C. H.
Green, E.
Green, F.
Green, F. H.
Green, G.
Green, J.
Green, P.
Green, T. W.
Greenhalgh, J.
Greenhalgh, J. B.
Greenless, J.
Greenough, L. V.
Greenwood, A.
Gregory, A.
Gregory, H. E.
Gregory, W.
Gresswell, C.
Grewar, W. C.
Grice, F.
Griffen, A E.
Griffen, T.
Griffen, T. J.
Griffin, A.
Griffith, J. F. J.
Griffiths, H. W.
Griffiths, W.
Grimsdale, W.
Grimsdell, G. W.
Grimshire, J. H.
Grisbrook, V.
Grist, C.
Griver, M.
Grose, T.
Gross, W.
Grove, W. A.
Groves, T.
Groves, W. S.
Grunshaw, A.
Guess, A.
Guess, C.
Guise, T. H.
Guise, W. F.
Gummer, S.
Gunn, J.
Gunn, P.

Gunnell, E. J.
Guntrip, F. G.
Guntrip, H.
Guntrip, J. J.
Guntrip, W.
Gurney, A.
Gurney, G.
Gurney, P.
Gutteridge, A.

Haffenden, J. H.
Haines, C.
Haines, F.
Hagger, A. L.
Hale, A.
Hale, C.
Hale, F.
Halford, F. W.
Hall, A. H.
Hall, E.
Hall, F.
Hall, J.
Hall, L. P.
Hall, P. P.
Hall, R. R.
Hall, R. W.
Hall, T.
Hall, W.
Hall, W. J.
Halladay, D.
Hallett, A.
Halsey, F.
Hamilton, W. H.
Hamlet, J. R.
Hampshire, A. S.
Hance, G.
Hancock, G.
Hancock, W. E.
Hancocks, W.
Hancox, O. P.
Hann, A. J.
Hardcastle, J.
Harding, A.
Harding, H.
Harding, J.
Hardy, P. T.
Harman, H. E.
Harman, J.
Harman, R.
Harper, H.
Harper, S.
Harrington, J.
Harris, A.
Harris, A. S.
Harris, C. J.
Harris, E. J.

Harris, J.
Harris, J. E.
Harris, R.
Harris, T. W.
Harris, W. E.
Harrison, A.
Harrison, H.
Harrison, P.
Harrison, P. E.
Hart, A. E.
Hart, A. J.
Hart, E. S.
Hart, J. G.
Hartley, H.
Hartley, W.
Harvey, E.
Harvey, F.
Harvey, G. W.
Harvey, P. E.
Harvey, W. B.
Haslem, C. S.
Hastings, C. W.
Hastings, G. G.
Hastings, S. J.
Hatch, H. G.
Hathaway, E. E.
Hatley, S.
Hatt, F. W.
Hatt, J. M.
Hatt, S.
Hatton, T.
Hatwell, J.
Hawes, J.
Hawkes, F.
Hawkins, C. R.
Hawkins, E.
Hawthorn, A. W.
Hayman, A. R.
Hayman, J. W.
Haynes, J. G.
Haynes, S.
Haynes, W.
Haysom, T.
Hayward, A. E.
Hayward, G. F.
Hazard, H.
Hazell, G.
Hazell, H. A.
Head, M. M.
Hearn, P. R.
Hearn, W.
Hearn, W.
Heath, A. C.
Heath, F. W.
Heath, L.
Heather, G.

APPENDIX VI

Heathcock, C.
Heaton, C. J.
Hearen, G.
Hedges, A. E.
Hedges, F.
Held, A.
Hellenburgh, A.
Henderson, W.
Henshaw, S.
Henson, H. G.
Herbert, A.
Herbert, F.
Herbert, W. C.
Hermon, G.
Hermon, R. E.
Hern, H.
Herring, T.
Hepworth, C.
Heseltine, R.
Hester, H. H.
Hester, W.
Hewitt, S.
Hewlett, F. H.
Hext, R. B.
Heyes, T.
Hickenbottom, W. C.
Hicks, A. E.
Hicks, A. W.
Hicks, C. J.
Hicks, F. A.
Hicks, H.
Hicks, J.
Hicks, T.
Hicks, W.
Higgins, G. H.
Higgs, F. W.
Hill, A. J.
Hill, A. T.
Hill, C.
Hill, F.
Hill, F. C.
Hill, J. F.
Hill, P. A.
Hill, R. F.
Hill, R. J.
Hill, W. W.
Hilliar, A.
Hills, H. H.
Hinchliffe, A.
Hinde, T. H.
Hines, W.
Hipgrave, A.
Hipson, N.
Bird, W.
Hitchman, H.
Hoare, A. O.

Hoare, J. B.
Hobbs, F. H.
Hobbs, W. J.
Hobden, C. G.
Hockaday, E.
Hoddor, A. W.
Hodgkiss, E.
Hodgson, C. W.
Hodgson, J. W.
Hodgson, J. W.
Hoey, C. R.
Hogg, J.
Hoing, W. R.
Holder, F. J.
Holdham, F. A.
Holdway, F. H.
Holland, W.
Hollingworth, A. S.
Hollins, W.
Hollis, A. W.
Hollis, F.
Hollis, W. C.
Hollomon, W. J.
Holloway, A.
Holloway, A. F.
Holloway, A. G
Hollyoake, A. G.
Holman, C. B. O.
Holmes, C.
Holt, A.
Holt, D.
Holt, S. G.
Holt, T.
Holt, W. A.
Honour, A. J.
Honour, P.
Honour, W. H.
Hooker, F. C.
Hooker, W. C.
Hookway, E. A.
Hooper, J.
Hooten, J. H.
Hopcroft, T.
Hopkins, S.
Hopley, J.
Hopley, W. G.
Hopper, F. W. W.
Horn, P. J.
Horne, A.
Horne, E.
Horne, F. C. T.
Horsler, W. A.
Horspool, W. E.
Horton, W.
Horwood, G.
Horwood, H.

Hough, F. W.
Hounsell, A.
How, W. S.
Howard, H.
Howard, H. E.
Howard, J.
Howard, T.
Howard, W.
Howe, C. A.
Howe, F.
Howe, J. L.
Howe, S.
Howell, R. L.
Howell, T. E.
Howes, J.
Hubbard, A.
Hucklebridge, H.
Hudson, A.
Hudson, F. A.
Hudson, J.
Hudson, R.
Huet, F. C.
Huggins, A. L.
Huggins, H.
Hughes, E.
Humphrey, C.
Humphrey, W. J.
Humphries, A. T.
Hunt, A.
Hunt, C. A.
Hunt, G. O.
Hunt, P.
Hunter, G.
Hunter, R.
Hurst, H. J.
Hussey, E.
Hussey, G.
Hutchings, H.
Hutt, A. C.
Hutt, W.
Hutter, G. R.
Hyde, E. V.
Hyde, F. H.
Hyde, F. W.

Illingworth, R.
Imber, H.
Impey, J.
Ing, A.
Ing, A. E. H.
Ing, F.
Ing, T.
Ingram, A. L.
Ings, W. J.
Ireland, W. C.
Irving, H.

ROLL OF WARRANT OFFICERS, ETC. 205

Israel, L.
Ivamy, F. C.
Ives, F.
Ives, F. R.
Ives, H.
Ives, W.
Ives, W.

Jackman, G.
Jackman, H.
Jackman, W.
Jackman, W.
Jackson, F.
Jackson, H.
Jackson, H. E.
Jacobs, A. A.
Jacobs, H.
Jacobs, M. V.
Jakeman, S.
Jakeman, W.
Jakes, J. H.
Jakes, T. W.
James, A.
James, A.
James, A. J.
James, E.
James, F. A.
James, F. T.
James, F. W
James, G.
James, J. J.
Jamieson, M.
Janes, A.
Janes, P.
Jarvis, H.
Jasper, A. C.
Jasper, E.
Javes, F.
Jaycock, F.
Jayne, H. F.
Jefferson, F.
Jeffries, E. H.
Jenner, J.
Jennett, A.
Jennings, B. T.
Jennings, P.
Jennison, H.
Jenns, L. J.
Jervis, J.
Jesty, L.
Jillion, J. F.
Jobling, J. D.
Johnson, A.
Johnson, C.
Johnson, E.
Johnson, E.

Johnson, F.
Johnson, F. J.
Johnson, S. J.
Johnson, W.
Johnson, W.
Johnson, W. F.
Johnston, A. E.
Johnston, R. W.
Joiner, A.
Jolley, R. F.
Jolliffe, B.
Jones, A. S.
Jones, E.
Jones, F. D.
Jones, F. E.
Jones, G. W.
Jones, H.
Jones, H.
Jones, H. J.
Jones, H. R.
Jones, J.
Jones, J. W.
Jones, R. E.
Jones, R. T.
Jones, R. W.
Jones, S. C.
Jones, W.
Jones, W.
Jones, W.
Jordan, A.
Joseph, J.

Kape, P. S.
Karmuck, A.
Kay, H.
Kearley, S.
Kearsey, E. S.
Keating, F.
Keating, M. C.
Keating, M.
Keen, E. C.
Keen, F.
Keen, H. R.
Keen, J.
Keen, S.
Keen, S.
Keen, T.
Keen, W.
Keep, W. G.
Kemp, A. S.
Kemp, W.
Kempson, W. R.
Kempston, A. E.
Kempston, W. E.
Kennedy, A.
Kent, G.

Kent, W. H.
Kerr, J.
Kerr, S.
Kettle, R.
Keys, H.
Kidnee, R.
Kilby, G.
Kilsby, H.
Kightley, R. G.
King, A.
King, A. J.
King, A. W.
King, C. E.
King, H. G.
King, R. C.
King, R. J.
King, W.
King, W. H.
Kingdom, E. J.
Kingfish, H.
Kingham, A.
Kingham, A.
Kingsland, J.
Kirby, L. G.
Kislingbury, W.
Knibb, A. T.
Knibb, W. G.
Knight, C. H.
Knight, E.
Knight, E. C.
Knight, G.
Knight, R. J.
Knock, E.
Kramer, I.
Krill, E.

Laband, H. J.
Lacey, C. E.
Lacey, F.
Lacey, F.
Lacey, F. R.
Lacey, W.
Lacey, W. A.
Lack, L. R.
Laird, W.
Lake, T. C.
Lambdin, P. H.
Lambert, H.
Lambert, W.
Lamberth, H.
Lambird, G.
Lambourne, A.
Lambourne, A.
Lambourne, T.
Lambourne, W.
Lane, W. S.

APPENDIX VI

Lang, W.
Langley, C. H.
Langley, G. T.
Langley, N.
Langston, P.
Large, W. J.
Latham, F. W.
Law, R. C.
Lawes, J.
Lawrence, A. D.
Lawrence, A. J.
Lawrence, E.
Lawrence, G.
Lawrence, W.
Lawrence, W.
Lawrence, W. G.
Lawrence, W. S.
Lawson, C.
Lawson, P.
Lawton, T.
Leach, H.
Leach, R.
Leader, J.
Lee, F. L.
Lee, G. A.
Lee, H.
Lee, P.
Lee, W. W.
Leeson, A.
Legge, J. E.
Leigh, T.
Leonard, J. H.
Lerew, J.
Letts, F. A.
Lewendon, J.
Lewis, A. C.
Lewis, E.
Lewis, F.
Lewis, H.
Leworthy, A.
Levart, E.
Levick, G.
Levy, I.
Liddiard, H.
Light, A.
Lindon, G. C.
Line, A.
Line, B.
Lineham, W. H.
Lines, F. G.
Lines, H.
Lines, J.
Linford, G.
Littlehales, J. W
Littlewood, A.
Lock, S. G.

Locke, W. J.
Lodder, T.
Lolley, A. V.
Long, E.
Long, E. M.
Long, G. E.
Long, W.
Longmore, J. W.
Looker, H. G.
Loosemore, R. F.
Loosley, F. J.
Lord, E.
Lord, F. W.
Lord, J.
Lord, W. J.
Loud, E. T.
Loveday, C.
Lovegrove, F.
Lovegrove, H.
Lovegrove, T.
Lovell, S.
Lovell, W. C.
Lovelock, F.
Lovesay, J.
Lowe, A.
Lowe, T.
Lucas, G. F.
Luck, G.
Lukies, W. J.
Lunnon, A.
Lunnon, A. W.
Lunnon, C.
Lunnon, W. A.
Lynes, H.
Lyon, J.

Macadam, A. J.
Mace, C. J.
Macfarlane, G.
Mackenna, M.
Major, A.
Major, W. T.
Malloy, J.
Malpass, T.
Manders, A.
Manning, C. J.
Manning, J. R.
Manton, T.
Marcham, R.
Marcham, R.
Marchant, L.
Markham, P.
Markofsky, E.
Marks, A. J.
Marks, A. W.
Marriott, E. J.

Marriott, J. W.
Marsh, C. A.
Marsh, W. L.
Marshall, E. C.
Marshall, F. A.
Marshall, F. W.
Marshall, S. C.
Marshall, W.
Martin, D. C.
Martin, G.
Martin, H.
Martin, J. W.
Martin, S.
Martin, T. H.
Mason, C.
Mason, P. W.
Massey, J. C.
Masters, G. H.
Matthews, S. A.
Matthews, V. G.
Matthews, W. J.
Mattin, P. W. G.
Maxfield, W. P.
May, A. S.
May, C. W.
Mayhew, S. F.
McBlain, J. J.
McBright, S.
McCoy, A. J.
McDermott, E. J.
McDermott, J.
McDermott, W. G.
McGregor, C.
McGregor, W.
McKay, W.
McLachlan, H.
McLaren, A. W.
McLaren, C. T.
McLeod, D.
McPhee, J.
McPherson, J.
Meachem, A. J.
Mead, R.
Mead, R.
Meads, T. H.
Mealing, M.
Meeks, L.
Meeks, W. J.
Meiklejohn, J. K.
Meldrum, R.
Mellor, R.
Mellor, W.
Merrick, H. F.
Merridan, A.
Merriman, H.
Merriman, R. C.

ROLL OF WARRANT OFFICERS, ETC. 207

Merry, J.
Messenger, H.
Messinger, J.
Metcalfe, H.
Middlebrook, A.
Middleton, W.
Middleton, W. H.
Miles, A. C.
Miles, S.
Miles, S. G.
Miles, W. R.
Millard, J.
Miller, G.
Miller, T. H.
Miller, W. J.
Mills, A. V.
Millward, B.
Millward, H.
Minchin, A.
Mines, A.
Mines, G. J.
Ming, G.
Mingay, R. W.
Mitcham, S.
Mitchell, A. W.
Mitchell, G. B.
Mitchell, J.
Mitchell, J. C.
Mobley, G.
Moffatt, W.
Mondon, P. C.
Monger, A.
Monk, J. H. W.
Monshall, G.
Montague, H.
Montague, T.
Montgomery, C. H.
Moon, E. A.
Moore, F.
Moore, W. G.
Morbey, S.
Moreland, H. J.
Morgan, A. H.
Morgan, C.
Morgan, C. R.
Morgan, F.
Morgan, J.
Morgan, W. J.
Morley, S.
Morrell, V.
Morris, A.
Morris, A. A. G.
Morris, H. E.
Morris, H. G.
Morris, J.
Morris, J.

Morris, J.
Morris, W. G.
Morrish, A. J.
Morrison, K.
Morrison, W.
Morse, F. C.
Morse, J.
Mortemore, E.
Mortimer, H.
Mortimer, J.
Moseley, E. J.
Moseley, F. C.
Mould, C. A.
Moyle, H.
Mudge, G. E.
Mullins, F. H.
Munday, A.
Munday, A. G.
Munday, A. J.
Munday, G.
Munday, H. L.
Murphy, J.
Murphy, J. G.
Murphy, P.
Murray, C.
Murrell, F.
Muxovitch, L. H.
Myers, T.
Mynott, J. E.

Nancarrow, R.
Napier, E. W.
Napper, W. E.
Nash, C.
Nash, E.
Nash, F.
Nash, F. G.
Nash, G.
Nash, G.
Nash, J.
Nathan, H. J.
Nathan, J.
Naylor, G.
Neale, F.
Neale, R.
Neale, S.
Neill, J.
Neilly, E.
Nepovent, M.
Neville, F. T.
New, R.
New, R.
Newell, A. W.
Newell, E.
Newell, J. O.
Newell, R.

Newman, A.
Newman, A. W.
Newman, P.
Newman, W.
Newnes, H.
Newns, F.
Newns, H.
Newton, F.
Newton, J. H.
Newton, S. W.
Newton, W.
Niblett, C.
Niblett, T. W.
Nicholas, S.
Nicholls, P.
Nichols, F.
Nicholson, D.
Nicholson, F. J.
Nicholson, S. S.
Niesigh, S. G.
Nightingale, C.
Nightingale, T.
Nixey, T. W.
Nobes, W. A.
Nolan, M.
Norcott, G. H.
Norris, E. J.
Norris, L. B.
North, C.
North, E. C.
North, T.
Norton, D.
Norton, F.
Novels, D.
Nunn, H.
Nutt, D.
Nutton, C. C.

Odell, G. H.
Odell, P. J.
Oliver, F. H.
Oliver, S.
Olliffe, T.
Orbell, F. J.
Orchard, E.
Orchard, R.
Ormes, H.
Osborne, A.
Osborne, L. C.
Osborne, R. H.
O'Shea, L. R.
Ounsworth, W. H.
Overshott, R.
Overton, A.
Owen, C. F.
Owen, C. R.

APPENDIX VI

Owen, E.
Owen, F.
Owen, W.
Owens, F.
Oxford, F. J.
Oxlade, A. J.
Oxlade, F.
Oxlade, L.
Oxlade, W. H.
Oxley, F.

Pace, E. J.
Packer, D. E.
Packford, R. B.
Packman, W. H.
Paige F.
Pain, G.
Page, A. E.
Page, C.
Page, F. D.
Page, G. W.
Page, N.
Page, S.
Page, S.
Pallett, C. A.
Pallett, G.
Pallett, R. E.
Palmer, F. J.
Palmer, W.
Papworth, B.
Pargeter, F.
Parker, B.
Parker, B. H.
Parker, H.
Parker, S.
Parker, W. J.
Parkin, J. R.
Parr, A.
Parrott, H. G.
Parrott, J.
Parrott, S. H.
Parsler, R. J. S.
Parslow, G.
Parsons, A.
Parsons, D.
Parsons, N. A.
Parsons, S. C.
Pass, F. W.
Patrick, W.
Paul, G.
Pauline, G. R. N.
Pawley, J.
Paxton, B.
Payne, A.
Payne, A.
Payne, A. J.

Payne, E.
Payne, E.
Payne, F.
Payne, F. H.
Payne, F. J.
Payne, G. E.
Payne, H.
Payne, R. H.
Payne, T.
Payne, W.
Pearce, A. E.
Pearce, D.
Pearce, H.
Pearce, S. G.
Pearce, W.
Pearce, W. G.
Pearlman, S.
Pearson, E. A.
Pearson, F. C.
Peart, A.
Peddle, A.
Pelham, J.
Pendery, W. C.
Penna, W. H.
Pennington, E.
Pennington, W.
Pentycross, D. B.
Peppercorn, H. J.
Perez, E.
Perkins, E. S.
Perkins, J.
Perkins, S.
Perry, C.
Perry, G.
Peters, G. W.
Philbey, F.
Phillips, A. G.
Phillips, E.
Phillips, F.
Phillips, F.
Phillips, H.
Phillips, H.
Phillips, J. H.
Phillips, R.
Phillips, W.
Phillips, W.
Phipps, T.
Pickering, A.
Pickering, G.
Pickles, H.
Pickston, S.
Piddington, F.
Pierce, E. H.
Piggott, J.
Pike, G.
Pinder, R.

Pinnell, E. W.
Pitcher, E.
Pitkin, E.
Pitt, E.
Pitt, G. R.
Pitt, J.
Pitwell, W.
Plank, H. T.
Plumridge, G.
Plumridge, P.
Plumridge, W. H.
Pocock, E.
Poliat, E.
Pollard, T. G.
Pollard, W.
Pond, A. J.
Pook, A. E.
Pook, W. A.
Pope, W. J.
Popkin, A. J.
Porterfield, V.
Portlock, A.
Portsmouth, W. J.
Posner, I. M.
Potter, A. J.
Pountney, T.
Powell, C.
Powell, E.
Powell, J.
Powell, L.
Powell, L. W.
Powell, S.
Powell, W. A.
Pratley, C.
Pratley, C.
Pratley, F. G.
Pratley, H.
Pratley, J.
Pratt, F. L.
Pratt, G.
Pratt, J. H. F.
Pratt, L. C. D.
Pratt, W. J.
Pratten, H. H.
Preece, H. A.
Prentice, W.
Pressley, E. G.
Preston, A. F. E.
Pretty, F.
Price, B.
Price, C.
Price, H.
Price, J.
Price, L. A.
Price, R. J.
Priest, C. G. T.

ROLL OF WARRANT OFFICERS, ETC. 209

Priest, W.
Primavesi, C. F.
Prior, L. E.
Pritchard, A. J.
Pritchard, E. J.
Pritchard, F.
Pritchard, T.
Pritchard, W. H.
Proctor, R.
Protherve, O. I.
Proudfoot, D.
Pryer, H.
Pryor, H.
Puckett, H.
Pulker, G.
Purcey, C. J.
Purchase, W. G.
Purden, A. J. E.
Pursey, W.
Puryer, H. H.
Pusey, B.
Putnam, A.
Putt, H.
Puttnam, C.
Pykett, G.

Quail, C. L.
Quarterman, W.
Quick, N. D.
Quirk, S. D.

Radcliffe, J.
Rainbow, G. W.
Raison, W. L.
Ralph, W. L.
Rance, F.
Randall, A.
Randall, A. E.
Randall, R.
Randall, T.
Randall, W.
Raphael, J.
Rashleigh, W.
Ratcliffe, R.
Rawlings, R.
Rawlins, A.
Ray, F.
Ray, W.
Rayner, J.
Read, A.
Read, A.
Read, A. H.
Read, E.
Read, F. H.
Read, J.
Read, R.

14

Read, W. S. J.
Redrup, J.
Reeve, P.
Reeves, R.
Reeves, W.
Reeves, W.
Reeves, W. E.
Regan, E.
Rendell, F. W.
Rendell, J.
Renn, W. T.
Revels, H.
Revels, H. J.
Reynolds, A.
Reynolds, A. S.
Reynolds, A. W.
Reynolds, E. G.
Reynolds, F.
Reynolds, G. H.
Reynolds, G. H.
Reynolds, J.
Reynolds, W. A.
Reynolds, W. F.
Rice, A. G.
Rice, B.
Rice, F.
Rice, H. W.
Rice, W. M.
Rich, G.
Richards, D. J.
Richards, E. J.
Richards, F.
Richards, T. K.
Richards, W.
Richards, W. M.
Richardson, G.
Richardson, G.
Richardson, N.
Riches, A.
Riches, A.
Riches, E. W.
Rickard, F.
Rickard, R. H.
Rickard, T.
Rickards, H.
Ricketts, F. C.
Riddell, E.
Ridgeley, W. M.
Ridgway, F. J.
Ridgway, R. J.
Ridgway, W. C.
Riley, B.
Ringsell, F. S.
Risdon, A.
Ritchie, J.
Rivers, G.

Rixon, J.
Rixon, J.
Roads, L.
Roads, W. J.
Robb, W.
Robbins, G. E.
Robbins, W.
Roberts, E.
Roberts, H.
Roberts, H.
Roberts, J.
Robertson, A.
Robertson, J.
Robertson, J.
Robertson, W.
Robertson, W. M. T.
Robins, J.
Robinson, A.
Robinson, A. E.
Robinson, H.
Robinson, J.
Robinson, T.
Robinson, W.
Robinson, W.
Robinson, W.
Robson, W. M.
Roche, T. B.
Rockell, F.
Rockell, H.
Rockey, G.
Rodd, R.
Rodwell, C. H.
Rodwell, W. J.
Roe, E.
Rogan, J.
Rogers, D. G.
Rogers, F.
Rogers, F. G.
Rogers, F. L.
Rogers, H. T.
Rogers, J.
Rogers, P
Rogers, R.
Rogers, S. G.
Rogers, W.
Rogers, W. A.
Rolfe, A.
Rolfe, A.
Rolfe, R.
Rolfe, W. M.
Rooke, F.
Rootham, G.
Rootham, W. H.
Rose, A.
Rose, C. H.
Rose, C. J.

APPENDIX VI

Rose, E. L.
Rose, F. G.
Rose, W.
Rosen, J.
Rosen, P.
Rosenbaum, S.
Rosewood, A.
Rosier, H.
Rosomond, P.
Ross, J.
Ross, J.
Rout, J.
Rowbottom, A.
Rowe, C.
Rowe, W.
Rowley, H.
Rowland, A.
Rowntree, R.
Rowse, F.
Royce, J.
Royce, M.
Ruddlesdin, L.
Rush, T.
Russell, J. S. H.
Russell, W. A.
Rutland, A. J.
Rutland, R. W.
Rutland, W.

Sabatini, A.
Sabatini, H.
Sadler, A. V.
Sails, W. N.
Salcombe, G.
Salmon, A. E.
Salter, C.
Sambrook, G.
Samways, W.
Sandall, F.
Sandell, T. E.
Sanders, F.
Sanderson, W.
Sansom, C.
Sansum, G. H.
Sargeant, J. H.
Sargood, H.
Sarney, W.
Sartin, E. F.
Saunders, A. J.
Saunders, E. C.
Saunders, H. J.
Saunders, H. W.
Saunders, J.
Saunders, S. R.
Saunders, W.
Saunders, W. G.

Savage, H. S.
Saving, E. W.
Sawyer, H.
Sayell, A. A.
Saywell, W. J.
Schew, E.
Schibl, R. A.
Schofield, H.
Schooling, A.
Schulman, B.
Scott, A.
Scott, J.
Scott, J.
Scott, W. A.
Scoulding, W. H.
Scragg, G.
Scragg, J. H.
Scragg, P.
Scrimshaw, A. W.
Scriven, E. W.
Scroggie, D.
Scutchings, R. C.
Seaman, C.
Seaman, E.
Seaman, H.
Sear, H.
Sear, J. A.
Sear, W. J.
Sears, H. G.
Sellers, J. A.
Selwyn, R.
Seward, G.
Seward, G
Sexton, W.
Seymour, A. E.
Seymour, P.
Shaer, I.
Shanks, H. J.
Sharman, H. J.
Sharp, J. W.
Sharp, T. J.
Sharpe, A.
Sharpe, C.
Shaw, F. T.
Shaw, H.
Shaw, J.
Shaw, R.
Shaw, W.
Shaw, W. J.
Shedd, F. H.
Shedd, H. W.
Shedd, P. J.
Shelley, G.
Shephard, W. J.
Shepherd, S.
Sheppard, T.

Sheppard, W.
Sherrell, E. P.
Sherwin, H.
Sherwin, R.
Sherwin, P.
Shillingford, J.
Shillingford, J.
Shorter, S. V.
Shouler, G.
Shouler, T.
Sibley, L.
Sillitoe, J.
Silverton, W. T.
Silvester, A. G.
Silvey, J.
Simmonds, C.
Simmonds, C. G.
Simmonds, E. J.
Simmonds, F.
Simmonds, H.
Simmonds, V.
Simmons, E. J.
Simmons, H.
Simms, B.
Simms, H. C.
Simons, I.
Simpson, A.
Simpson, J. L.
Sinclair, F.
Sinclair, N. S.
Sirett, A. G.
Skeet, P.
Skey, G.
Skuce, E. F.
Slade, A. H.
Slade, F.
Slade, W.
Slawson, A. E.
Sloper, W. G.
Small, A. T.
Small, E. W.
Small, H. G.
Small, J.
Small, J. A.
Small, W. J.
Smart, C. W.
Smart, F. H.
Smedley, R. W.
Smewin, C.
Smewin, G.
Smewin, P.
Smewin, R.
Smith, A.
Smith, A. H.
Smith, A. H.
Smith, A. J.

ROLL OF WARRANT OFFICERS, ETC. 211

Smith, A. J.
Smith, A. W.
Smith, A. W.
Smith, A. W.
Smith, C.
Smith, C. D.
Smith, D.
Smith, E.
Smith, E.
Smith, E. E.
Smith, E. F.
Smith, E. F.
Smith, F.
Smith, F.
Smith, F.
Smith, F.
Smith, F. E.
Smith, F. G.
Smith, F. J.
Smith, G.
Smith, G.
Smith, G. F.
Smith, G. H.
Smith, H.
Smith, H. S.
Smith, H. W.
Smith, J.
Smith, J.
Smith, J.
Smith, J.
Smith, J. E.
Smith, J. E. L.
Smith, J. T.
Smith, M. W.
Smith, R.
Smith, R. J.
Smith, S.
Smith, S.
Smith, S.
Smith, S. W.
Smith, T.
Smith, T.
Smith, W.
Smith, W.
Smith, W. A.
Smith, W. E.
Smith, W. F.
Smith, W. L.
Snell, W. H.
Snitch, H. B.
Snowden, G.
Souster, W. B.
Souster, W. J.
Southall, E.
Southam, A.
Southam, A. W.

Southam, S.
Snapes, H.
Snapes, W.
Spencer, P. W.
Spicer, O.
Spicer, T.
Spiller, T. B.
Spittles, E. G.
Spittles, S. F.
Spong, A. H.
Spooner, T.
Spriggs, F.
Spurge, W. H.
Spurr, F. J.
Stacey, H.
Stacey, H. C.
Stagg, J.
Stallwood, H.
Stallwood, J. W.
Stammers, G.
Standing, C. R. T.
Stanford, J.
Stanners, G.
Stanners, R.
Staughton, C. A.
Steele, H.
Steele, R. E. H.
Stephens, G. J.
Stephenson, C. A.
Steptoe, F. J.
Steptoe, J.
Steptoe, W. F.
Sterry, J.
Stevens, A. E.
Stevens, C. F.
Stevens, C. W.
Stevens, G. W.
Stevens, H.
Stevens, J. E.
Stevens, J. H.
Stevens, R. H.
Stevens, T.
Stevens, W.
Stidworthy, J. E.
Stiles, R. A.
Stilton, W.
Stimpson, H.
Stimson, P.
Stocker, J. P.
Stockley, J.
Stocks, A. H.
Stockwell, E. F.
Stokes, A.
Stokes, J. T.
Stollard, A. R.
Stone, B.

Stone, E. J.
Stone, G.
Stone, G. W.
Stone, G. W.
Stone, H.
Stone, H.
Stone, H. E.
Stone, N. J.
Stone, S.
Stone, W.
Stone, W.
Stonehill, F.
Stonehill, F. T.
Stonehill, S.
Stoneman, A.
Stopps, G. S.
Storey, W.
Storr, E. R.
Storr, H.
Stott, W.
Strange, F.
Strange, H. R.
Stranks, A.
Stratford, F.
Stratford, F. J.
Stratford, S.
Stratfull, F.
Stratton, H. S.
Stretton, W.
Strickson, W.
Stronnell, W. L.
Strudwick, P.
Stuckfield, G.
Sturgess, G.
Sturgess, W.
Styles, B.
Styles, W.
Swadling, C.
Swadling, P.
Swadling, T. E.
Swatton, C. H.
Swindle, V. V.
Sullivan, H.
Sulston, E.
Summerfield, C.
Summerfield, E.
Summerfield, E.
Summerfield, G. W.
Summers, F.
Summers, H.
Sumpter, F. H.
Sutton, A.
Sutton, H.
Symonds, E. J.
Symons, I.
Symons, J. R.

APPENDIX VI

Symons, S.
Syratt, A. T.

Taberner, T. M.
Tack, G.
Taffier, A.
Talmer, H.
Tandy, H. A.
Tanner, F.
Tanner, F. J.
Tapping, F.
Tapping, T. W.
Tarbox, E. J.
Tarr, R. G.
Tasker, A.
Tattam, W.
Tattman, C. F.
Tavroges, M.
Taylor, A. B.
Taylor, A. C. H.
Taylor, F.
Taylor, F. A.
Taylor, G. S.
Taylor, H. P.
Taylor, J.
Taylor, J. A.
Taylor, J. W.
Taylor, M.
Taylor, R. G.
Taylor, T.
Taylor, W.
Teagle, C. S.
Tearle, J.
Tewkesbury, C.
Thatcher, W.
Thomas, D.
Thomas, F.
Thomas, T.
Thomas, W.
Thompson, B.
Thompson, F. W.
Thompson, H. B.
Thompson, H. E.
Thompson, J. M.
Thompson, P. J.
Thompson, R. F.
Thompson, V.
Thomson, W.
Thorburn, W. S.
Thorne, J.
Thorne, J.
Thorne, J. H.
Thorne, O.
Thornewell, R.
Thrussall, A.
Thurgood, A.

Thurley, H. J.
Thurley, J. T.
Thurley, P. A.
Tibbetts, A.
Tibbetts, A. T.
Tibbles, F. H.
Tilbury, F.
Tilbury, J.
Tiller, G. J.
Timms, F. G.
Timson, F.
Tingle, H.
Tippett, R. J.
Tippett, W. H.
Tipping, F.
Tipping, F.
Tippler, T.
Titman, C. J. W.
Todd, B.
Todd, B.
Todd, E.
Todd, F. T.
Todd, G.
Todd, J.
Todd, S.
Todd, W.
Tofts, F.
Tolley, W.
Tombs, R. L.
Tompkins, F. J.
Toms, H. C.
Tonks, T. A.
Toogood, J.
Tooley, H. J.
Topper, H. B.
Topple, H.
Toseland, G. F.
Toseland, J.
Tout, G. G.
Towersey, F.
Townsend, G.
Townsend, H.
Townsend, L. E.
Townsend, W. T.
Toy, H. E. F.
Tozer, S.
Trace, J.
Tranter, E.
Tranter, J. M.
Treadwell, G. S.
Treadwell, J.
Trewin, E. J.
Trimby, C. W.
Trimmings, G.
Trodd, W.
Trodd, W. W.

Trott, F.
Trump, T.
Tubb, T. C.
Tuck, D. G.
Tucker, G.
Tucker, J.
Tucker, J. D.
Tucker, P. W.
Tunn, P.
Turner, J. C.
Turner, J. H.
Turner, L.
Turney, F.
Turney, J.
Turney, W.
Turnham, W. J.
Turvey, A.
Tustain, J. H.
Twigg, F. G.
Twitchen, G.
Tyas, G. K.
Tyrrell, F.
Tyrrell, W.

Uff, C.
Underdown, O.
Underwood, G.
Underwood, W.
Usher, H. T.
Utton, S. H.

Vacher, A.
Vallance, J.
Varcoe, W. H.
Varney, F. H.
Varney, J.
Vatcher, J.
Veale, E.
Vears, H. W.
Veitch, A. C.
Venables, V. A.
Viccars, F.
Vickers, R. H.
Vickers, W.
Vickery, J.
Vigurs, F. J.
Vigurs, W. J.
Vincent, A. A.
Vincent, H.
Vincent, H.
Vincent, J.
Vincent, T.
Viner, C. E.
Vizor, F. W.
Vlcek, V.

ROLL OF WARRANT OFFICERS, ETC. 213

Wadelin, A.
Wadlow, F. H.
Wagstaff, W. F.
Waine, A. E.
Waine, H.
Waine, H. T.
Waite, G.
Waite, G. W.
Waldock, C.
Waldock, S. G.
Walker, A.
Walker, A.
Walker, A. T.
Walker, A. T. E.
Walker, C.
Walker, G.
Walker, H.
Walker, J. O.
Walker, R.
Walker, W. C.
Wall, G.
Wall, J. R.
Wall, N.
Wallace, A.
Wallace, E.
Waller, G.
Wallington, G.
Wallis, A.
Wallis, A.
Walsh, H. T.
Walton, H. N.
Warburton, F. A.
Ward, A.
Ward, A. J.
Ward, T. J.
Wardell, E. J.
Warden, H.
Ware, W.
Waring, W. C.
Warlow, H. G.
Warne, E.
Warner, C.
Warner, G. S.
Warner, H.
Warner, J. D.
Warren, A.
Warren, G. R.
Warren, S.
Warren, W. E.
Washington, V.
Waters, S. L.
Waters, S. R.
Waters, T. H.
Watkins, G. J.
Watkins, H. T.
Watkins, J.

Watkins, R. S.
Watson, A. J.
Watson, C.
Watson, E.
Watson, E.
Watson, G.
Watson, J. W.
Watson, K. B.
Watson, P.
Watson, W.
Watts, F.
Watts, H.
Watts, P. A.
Way, H. J. R.
Weaver, A. G. E.
Weaver, W.
Webb, A.
Webb, F. W.
Webb, H.
Webb, J.
Webb, J. H.
Webb, W. A.
Webb, W. S.
Webster, J.
Weedon, C.
Weedon, J.
Weedon, W.
Weeks, W.
Weinbaum, H.
Weiner, L.
Weller, B. O.
Weller, C.
Weller, T.
Weller, W.
Wellington, R.
Wellman, A. J.
Wells, A.
Wells, A.
Wells, R.
Werrell, C.
Werring, W. S.
West, A.
West, B.
West, H.
West, J.
West, J.
West, P.
West, P. B.
West, R. A.
West, T.
West, W.
Westbrooke, G. R.
Westley, F.
Westley, F. R.
Weston, A.
Weston, A. D.

Weston, S.
Westrup, A.
Westrup, A. G.
Westrup, R.
Whale, G.
Whale, W. A.
Wharton, J.
Wheadon, L. C.
Wheeler, C. J.
Wheeler, D.
Wheeler, G.
Wheeler, G.
Wheeler, J.
Wheeler, O.
Wheeler, P. H.
Whelan, M. J.
Wherry, H.
Whichelo, T. H.
Whike, S.
Whipps, A.
Whitby, E.
White, A.
White, C.
White, C.
White, C.
White, C. E.
White, C. W.
White, E.
White, E.
White, E.
White, F.
White, F.
White, F.
White, G.
White, H.
White, J.
White, J. H.
White, O. W.
White, P. B.
White, R.
White, R.
White, S.
White, S. T.
White, T.
White, T. C.
Whitestone, D. G.
Whiteway, H.
Whitfield, E. E.
Whiting, O.
Whitley, W. P.
Whitman, H.
Whitney, F.
Whitney, F. S.
Whitsey, J.
Whittaker, F.
Whittingham, A.

Whittlesey, G.
Whitty, E.
Why, W. J.
Whyatt, E.
Wicketts, W. J.
Wicks, S.
Wigglesworth, J. W.
Wilde, W.
Wiles, F. J.
Wilkes, J. H.
Wilkins, O.
Wilkins, O.
Wilkinson, A. E.
Wilkinson, G.
Wilkinson, G.
Wilkinson, J.
Williams, F.
Williams, G.
Williams, G.
Williams, H.
Williams, H.
Williams, H.
Williams, T.
Williams, T.
Williams, W. H.
Williamson, J.
Williamson, W.
Willis, A.
Willis, A. H.
Willis, C.
Willis, H.
Willis, J.
Willmott, A.
Wills, F.
Wills, F. J.
Wills, W.
Willson, A. J.
Wilsdon, F. A.
Wilson, A.
Wilson, F.
Wilson, F. H.
Wilson, G.
Wilson, H.
Wilson, T. A.

Wilton, J.
Wilton, W. S.
Wimms, J. B.
Windsor, R.
Wingrove, S.
Winn, W. A.
Winsborrow, G.
Winsper, T. J.
Winsor, W. F.
Wisbey, G. W.
Wise, O.
Wise, W.
Witney, F.
Witty, T.
Wood, C.
Wood, F.
Wood, H.
Woodford, G.
Woodford, J. W.
Woodgates, H. J.
Woodham, F.
Woodham, S. T. H.
Woodley, E.
Woodley, J. H.
Woodley, W. B.
Woods, A. E.
Woods, A. F.
Woods, E.
Woods, H. F.
Woods, T.
Woodward, F. W.
Woodward, R.
Woodwards, H.
Woollard, E. S.
Woolley, W. V.
Woolven, W.
Wooster, G.
Wootton, A.
Wootton, J.
Worden, T.
Worker, C.
Worker, W.
Worley, A.
Worley, J.

Worley, J. E.
Worley, W. E.
Worling, A.
Worraker, A.
Worrall, W.
Worsh, J. E.
Worth, E. J.
Wright, A.
Wright, A.
Wright, A. C.
Wright, A. G.
Wright, E.
Wright, F. C.
Wright, H.
Wright, J.
Wright, J. F.
Wright, R.
Wright, S.
Wright, S. H.
Wright, W.
Wright, W. J.
Wyatt, G.
Wylie, R.

Yates, F.
Yates, W.
Yeo, A. C.
Youers, A.
Youers, B.
Youers, J.
Youers, P. T.
Youers, W.
Youers, W.
Young, A.
Young, A. E.
Young, A. J.
Young, A. V.
Young, E. A.
Young, J. C.
Young, J. E.
Young, W.

Zusman, J.

APPENDIX VII

(A) COPY OF WAR OFFICE LETTER

WAR OFFICE, LONDON, S.W.
27th July, 1920.

SIR,

I am commanded by the Army Council to inform you that they have recently received through the Foreign Office for distribution to the Army seven bronze reproductions of a Gold Medal which was presented to His Majesty the King of Italy by a National Committee in commemoration of the War. Four others, it is understood, have been allotted to the Navy, and one to the Royal Air Force.

The Council, after consultation with Lieutenant-General the Earl of Cavan, have selected the following units to receive these medals, as representatives of the British Military Forces which were engaged on the Italian Front:

> Northamptonshire Yeomanry.
> Bucks Battalion, Oxfordshire and Buckinghamshire Light Infantry.
> 1st Battalion Royal Welsh Fusiliers.
> Royal Artillery Mess, Woolwich.
> Royal Engineer Mess, Chatham.
> Honourable Artillery Company.
> Royal Army Medical Corps Mess, Millbank Hospital.

I am accordingly to transmit herewith a copy of the diploma which accompanied the medals, together with a translation of the same, and to inform you that the medal will be forwarded to you forthwith by registered post. I am at the same time to request that you will be good enough to furnish a formal receipt at your earliest convenience.

          I am, Sir,
               Your obedient Servant,
                   H. J. CREEDY.

The Officer Commanding
  Bucks Battalion,
    Oxfordshire and Buckinghamshire
      Light Infantry.
    14, Temple Square, Aylesbury.

(B) TRANSLATION OF THE ITALIAN DIPLOMA

THE NATIONAL COMMITTEE OF THE ARMY AND NAVY COMMEMORATIVE MEDAL, instituted in Rome with the object of offering to His Majesty the King of Italy, Vittorio Emanuele III, as Supreme Head of the Army and Navy, a large medal in gold, in memory of the War fought in the cause of Freedom and Civilization, presented this medal to the August Sovereign on the 10th December, 1919.

The National Committee has also offered a facsimile of the medal to all the Ships and Regiments which took part in the Great War, and each individual Italian soldier and sailor who distinguished himself on active service.

With the desire that this medal should also be a solemn emblem of distinction for the Armies and Navies of the Great and Valiant Allied Nations, the National Committee has decided to present to them reproductions of the same as a token of the profound sentiments of fraternity by which it is animated.

This diploma, together with a facsimile in bronze of the medal, is presented to:
            The Bucks Battalion,
   Oxfordshire and Buckinghamshire Light Infantry.
           For the Executive Committee,
                  THE PRESIDENT.

ROME, 28*th March*, 1920.

Il Comitato Nazionale per la Medaglia d'onore all' Esercito e all' Armata,

istituito in Roma per offrire alla Maestà del Re d'Italia Vittorio Emanuele III, quale Capo Supremo dell' Esercito e dell'Armata, una grande Medaglia in oro celebrante la Guerra di redenzione e di civiltà, ne fece consegna all'Augusto Sovrano il 10 Dicembre 1919.

Il Comitato Nazionale ha inoltre offerta una riproduzione-ricordo della stessa Medaglia a tutte le Navi ed a tutti i Reggimenti che hanno partecipato alla Grande Guerra, nonchè singolarmente a soldati e marinai italiani, che maggiormente si sono distinti in fatti d'armi.

Volendo il Comitato Nazionale che l'omaggio sia anche una solenne testimonianza di plauso per gli Eserciti e le Armate delle forti e valorose Nazioni alleate, ha deliberato ancora di offrire Loro delle riproduzioni-ricordo a conferma di sentimenti di sincera fratellanza.

Il presente attestato con una riproduzione in bronzo viene rilasciato a *The Bucks Battalion, Oxfordshire and Buckinghamshire Light Infantry*

Roma, li 28 Marzo 1920.

168

per la Giunta Esecutiva
Il Presidente

Il Presidente

ITALIAN MEMORIAL CERTIFICATE.

Map No. 4. THE ASIAGO PLATEAU. April—November, 1918

SCALE OF YARDS

www.ingramcontent.com/pod-product-compliance
Lightning Source LLC
Chambersburg PA
CBHW071814230426
43670CB00013B/2457